THE JOE WILLIAMS
BASEBALL READER

THE JOE WILLIAMS BASEBALL READER

The Glorious Game, from Ty Cobb
and Babe Ruth to the Amazing Mets

50 Years of Baseball Writing
by the Celebrated Newspaper Columnist

Edited by Peter Williams

ALGONQUIN BOOKS OF CHAPEL HILL 1989

Published by Algonquin Books of Chapel Hill
Post Office Box 2225
Chapel Hill, North Carolina 27515-2225

a division of
Workman Publishing Company
708 Broadway
New York, New York 10003

Material from Joe Williams' columns originally appearing in the
New York World-Telegram is used by permission of Bell & Howard, Inc.

Photographs throughout credited to *NBL* were furnished by the National Baseball
Library, Cooperstown, New York. Grateful thanks are extended to
Ms. Patricia Kelly, photo collection manager, for her help.

Photographs credited to United Press International are used by permission of
UPI/Bettman Archives; those credited to the Associated Press and Wide World are used
by permission of Wide World Photographs; and the photograph of Johnny Mize
is used by permission of *Chicago Today*.

The cartoons by Willard Mullin are reproduced by permission of his daughter,
Ms. Shirley Rhodes, of Corpus Christi, Texas.

Library of Congress Cataloging-in-Publication Data

Williams, Joe, d. 1972.
The Joe Williams baseball reader.

Bibliography: p.
1. Baseball—United States.   2. Newspapers—Sections,
columns, etc.   I. Williams, Peter. 1937 Jan. 30–
II. Title.
GV863.A1W55   1989   070.4′49-96357′0973   88-24110
ISBN 0-945575-07-6

First Printing

10 9 8 7 6 5 4 3 2 1

Contents

35. ASSORTED DODGERS 183

36. THE SHOT HEARD ROUND THE WORLD 193

37. SATCHEL PAIGE 198

APPENDIX 202

Illustrations

Acknowledgments

Since this remains, as Madonna has pointed out, a material world, first credit should be given to two funding agencies: the Scripps-Howard Foundation gave me a grant to begin work on this project, and County College of Morris awarded me a sabbatical to finish it. Without their help it would have taken much longer.

The following libraries and librarians were invaluable: Cleveland Municipal Library (Charles Novak); the Western Historical Society; Shelby County Library in Memphis; County College of Morris Library (Helen and Steve); and especially Drew University Library (Josie Cook, who proves that stereotyping librarians as stuffy and unattractive is foolish). At least one academic, Joe Dorinson of Long Island University, was both very encouraging and supportive. I'd also like to thank a few personal friends whose enthusiasm for the game and the people who write about it helps feed my own: Jim Gorman, Bruce Palamountain, Sandy Zulauf, Evan Coaker, and Janet Eber.

Also, there are a few members of the old *World-Telly* staff (and some who worked or work elsewhere) who liked the idea from the beginning and helped enormously: Zander Hollander, Bill Bloome, Lester Bromberg, Jack Caldwell, and Paul MacFarlane of *The Sporting News*.

I'm particularly thankful for the gracious help and wonderful stories I got from the following major league players and officials: Al Lopez, John Mize, Yogi Berra, Ted Williams, Bill Terry, Buddy Hassett, Bob Thomson, and Happy Chandler.

Finally, while there were some prominent contemporary journalists who chose not to encumber me with help (you know who you are), there were also a number who did. Wilfrid Sheed took the time to help support the project in its early stages. Roger Angell, whose father probably saw Lajoie play in some of the games my father covered in Cleveland, put me in touch with Bob Creamer, who was tickled by the clippings I sent him. Bob, in turn, introduced me to Louis Rubin, baseball writer, novelist, literary critic, and the only D.Litt. of my acquaintance, and it's Louis who must be thanked last but most. The final editing of this book, as well as the selection and arrangement of the photos and cartoons, are entirely his. More important, it was his decision that the columns were worth preserving, and his choice to take a chance on publishing them, and it's my closing hope, Dear Reader, that his faith in you is not misplaced.

Introduction

by Peter Williams

On the night I was born Joe Louis was fighting Bob Pastor in the Garden and my father, loyal to the code, was at his post at ringside. After the fight, which went the distance, he walked over to Leone's, wrote the story and sent it by messenger to the *World-Telegram* office. After that he took a cab to Leroy Hospital on 61st between Park and Madison.

"How is my son?" he asked the floor nurse when he got there. She took a look at him, and she probably got a whiff of him.

"He's in much better shape than you are, Mr. Williams," she said.

Of course I have no memory of this —nor of the crack made by Hazel Weiss, George's wife, who, on the same occasion, was asked by my mother what she thought. I was a notably unattractive baby, bordering, I've been told, on the repulsive. "Oh, well," Hazel said, "maybe he has personality."

Psychologists might call these events, though they're unremembered, formative; at times I tend to think so. Once, as I was showing a few friends archival home movies my mother had rediscovered after a cou-

ple of decades, I was startled to see myself, two years old, being dandled by a uniformed Lou Gehrig. Since this was the first time I'd heard of that, I have to wonder what else is hidden beneath my particular surface. If I could locate a therapist with an interest in baseball, I might find out; at least I'd have a motivated therapist.

At any rate, mine was an odd upbringing, an embarrassment of sports riches. Whereas other kids would line up to get a chance to use the four free passes Dad was sent for every event at the Garden— including the Stanley Cup, the N.I.T., the Millrose Games, all the championship fights and even the rodeo—I could care less. Sometimes I sold them for a quarter or so apiece. Once, at the rodeo, I stiffed Roy Rogers when, during intermission, he was followed by a spotlight to my seat, glittering like a premonition of rock. He's still waiting to shake my hand. And when Joe DiMaggio and Casey Stengel came out to our home in Jersey as the guests of honor at my eighth grade graduation, a picture was taken of DiMag with my brother and myself. Joe has his arm around my shoulder; I'm looking away, mortified. As far as

the other guy went, the old guy, I had no interest in him at all.

Most of my memories of ballplayers I met through the offices of my old man dated from the late '40s and early '50s. I recall a grade-school trip to Yankee Stadium. My class got there in time for batting practice. Frank Scott, the Yankees' press liaison, was showing us around, and he asked Gene Woodling to come over to the boxes just above the Yankee dugout to talk to us. Woodling said nothing and just walked away, shooting us what I remember as a downright nasty look. A little later, in the locker room, we met Ralph Houk. Houk was then a third-string catcher halfway through an eight-year career total of 44 hits (no home runs). He was sitting in a

large whirlpool bath and the girls got quite giggly. He talked to us, very cheerfully, for what seemed a very long time. Of such moments are a kid's heroes made, and his goats. Even now I'm pleased that Houk, not Woodling, was heard from again.

My greatest hero as a kid, though, was Johnny Mize. In '48 my father took me west with him to the Giants' training camp in Arizona. For a while my time was taken up with the six weeks of homework I had been given as the price of the trip, but eventually I got it all done. A baby-sitter of sorts was needed one afternoon, and Mize either volunteered (he was the kind who might have) or was conscripted. I sat with him on a wall or a bench, and I think he must have talked with me as much about

Left to right: Christy Walsh, Babe Ruth and Joe Williams.

my own kid's interests as about his adult ones. I know he didn't condescend to me at all.

Shortly thereafter he was traded to the Yanks, and after he made the trip across the Harlem River it seemed to me he hit three homers in a game every other week. I kept rooting for him to take the first-base job permanently away from the much younger Joe Collins, with whom he shared it. I whooped gleefully once when Casey put on the steal and big Jawn, to my romantic soul an aging Porthos, went down to second with all the speed and grace of an earth mover—and there wasn't even a throw. When I met him again some time after his retirement he hadn't changed. If there is any truth in what one of his old foremen is supposed to have said about

"nice guys," Mize is the welcome exception.

I saw Ruth once, when I was 10. My father and I were filing out of the Stadium along the third-base line after one of the games in the '47 World Series. Ruth, in the camel's-hair coat and cap, thin, was walking toward the home-plate exit on the first-base side.

I knew my father was very close to Ruth, and I asked him for an introduction. After all, we were probably going to end up going down the same ramp at the same time. I was turned down, but I wasn't told why. Maybe my father wanted to shield me from the knowledge that Ruth was dying.

More likely, he wanted to shield himself. The following summer we rented a cottage on Cape Cod. The word came through

Lou Gehrig and Joe Williams, St. Petersburg, Florida.

that Ruth was dead, and a telegram to my father arrived. He had been named a pallbearer.

He chose to pretend he hadn't been reached in time to get to the funeral, saying he didn't want his vacation interrupted. Now, though, I believe that he just couldn't handle it: that, probably even more than the rest of the country, he was imaginatively incapable of making the paradoxical connection between Ruth and death.

I have a mental picture of a gathering at the family house in about 1950. A tournament had just been held at the local golf course, less than a block away, and my father had invited his peers over for a drink. About half a dozen of the best and best-known writers were there. I remember meeting Bill Corum and Arthur Daley, and I remember Dan Parker towering over everybody else. They seemed pleased to be all there together, like kids enjoying Jimmy Cannon's "toy department" or old-timers at a college reunion. It's pleasant, in retrospect, to recall all of them gathered in one room. They probably didn't know how good they were.

These men were the last of a group who had to be inventions of Hecht and MacArthur, who couldn't be real. Take Harry Grayson, who once ran the night desk for my father. He crashed Owney Madden's suite one night and browbeat the mob boss until Madden promised to help look for the Lindbergh baby's killer, all because Grayson himself had a son the same

Left to right: Willard Mullin, Gene Leone, Joe Williams and Grantland Rice.

age. Another time, annoyed by the night copy editor because he never took off his hat, he came back to the office with a hired speakeasy band and had them play "The Star Spangled Banner." Once he allegedly stole the corpse of a miniscule pal who had just died, took it to the Stork Club and begged to be let in because, he said, his friend was "only a little stiff."

In Tim Cohane's book *Bypaths of Glory* Harry is called the "sportswriter from Mars," and once I had a conversation with Red Smith in which I was told that "two sportswriters can't get together for more than twenty minutes without Grayson's name coming up." I remember having a beer with Harry in Gilhuley Brothers near the Garden on a night when

he had a blonde on his arm, a lady distinctly past her prime who had bleached her hair a couple of shades beyond white, and one time when he was past seventy and in an endearingly drunken state he propositioned my fiancée. He offered her a free ride to Florida during spring training, adding, "but don't tell Joe." My reaction wasn't important; she just couldn't tell Joe.

Joe was himself, God knows, consistent with this profile or what he preferred to call a "sporting writer." He grew up in a raucous city, listening to Handy help invent the blues, and ended up in an even more raucous one. In the Manhattan of the prohibition era he played handball with Jimmy Walker on the private courts which speakeasies like the Stork Club and Leone's

Joe DiMaggio, 1950, with Michael Williams, left, and Peter Williams, right.

had built for the mayor, thus insuring an uninterrupted supply of authentic hooch. He had a falling out with Tunney after suggesting Gene's interest in books was snobbish fakery, and Dempsey, offended by something he'd written, slipped him a mickey at a party. When Ruth spent several days in the hospital with gonorrhea and convinced even his wife it was ptomaine, he kept the secret.

In the '30s, he and two buddies, one of whom would later write *The Poseidon Adventure*, got Eleanor Holm loaded on champagne in the bar on the S.S. *Manhattan* en route to the Nazi Olympics; she was kicked off the squad before the boat docked. At the games themselves, when Hitler and the rest stood to sing "Deutschland Uber Alles," he and Henry McLemore sang "Dixie"; although nothing was said, then or at Goebbels' press reception, when

they got back to their hotel they found their rooms had been ransacked.

During the Truman administration he and Willard Mullin were en route to the Army-Navy game on a special train when Willard realized he didn't have the game tickets. My father refused to panic. When they got to the stadium the president's entourage was just going in. Two secret service men walked in front of his convertible, two behind. When the car appeared on the field there were four secret service men bringing up Truman's rear, and the crowd cheered Willard and my father all the way to the 50-yard line, where everybody took their seats, although two of the group continued up to the press box. And in the '50s he told off Benny Siegel in no uncertain terms and in a public place, and when Bugsy was murdered the following

Lefty Gomez and Peter Williams.

day the FBI investigated him. Throughout all this, like all the other sportswriters, he remained unscathed. They seemed able to move through their dramatic lives like corpsmen on a battlefield.

He was born in Memphis, probably in 1889, or possibly even earlier, despite the 1891 he claimed and which was used in his obituary. Red Smith once wrote that he was "kittenish" about his age and the comment, although coming after his death and therefore somewhat unkind, was probably valid. Still it's my suspicion that any date-fudging was less a question of vanity than one of job security.

At any rate, when he was a kid, the Mississippi was still crowded with stern-wheelers. There's a photomural in the Shelby County Library taken in 1903 which shows the Memphis riverfront, and

you can count seven of them. As an old man he'd tell us about a girl who must have been fast for an 11-year-old—she had a tent in her back yard, and she'd invite the boys in one at a time for what presumably was a little innocent spooning. Her nickname was Red Mike. My father remembered he was usually the one asked in first.

He shared a room and a Huck-like boyhood with his brother, Bill, with whom he'd swim in the muddy Wolf River, trying to catch snakes by the tail, unaware that they were water moccasins. One day he was catching in a kids' ball game and his passed ball gave the other team the lead in the top of the ninth, but Bill got him off the hook with the winning hit in the bottom half. Another time he and Bill were forced to quit their jobs as vendors at the Red Elm Park because my grandmother felt that all ballplayers were "drunkards or worse," and that the brothers were in grave danger of irreversible contamination.

One payday my grandfather was very late getting back to the small family house. Bill and my father stayed awake and watched their mother in the kitchen through the crack in the bedroom door, anticipating the Big Scene. "Pop" was weaving when he walked in, but when she confronted him, instead of flinching he grinned. She was astounded, of course. He told her to hold out her apron, and the kids watched as he dropped, bill by bill, a large quantity of U.S. currency into it. He had been to the track. The next day the family went out and bought a new, larger house in a better section of town. My father never forgot the name of the horse: Rustling Silk.

By 1910 my father was working for the *Memphis Commercial Appeal* and meeting established players like Cobb, Chance, and Joe Jackson, whose teams frequently barnstormed through town. He even met some youngsters like Casey Stengel who hadn't made it to the big show yet. He began to live more glamorously. He and Bill, who still shared a room, bought a suit to share, too. The night before a function for which my father felt he'd better dress, he would press the pants by slipping them between the mattress and the spring and sleeping on them all night.

But sometimes the new high-life required more informal garb. At the bordello to which he was introduced by an older editor who had taken him under a libidinous wing, the customers were required to strip and dress in smocks. His girl turned out to have been Stanley Ketchel's choice when he was in town, and when she found that my father had also been distraught on hearing of the fighter's murder and that they were fellow mourners similarly afflicted, she let him wear Ketchel's smock, which until then had been retired in the manner of Ruth's uniform. Although Ketchel never fought in Memphis, my father saw him once, between trains, stand-

ing on the platform, just before he was killed. He said Ketchel was the best-dressed man he'd ever seen. Ketchel, sad to say, caught his train.

In April, 1913, my father saw one more hero in his last moment of glory. Covering a minor league game between Memphis and Minneapolis in Hickman, Kentucky, he went to watch volunteers try to sandbag a weakening levee during a dangerous spring flood. There was only one white back among the laborers, who were stripped to the waist and working in heavy rain. The man was Rube Waddell, who shortly thereafter developed the illness that would kill him within the year.

In 1914 my father left Memphis to write for *The Cleveland News*. Although he returned to Memphis briefly, he was primarily a Cleveland writer from then until 1927. In Cleveland he knew and grieved over Ray Chapman, nicknamed Tris Speaker "The Gray Eagle," and scooped the rest of the country when George Sisler nearly went blind.

In 1927 he was sent to New York, where I was born, 10 years later, when he was nearly 50. As a result many of my personal memories of him as an energetic man, like my memories of ballplayers, are the memories of a kid. There is a kid's recollection of a New Year's Eve party when the sports staff put on a skit ribbing him. Joe King played him, sitting at a typewriter, drinking scotch and desperately trying to think up something to write to beat the daily deadline, and Jim Burchard, in bathing trunks and sneakers and somebody's son's borrowed boxing gloves, danced in and out as the ghost or hallucination of Johnny Kilbane, my father's favorite subject when he was too loaded to think of anything else. There was a terrific old-fashioned, guys-out-on-the-town warmth to that evening, as there was to the Christmas morning a year or so later, when Dad and Bill Bloome picked up the Daisy Tar-

Joe Williams in dialogue with Casey Stengel.

geteer air pistol I'd been given, measured off a suitable number of paces, assumed the proper duellist's stance and started shooting the balls off the Christmas tree.

I began to lose touch with him soon after that. I was in high school, and he was old enough to be my grandfather, and these were two very good reasons for an adolescent mind to dismiss a parent. He still made a point to keep Christmas in the best Fezziwig tradition, and he still occasionally brought back the winnings from a bet he had put down for me at the Derby, but when I went away for the usual lengthy periods to college and then to grad school I felt no particular loss of kinship. Nonetheless fathers are supposed to be invulnerable, and especially, I'd been taught, this one, and when in 1964, at 75, he was

finally handed his notice by the *World-Telegram* I was jarred. In 1965, helped by Lester Bromberg and Bob Sullivan, he put out a newsletter with an emphasis on the track, and he wrote a weekly note column for the *The Morning Telegraph*. Then, at 76, he had his first small stroke, which the doctor called a cerebral episode, using a euphemism which, under other circumstances, might have amused him.

Since the doctors told us the prognosis for rapid recovery was good, we chose to keep everything quiet. I found his notes and wrote his column for the *Telegraph*. I thought I'd done a good job—in fact, a very good job—but he came out of his fog after a day or so and rewrote the column completely. What's worse, and in all objectivity, he made it much better. When it came out in the paper he clipped it and left it on my desk with this note: "This is how it looks."

He had these mini-strokes frequently after that, and recovered each time, but each time a little more was lost. He got so that he would drift in and out of lucidity, and during the lucid moments he'd understand what was happening to him. He once told me it was like being outside on a fine day, the grass bright green in the sunlight, when suddenly a cloud would cover the sun and the grass would get dark. Shortly after he made that observation he forgot where he was.

He would keep up a front with men, but my mother says he frequently cried when he was alone with her. Nonetheless, he went down tough. When I talked my mother into hiring a practical nurse so that she could leave the house for a few days, he convinced the woman he could have as many martinis as he wanted and ended up breaking his hip. Just before the doctor told my mother he'd have to go into a nursing home he almost set himself on fire because nobody was going to tell him he couldn't smoke. And when Bill Bloome saw him in the nursing home just before he died Bill reported that they had had a good talk about the old days.

He died at 82 in 1972, six years after the first stroke, on Valentine's Day.

Although Ted Williams has said (both in print and in conversation with me) that when he met my father in the late '30s he thought he was "real New York," the emphasis on that city's people, athletes and teams in what follows comes less from regional chauvinism than from the fact that New York was his home base. He worked out of New York for the last 37 years of his career, and when he was fired, he was fired by the New York *World-Telegram*.

The firing (officially, he was told to resign) had been mechanical and summary, and he got many letters from colleagues and fans who were as startled as he was.

He kept the letters in a manila folder, sometimes underlining phrases that supported his sense of betrayal, and after his death I found them. Joe Cronin felt "much regret." Red Blaik "neither liked [his] being retired or the casualness of the announcement of the fact." Walter O'Malley put the word "retired" in quotes, and Fred Lieb came right out and said "fired," condemning the paper's "lack of appreciation or sentiment." Pegler ended by saying "you reigned long at the top of a great elite," adding that theirs had been "the greatest day of our journalism." When Moe Berg told friends that younger writers had taken over for Williams, they told him, "they can't carry Joe's pen." Ford Frick wrote a letter from the commissioner's office which concluded, perhaps a little comically but certainly in the best executive manner, "let's get together for lunch soon."

There was also a note from Willard Mullin. Dad had "discovered" and hired Willard in the early '30s, and Willard had always been a very close friend—a virtual member of the family—of whom I was particularly fond: he took me fishing at the Marciano Camp in Greenwood Lake (I caught a sunny); he taught me cribbage, introduced me to German food and let me watch him draw. He was a terrific chess player, which he once proved to me by trouncing me when he was far from sober. He was a very emotional man, who cried at my wedding and again when my father died—in fact, on the latter occasion he was too upset to come to the phone, and his wife had to deliver the condolences to my mother.

In his note to my father Willard said he wanted to "excoriate the 'powers that be,' solid brass as they have so uncompromisingly proved"; he thanked "the one who shoved the door ajar for Willard," and he anticipated "a book which must be written, earthy and forthright . . . on the beat we travelled together, by the only guy I ever listened to, even with one ear."

This is the book.

THE JOE WILLIAMS
BASEBALL READER

Prelude

Charley Shields at Memphis

September 5, 1953. About the only justification this essay has is that Charley Shields was an early baseball idol and back home the other day the old left-hander died and he even made the *Times* obit column. This was probably the first time the Old Gray Lady of West 43rd Street ever gave him a tumble, an understandable hauteur at that, since Charley was no Hall of Famer and maybe the only reason he broke in at all is that it was a dull night on the cadaver desk.

The obit said Charley pitched for McGraw in Baltimore and with the two St. Louis clubs which made him sound bigger than he was, because he was in and out quick. Once in Seattle, however, he did have a big day, striking out 19 in a nine-inning game which was a record.

Charley didn't seem to care much about fame or money and one summer he quit a team up North and came home and spent the rest of the season in the bleachers at old Red Elm Park watching the Southern Leaguers. People said if Charley took better care of himself he'd be another Rube Waddell or Eddie Plank. They said he wasn't ambitious.

Charley's friends laughed. Then they'd tell about a fellow who once lived in the neighborhood, a bookkeeper, who came home singing every night. His wife had a lot of cats and a parrot that was always boasting "The Lord loves me." The wife said it was a pity because if her husband shunned the demon he'd own the store and the sympathizing womenfolk agreed.

Well, she finally got him to sign the pledge or maybe the fellow got to believing he'd really own the store, but nothing happened except he stopped being neighborly and a few months later when the police came they found his wife shot dead, the cats and parrot poisoned and he was sitting on a bed with a bottle and singing again.

As youngsters this philosophic defense fortunately was lost on us and whether the story was true or not we didn't care. All that mattered was that Charley was a swell guy who would hit fungoes, umpire or play for both sides and stand treat all around with a new drink called Coca-Cola. A nice, simple, friendly man.

Some five or six years passed and suddenly everybody had grown up, or so it seemed, even the town, with a new skyscraper, horseless carriages in the streets, full-length movies with illustrated slides and a home-grown song, "The Memphis Blues," even Broadway was singing—and Charley had quit roaming and was pitching for the home team. He'd win some and lose some and those same people, grown older too, were still saying it was a shame about Charley because he could have been a real big-leaguer. But to the youngsters who knew him in other days Charley was still our guy and it hurt when he got beat and it was a wonderful feeling inside when he won. Those days and times were particularly exciting to a youngster who was crazy about baseball, whose head was full of batting averages and pitching lore, who had just got a job on the morning paper and a fierce loyalty for everything about the old Southern League. In those days, more so than in any other minor, the league was a crossroads at which young players coming up met old ones going back. You'd see Lave Cross, who was older than Satchel Paige is now. Scoops Carey was famous in

the '90s but still digging them out of the dirt and young Jake Daubert stood back of him to see how he made the plays. New Orleans had an outfielder who couldn't read or write but the pitchers couldn't get him out and it was no surprise when he went up to Cleveland. Joe Jackson.

There was a center fielder in Little Rock who seemed to cover the entire outfield, Tris Speaker, and he went to Boston. Chattanooga had a spitball pitcher who was unhittable when he could get the ball over and years later Burleigh Grimes was to win 13 straight for the Giants. And Montgomery had an outfielder who clowned it up and made the fans laugh and old-timers down there must be pulling for Casey Stengel to make it five in a row with the Yankees.

There were always two or three big-league scouts around making notes and pricing players but by then if they ever gave Charley a thought it was to say it was too bad he didn't take better care of himself.

1

Honus Wagner

The Greatest Shortstop of His Generation

September 24, 1938. It was interesting, sitting around with Honus Wagner the night the Pittsburgh Pirates left town. He was smoking a cigar, sipping a glass of beer and talking about the old days—the days when baseball knew him as the Flying Dutchman and the greatest shortstop of his generation.

He recalled the day he broke in as a shortstop. . . . "That's a funny story," he said, flicking ashes off his brown vest. "A fellow named Ely, Bones Ely we called him, was playing the position. One day he came up to Fred Clarke and said he wasn't feeling well, and wanted to be excused from the lineup. Clarke had just been made manager. Ely resented this. He thought he should have had the job. So Clarke figured Ely was scheming to let him down, make him look bad as a manager.

Here old Honus, now in his 60s, gray as a London fog and looking in profile astonishingly like Nance Garner, vice president of the United States, paused to wet his whistle.

"Well, I'd been around playing this position and that position when I wasn't in the outfield, which was my regular spot, and Clarke comes to me and says, 'This guy's trying to show me up. You get in there and play short. We don't need him.'"

The first day Mr. Wagner played shortstop he made three errors in one inning. "And you should have heard those Pittsburgh fans give me the razz," he smiled. "You see Ely was a real good shortstop, and pretty popular, too, so when I started out by kicking the first three chances I was a bum in spades.

"But before the inning closed I had a lucky break. And it was just dumb luck. There were men on first and second. I gave the pitcher the sign to make a quick throw to second to catch the runner off base, but he didn't get it. Instead, he pitched and the batter hit the ball. By this time I had run over to second; in fact, I was a few feet on the far side of second when I saw the ball burning through the box. I just stuck my glove down, squeezed the ball and had a made-to-order play for myself. All because I was out of position. The fans seemed to think that was all right, and the razzing stopped. I guess that was the best play I ever made in baseball."

Old Honus told how he happened to sign with Ed Barrow to play with Paterson,

Wagner and Ty Cobb at 1909 World Series.—*NBL*

N.J. One of Barrow's distinctions is that he "discovered" Wagner. Which is hardly the correct word. Wagner was already the property of the Pittsburgh club.

"They wanted to send me to Kansas City," he explained. "I was about 20, and I know it sounds awful to tell it now, but I didn't know where Kansas City was. I know I had a feeling it was mighty far off. Almost like crossing the ocean.

"I wouldn't go. I stayed home with my two brothers in Carnegie, Pa. One day we were down at the creek throwing stones, my brothers and myself, and Barrow came along. It seemed he had been looking for me, and he asked me if I would like to play with Paterson.

"Well, if Kansas City seemed far away, you can imagine what Paterson meant to me. A complete total of nothing. I had never heard of Paterson, or New Jersey, for that matter.

"'But you know Mike Swift, don't you?' asked Barrow. I did. 'And you know Joe Doques?' I did. And he mentioned several other fellows I knew, and I was satisfied. No matter where Paterson was, I concluded it must be in America, or else these other fellows wouldn't be there. And so that's how I happened to go with Barrow."

Old Honus is the last survivor of the frontier days of the World Series. He's the only man left in baseball today who played in the first World Series. This was the series in which the Boston Red Sox beat the Pirates. It was held in 1903.

But the Series Old Honus likes to remember is the 1909 set, which brought the Detroit Tigers and the Pirates together. At that time the two most talked-of men in baseball were Old Honus and Ty Cobb. This was to be a clash not only of great teams but great individuals. It was the Tigers against the Pirates and Wagner against Cobb.

Wagner shaded Cobb in every department, out-hit him by almost 100 points, and stole six bases, to tie a World Series record which still stands, and since base-stealing is now outmoded, probably always will stand.

Cobb stole home in the first game to score the Tigers' only run. And he stole second in the second game, for his last steal of the Series. "We had him out at second," recalls Old Honus. "We put up a squawk, but Silk O'Loughlin, the umpire, overruled it. We kept the squawk going for a minute or so, making no headway, of course, and then Cobb spoke up. He turned to O'Loughlin, an American League umpire, by the way, and said, 'Of course I was out. They had me by a foot. You just booted the play, so come on, let's play ball.'"

By the way Old Honus related this incident, you could tell he still has a certain amount of admiration for Mr. Cobb.

———

2

Frank Chance's Cubs

Tinker, Evers and Chance

December 9, 1936. We got to talking about the old Cubs—the Cubs under Frank Chance. Many legends have grown up around that club, one of the most romantic clubs the game has known. There was the story, for instance, about Evers and Tinker, one of the greatest second-base combinations in baseball—the story was they didn't speak for several years.

"That's right," admitted Mr. Evers. "We didn't even say hello for at least two years. We went through two World Series without a single word. And I'll tell you why. I'm 55 years old now and Joe is 56. Poor fellow, they tell me he is dying down in Florida. A great fellow and a great ballplayer.

"But one day—it was early in 1907 —he threw me a hardball. It wasn't any further than from here to there (Mr. Evers pointed to a bridge lamp about 10 feet away). It was a real hardball. Like a catcher throwing to second. And the ball broke my finger. This finger here (he showed a gnarled finger on his right hand). I yelled at him, 'You so and so!' He laughed. That's the last word we had for—well, I just don't know how long."

But how about the time they trapped Ty Cobb off second base in the 1907 World

Series? You two guys must have been speaking then.

"No, we weren't. We still took signs, but we didn't speak. I remember that incident very well.

"Cobb was on second. Johnny Kling was catching for us. I think he was the first Jewish player in the majors. Cobb took a lead off second. Tinker said to him: 'Don't get too far away from that bag or the Jew will nip you off.' With that he gave me a signal to take the throw. Cobb turned to sneer at Tinker, and as he did I rushed in to cover. Kling threw the ball. We caught Cobb by two feet. It helped win the ball game and the Series."

To me this was interesting in connection with the theory of team harmony and its importance in winning ball games. Mr. Evers had an answer to that. It seemed quite logical. "What one guy thinks about another guy on a ball team doesn't mean a thing. That's a personal affair. What a guy thinks about the team as a whole is something else. Tinker and myself hated each other, but we loved the Cubs. We wouldn't fight for each other, but we'd come close to killing people for our team. That was one of the answers to the Cubs' success."

Frank Chance.—*NBL*

Three-Fingered Brown

December 2, 1942. PEORIA—It took us back a long stretch. We were in summer school across the lake from Chicago. A Saturday came and there was a trip for the "merit students." Somehow we were included. The big belt of the trip was a baseball game. Cubs against the Giants. Brown against Matty.

Now a fellow who was seeing his first big-league game and who later turned out to be a sportswriter should have found that an unforgettable adventure. And it was all

of that. But more, he should have remembered every play and to this day should be able to repeat all that happened in detail. All we remember is that the Cubs won, Matty was beaten, Brown didn't start.

Brown came into the game in the third or fourth inning. What we remember most about him, besides his pitching, of course, is that he wore a red woolen undershirt with sleeves that came down to his wrists. We remember seeing him come from the

Poster, Chicago, Labor Day, 1916. — *NBL*

old Cubs' clubhouse and make the long walk to the pitcher's box.

That was so many years ago it is tortuous to try to fix the exact date. We suppose Brown was our first baseball hero. But it wasn't until last night that we first met the great Three-Fingered Brown.

Mr. Brown is now 66 years old. He is gray, sharp-featured, vibrant and thin. He has the biggest filling station in Terre Haute, Ind. He has saved his money and is in a position to give the wolf a vigorous hand-to-hand rassle. In the evening we went with our old hero to his hotel room and played over some of his more spectacular chapters in baseball. We were still puzzled that he came from the clubhouse that day, the day he beat Matty. Why wasn't he on the bench?

For some reason he didn't want to discuss it. He tried to dismiss it with a wisecrack. But in due time the truth came out. You never hear Mr. Brown's name mentioned when they get around to talking about the great pitchers of all time. It's always Mathewson, Johnson and Alexan-

der. . . . And in more recent years, Grove. But there was always one guy Matty had trouble beating.

The reason Mr. Brown didn't start that day was that John McGraw, who managed the Giants at the time, no longer wanted any part of Mr. Brown. Matty could whip anybody else but he couldn't beat Mr. Brown, who had won nine consecutive decisions against the New York idol. So the Cub strategy was to wait until Matty had started the game before putting Brown in the box. It was too late then for McGraw to do anything about it.

"It wasn't that I was a better pitcher," Mr. Brown told us, sipping his highball slowly and looking at us over his glasses. "It was just one of those things. It seemed I always was at my best against Matty. In the beginning he would beat me all the time; in the end I would beat him all the time. McGraw finally got around to playing the percentage. He must have said to himself: 'Why waste Matty against that lucky bum.'"

3

McGraw's Giants

John McGraw's Anniversary

April 20, 1927. Today New York helps John Joseph McGraw celebrate his 25th anniversary as manager of the Giants. Back in 1902 a young, vibrant Irishman stepped off a Baltimore train, got into a sombre-looking hack, rattled down to the club offices and affixed his signature to a contract that has endured for a quarter of a century.

That was a long time ago. A lot of dandruff has settled on the coat collars of the nation since that day. A cross-section of the metropolis that greeted this 29-year-old genius of the diamond 25 summers ago may interest you.

That day after McGraw took command of the Giants the *Herald* man commented:

"McGraw is a peppery, argumentative man on the field, but he is a competent baseball manager and knows the game thoroughly. If he can do nothing more he can inject sufficient vigor into the players to enable them to grasp the fact that lack of backbone never won a championship. The salary of the new manager is $10,000 per annum."

Dan Patch was pacing miles in around 2:06, and James J. Jeffries was training for a forthcoming fight with Bob Fitzsimmons in San Francisco. The newspapers commented that the East manifested little interest in the fight, while the West was quite enthusiastic.

On the day McGraw signed with the Giants President Roosevelt began his outdoor summer life at Sagamore Hill, beating his sons Archie and Kermit at tennis and rifle practice. Later he led the two boys in a horse race around the countryside and returned in time for a big supper feeling "bully."

Ethel Barrymore created considerable publicity for herself at about the time McGraw was winning his first games here by announcing that she would appear in a drama wearing loose blouse and trousers, after the style of the French peasant. Girls appearing on Broadway today without either blouse or trousers create far less stir than did the daring Ethel a generation ago.

A cable from Berlin quoted J. Pierpont Morgan as saying: "The Kaiser is a great man."

The same cable reported that in Berlin Morgan retained a bodyguard "some-

Rube Marquard and wife. —*NBL*

thing like the prize fighter Jim Corbett, or worse, whose grimace was sufficient to frighten the boldest mendicant."

I can imagine that the aristocratic Mr. Corbett on reading this cable immediately checked Morgan off his social list.

Rube Marquard

February 1, 1964. "You're a sportswriter and wish to interview me?" Mrs. Richard William Marquard said she'd be delighted. "Some of my best friends are sportswriters."

The interview was conducted backstage at the famed Hippodrome Theater in Cleveland. Mrs. Marquard's stage name was Blossom Seeley. She was one of vaudeville's most popular and highest-paid headliners. The actress had immediately made it clear she never referred to her husband as Rube. Always, meticulously, it was Richard.

Just at what point I got lost in total confusion is no longer remembered. It must have been when the musical comedy star, in answer to a question, said, no, Richard

hadn't accompanied her, he was in New York.

"I talked with his nurse moments before you arrived," she continued. "I wanted to be sure she was watching him closely. You see, the instant you turn your back Richard starts nibbling at his toes. A most distressing habit and it's high time we broke him of it."

High time indeed, I agreed. Yet I was puzzled. The rap on left-handed ballplayers, especially pitchers, has always been that they are congenital screwballs. But nibbling his toes? There had to be a limit somewhere, even for left-handers. It wasn't until Miss Seeley directed my attention to a framed picture on her dressing room table that the fog began to lift. A cuddly tot, toes protectively encased in tiny boots.

Richard W. Marquard was about as much a rube in dress, manner and diction as Jimmy Walker. On the contrary, he was tall, handsome, articulate, a patron of the smartest Times Square restaurants and obviously no stranger to the bright lights. Touring sportswriters unfailingly found him easy of access and enjoyably reminiscent.

Sooner or later he'd get around to the game he liked best to recall. It was against the Pirates, always a soft touch for him. "Just get me one run," he told his teammates. "That's all I need to beat these guys."

It was tied until the 21st when Larry Doyle hit an inside-the-park homer. "Next time you say you need only one run to win," laughed Larry, "be specific. Name the inning."

Mathewson and Marquard

December 26, 1961. Frank Baker, critically ill at 75 and the original symbol of the home run, was the central figure of a rancorous yet hilarious cause célèbre, involving two star pitchers, Christy Mathewson and Rube Marquard of the Giants.

It subsequently developed neither of the teammates was wholly responsible for the exchange of unpleasantries in which they publicly engaged, and one of them, Marquard, was totally unaware of his role until so informed by the sports pages.

A young sportswriter, recently graduated from Columbia, and probably unmindful of the historical significance of his assignment, one which was to immortalize him as baseball's first ghostwriter, contributed no little to the spurious feud.

John Wheeler, whose stately white mane gives him more the appearance of a Dean of Philosophy than boss of a national news syndicate, breaks down and tells all (very likely by way of atonement), in his new, lively, absorbing book, *I've Got News for You.*

The gentleman's confession: "I was travelling with the Giants in 1911 when I got a wire from the sports editor: 'Sign Mathewson to cover the World Series. Offer up to $500, but try to get him for less.' I offered Matty $500 and he accepted. I was to confer with him after each game, then turn out the masterpieces. All went well

until Baker, the Athletics' third baseman, hit one out of the park off Marquard. Matty and I turned out a very informative piece, pointing out that Rube had pitched wrong to Baker, inside instead of outside."

The original ghost had reasons to feel quite proud of his spectral prose. Marquard's stupidity was prominently featured in the *New York Herald* and subscribing papers elsewhere. But within hours the fledgling wraith was to discover pitfalls exist even in Ghostland.

The piece stood up well until the next afternoon when Matty, the old master himself, was in the box and up came Baker with two on. The last seen of the ball was when it disappeared over the center-field bleachers.

"There was considerable razzing by the fans who evidently had read the article on the proper way to pitch to Home Run Baker by Christy Mathewson. We had a tough time working out a story that night. Finally Matty decided the best way out of our embarrassment was to write that he had pitched wrong to Baker, too."

You may be interested in the details which led to this comic controversy, especially since our repentant phantom trips over a fact here and there. Baker's two-run homer off Marquard came in the sixth inning of the second game and won it, 3-1.

There was nobody on when Baker hit his homer off Matty in the ninth with the Giants leading 1-0. The wallop tied the game and sent it into extra innings, the A's eventually winning in the 11th.

This was the Series in which the Maryland farmer won the sobriquet Home Run Baker. He didn't stop at home runs, though. His .375 led both Series teams at bat.

The Merkle Boner

March 13, 1934. Some of the boys were talking about McGraw and the old Giants. Mr. Jack Doyle chuckled. When Mr. Doyle chuckles the effect is startling. It is a cross between a barnyard cackle and a mailman's whistle. Mr. Doyle went back to the 1908 season when the Giants lost the league championship because of Fred Merkle's failure to touch second base in a game with the Cubs.

"McGraw thought he might still be able to overthrow the decision," related Mr. Doyle, "provided he could summon up enough pressure to make an impression. Immediately he got his men to sign an affidavit testifying that Merkle had touched second base, despite the fact that everybody in the park knew he didn't.

"Mathewson, who had been coaching at first base, didn't want to sign it. He hadn't seen Merkle touch the bag so how could he sign the affidavit? McGraw arranged a device by which it became less agonizing for Mathewson to wrestle with his pliable conscience.

"Merkle had left the park. By the time they fetched him back darkness had fallen. A lantern was lighted. McGraw ordered Merkle to run from first to second and touch the bag. Mathewson watched the eerie operation. When it was over he signed the affidavit affirming that on this day and date he had seen Merkle touch second base."

McGraw Steps Down

June 4, 1932. After 30 years of continuous services John Joseph McGraw has resigned as manager of the Giants. At the age of 59 Mr. McGraw steps down because of failing health, with his Giants in last place, apparently headed for no place in particular—an ironical climax of a career marked by many successes and a stern intolerance for mediocrity. To quit with his team on the rocks must have been a terrific sacrifice to his pride.

The truth is Mr. McGraw has not been the Giants for a long time, and by the same token the Giants have not been the Giants. Mr. McGraw began to fade as a leader when two of his star players, Rogers Hornsby and Burleigh Grimes, were sent away in mysterious deals justified only by a meagre bulletin from the business office that the men were disposed of "for the best interests of the team." The transactions moved one of Mr. McGraw's followers to inquire: "For the best interests of which team?"

Since that time the Giants have been consistently unsuccessful as championship contenders, and Mr. McGraw has been little more than a fat, elderly gentleman sitting in the dugout, plagued with recurrent

John McGraw and his replacement as New York Giants manager, Bill Terry.—*NBL*

ailments of a nature to which fat, elderly gentlemen are susceptible.

I am glad he has decided to resign. For one thing, he owes it to his failing health. For another, the Giants as he knew them no longer exist.

The game offered no more stirring spectacle in the old days at the Polo Grounds than the short, stocky figure of Mr. McGraw moving toward the home-plate umpire with a chip on his shoulder. It was, somehow, a natural part of the Giant picture. It is not a part of the re-cords that he ever won one of these bat-tles, nor is it in the records that he ever quit trying. To the end Mr. McGraw was faithful to his truculent creed. The last official act he performed as manager of the Giants was to file a protest with the league president against Bill Klem, the umpire.

Mr. McGraw was a product of the old school of baseball, when fistfights were common, when red liquor was sold at all the parks, when only ladies of question-able social standing attended the game. He was a black-haired, pasty-faced young Irishman to whom roughhouse tactics were merely a part of the trade. It was a fighting game in which only fighting men survived. Mr. McGraw became distinguished for his fiery exploits, which bordered on rowdy-ism. Somebody tagged him Muggsy. But as the game gradually emerged from its primitive crudeness Mr. McGraw softened and changed with it.

4

Ty Cobb

The First and Only

June 30, 1925. Ty Cobb says this will be his last year as a player and the pitchers hope so. Cobb was a star when Niagara was a mill pond, but he's still harder to fool than a widow with a purpose.

Ty was one of the first ballplayers to experiment with the hazardous science of thinking. Cobb used to startle the buyers by dashing from first to third on an infield fumble. When he wasn't doing this he was going all the way home. Baseball has never known a more daring or colorful base run-ner. They tell you base-stealing is an art. With the Peach it was a habit, like walking in an upright position and using soap on the back of the neck.

Smart crackers used to say Jennings had a great ball club in Cobb. They could have gone further and said Ban Johnson had a great league in him. It will be a long time before the game develops a second Cobb, and then it will be just that—a sec-ond Cobb. You've seen the first and only.

Cobb Sets a Record

April 30, 1927. History was made at the Yankee Stadium yesterday. Ty Cobb went around the bases in the sixth inning of the opening game. It was a world record for the Georgian. It marked the 2,057th time he had circled the bases since he came to the big leagues.

No other ballplayer in modern history has been around the bases as often as Cobb. In Cobb's own league Tris Speaker is closest with 1,782, followed by his pres-ent teammate, Eddie Collins, with 1,765. Every time Cobb get to first base these days it constitutes a new record, likewise every time he scores.

I don't know whether this is impor-tant. I don't know whether it means any-thing to Cobb or not. Very likely it doesn't.

The Cobb run came in typical Cob-bensian fashion. Opening the sixth inning he laid down a bunt. Joe Dugan looked at

Ty Cobb on deck. — *NBL*

it. That was all he did. I think it took him somewhat by surprise. Cobb slid into first base. This was unnecessary. No play was made on him. Those of you who are getting along in life should find encouragement in this episode.

To my simple mind Cobb's run was the big thrill of the ball game. It came this way. He bunted and was safe. Hale produced a short hit to center. The average player would have stopped at second. Cobb has never been an average player — not in his own mind, anyway. Instead of stopping at second he continued to third.

There was a geyser of dust as the Georgian hit the dirt. Everyone expected Evans to wave Cobb out, but he didn't. With both arms extended in the time-honored umpirical manner, he fluttered him safe. And he was right. Cobb had pulled one of his old

tricks. He had overslid the bag with his feet to evade Dugan's tag, but he had twisted his body and come back to touch it with his hands — a subtle heritage from the base-running days of a more romantic period.

Having reached third in safety, Cobb gave every indication of a desire to steal home. Once he worked his way almost to the plate on Hoyt's windup. Finally he scored on an infield out.

Cobb was the most interesting figure in the ball game, not excepting Ruth. When he laid down the aforementioned bunt and beat it to first, he was the Cobb your Dad knew — a vibrant, impetuous base runner, asking no quarter and giving none, a 40-year-oldster thumbing a matured nose at the unskilled robustness of youth.

Everybody's Hall of Fame outfield for the first three decades of the 20th century:
Ty Cobb, Babe Ruth, Tris Speaker. — *NBL*

Cobb Quits for Good

January 19, 1929. Cobb announced his retirement at the end of the 1928 season. He announced it again today. Maybe he means to stay retired. There will always be doubt about his intentions until he is too old to throw a ball.

He is a restless fellow; baseball has been his life since he was a youth; he has spent the last 23 years in the big leagues.

It is not easy for a nervous type with an active, imaginative mind to stay out of the fight. Where October palls, April enchants. Under the witchery of spring these permanent retirements often melt and disappear for another twelvemonth.

There have been faster men in baseball than Cobb and stronger men and men with more mechanical ability, but there never was another whose mind coordinated so perfectly with his body. He proved the power of the mind. Because his brain was better developed than the brain of any predecessor or contemporary Cobb established the greatest baseball records in the books. He had a flaming ambition and the intelligence to achieve it. His will was strong enough to carry him over any and all obstacles.

One of the finest tributes to Cobb's genius came from a ball player, a star himself, Everett Scott: "He is the only man in baseball who ever gave me a thrill. In retiring from the game I'll carry one picture with me always, Cobb tearing down the base line. If I live to be 100 I'll never see a more fascinating picture than he made. He was a cyclone, a tornado, a typhoon all rolled into one."

The Arch Egoist

March 31, 1931. Ty Cobb was the arch egoist of baseball. From the start he believed himself better than any ballplayer that ever drew on a pair of spiked shoes. Most of his early conflicts grew out of a sense of extreme superiority as a performer. He believed there was nothing that could be done on the diamond by human hands that he couldn't do just as well if not a great deal better.

Cobb was an egoist with brains. When he talked he said things. Once he told me: "When you go to bat in a tight ball game with runners on base all you've got to remember is that the pitcher's more worried about you than you are about him. Keep that in mind, make him get the ball over, and when he does, smack it. The advantage is all on your side."

Setting the Record Straight

January 27, 1960. Cobb's immediate project is a story of his life.... "Mostly I'm interested in setting the record straight. A lot of things that have been written about me aren't true. I played the game for keeps all right, but I never provoked a fight or deliberately spiked a man.

"Just the other day a fellow wrote how I'd tear into home plate with my spikes high as if I intended to cut the catcher in half. What he didn't mention was that the catcher would put his mask in front of the plate, and the bat, too, if he had time to reach for it. Paul Krichell of the Browns did that once too often."

What happened?

"I slid in high, scissored him between my legs, a bone snapped in his shoulder and the guy never caught another ball game in his life."

[Krichell later became a well-known and successful Yankee scout, best known for landing Gehrig and missing out on Greenberg. — P. W.]

5

Connie Mack and the White Elephants

The $100,000 Infield

November 28, 1939. The other night we sat around chinning with Harry Davis, who played first base for Connie Mack in the days when the Athletics were known as the White Elephants. This was some 30 years ago. Davis finally gave way to a young fellow named Stuffy McInnis, and that was the birth of a famous legend—the $100,000 Infield.

A lot of foul balls have been driven into the screen since that era, and a number of fine infields have been developed, including the Yankees quartet of 1939, which had Dahlgren at first, Gordon on second, Crosetti at short and Rolfe at third. More than one critic thought this was probably the greatest infield of all time, especially from a defensive point of view, so we wondered how Mr. Davis rated it in comparison with the storied $100,000 Infield of his time.

It didn't take long for the red-faced, soft-spoken old-timer to answer. He'd take the old one, position for position, group for group, or what have you.

"Let's start with first base," he suggested. "I'll grant you Dahlgren's a fine fielder, but there isn't anything he can do around the bag that McInnis couldn't. Remember McInnis still has the highest fielding average of all time for one full season, .999. You can't come any closer to perfection than that. What's more, he was a solid .300 hitter, which Dahlgren certainly isn't.

"The Yanks have another brilliant performer in Gordon at second base. All we had was a fellow named Eddie Collins. It will be time enough, if ever, to talk of Gordon in the same breath with Collins when he has been around a dozen years. Look up the records on Collins and you will find he led the second basemen in fielding more times than any other player in the history of the game. Nine times all told, if my memory's right. He led 'em first in 1909 and he was still good enough to lead 'em as late as 1924. And I don't have to tell you what kind of a hitter Collins was. His all-time batting average for 25 years was .333. And don't forget he didn't even get to hit against the lively ball very long. Two or three years at the most."

Black Jack Barry was the shortstop on the infield, and if you want to ride along with Mr. Davis, who seems to strive ear-

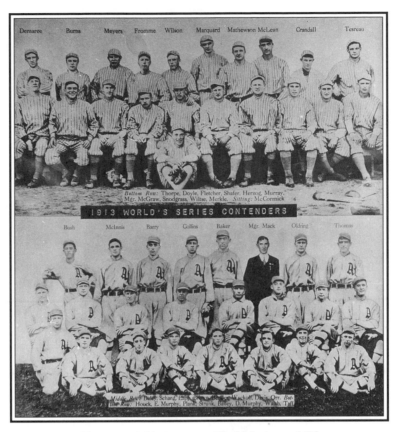

Giants vs. Athletics, 1913 World Series.—*NBL*

nestly for authentic comparisons, he was better than Crosetti.

This brought the discussion around to Home Run Baker at third base, and Mr. Davis said he'd have to take him over Rolfe. He says Baker's fielding skill was underrated, because he wasn't showy, but insists he was a great third baseman who had the added merit of being able to whip the ball across the infield with bulletlike speed.

"We won't even bother going into his hitting," smiled the old-timer. "People laugh nowadays when they hear Baker led the league in home runs with 12, but he was hitting against a cabbage. He'd have hit the lively ball as far and often as any of the moderns."

Including Ruth?

The old-timer paused reflectively and studied the ashes on his cigar. . . . "Well, maybe not Ruth. Say, he was one hell of a ballplayer, wasn't he?"

Rube Waddell

January 28, 1930. One of the greatest games the Rube ever pitched was against Detroit when he was with the Athletics. He had been out all night chasing fire engines—which, next to chasing firewater,

was his most soul-consuming pleasure.

Connie Mack had a way of handling the Rube. He tried to shame him into reform. When he knew the Rube had bro-

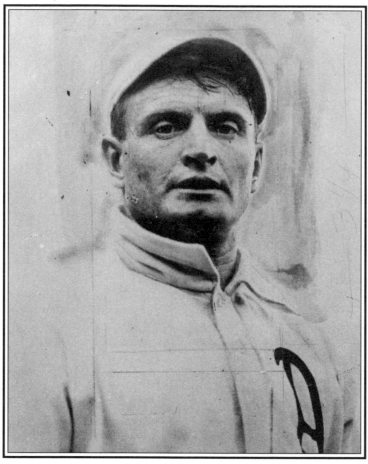

Rube Waddell. — *NBL*

ken training he would send him out to pitch. The Rube was always scouted. Connie knew when he had been on a twister.

"You pitch today, Rube," Connie told him after the all-night siege.

And Rube pitched. This was in the early days of Cobb's career, and Cobb at the time was the lead-off man for the Tigers. First up, he dragged a bunt down the third-base line and, because of his extraordinary speed, beat the throw to first, and it was scored as a base hit. It was the only hit the Tigers got.

"I saved the town for you"

January 28, 1930. The headlines tell of the fight Joe Cantillon is making for his life.

And that reminds me:

The last time I saw Cantillon was in the little town of Hickman, Kentucky, where his ball club, Minneapolis, was doing its spring training. One of the members of the club was a fairly distinguished left-hander—Rube Waddell by name.

Generously they called Rube eccentric. Actually he was a simple-minded giant with few scruples, a great fastball and a tremendous thirst. He had spent the glory of his big-league career at the time Cantillon took him on. He was set in his ways, and his ways ran largely to barroom soirees, indiscriminate fistfights and miscellaneous loves.

During this particular spring there had been unusual snows in the North, and the Mississippi River at this point was swollen to the breaking stage. Another tumultuous day and the clay-banked levee would break. Such a day came. It came late in the night after a warm spring sun had settled over the community and the householders had gone to their beds.

An alarm for volunteer workmen was sounded. Most of these volunteer workmen were Negroes. Under the lashing commands of whites they sloshed out into the angry waters and threw up a temporary barricade of bags filled with sand.

There was one white man among them—and it was the Rube. He had come lickety-split from the village inn when the alarm was sounded, a little bit shaky. This was an assignment he could measure up to. It required a strong back and a mechanical procedure. All through the night the Negroes and the Rube worked throwing up sandbags that were to divert the stream, and thus save a whole township. The dawn came, and the Rube went back to his favorite brass rail.

"You look as if you had been up all night," said Cantillon.

"I have; I saved the town for you," he answered.

The Rube's gallant gesture in the little Kentucky village cost him his life. He contracted a cold, which developed into pneumonia and later into a fatal lung trouble. He succumbed and died in San Antonio, where, I believe, he was buried.

"He had more stuff than any pitcher I ever saw," Connie Mack will tell you. "He had everything but a sense of responsibility."

Which may or may not have been an handicap.

"I was partially responsible for the Rube's not pitching"

August 16, 1932. Mr. Andy Coakley has an interesting background in baseball. He belonged to the era of Waddell, Mathewson and Brown. He pitched in the first official World Series. He discovered Eddie Collins. He was in the Chicago dugout the day Merkle failed to touch second.

Back in the early days of the present century Mr. Coakley was the leading college pitcher of the game. In 1905 he became the ace of Connie Mack's pitching staff. The Athletics got into the World Series that year. They met the Giants and were beaten in five games, each a shutout —a pitching record that has never been equalled. Mathewson alone pitched three shutouts, one of them against Mr. Coakley.

There was great mystery surrounding the failure of Rube Waddell to appear in the Series. The Rube didn't pitch a ball. It was generally believed he had gone away on one of his whoopee whirls.

"The truth is," relates Mr. Coakley, "I was partially responsible for the Rube's not pitching. A few days before the Series was due to open the Rube tried to smash my straw hat. We wrestled. The Rube fell, injured his shoulder and was out until the following year."

The eccentric Rube and the college-bred Mr. Coakley got along very well. The Rube wanted him for his roommate —a high but perilous distinction for a youngster.

"I balked," says Mr. Coakley, "when I

Home Run Baker swings at a pitch. The catcher is Roger Bresnahan. —*NBL*

found the Rube sitting at the foot of the bed one night with two revolvers pointed at his reflection in the mirror and talking about his control."

[Like many other early stars, Waddell worked for years in the minors after his *big-league career was over. His last year in the majors was 1910, when he was 3 and 1 with the Browns. His lifetime ERA of 2.16, however, is the sixth best ever.* —*P.W.]*

Home Run Baker

December 26, 1961. Frank Baker was contemporaneous with the deadball, trick-delivery era and his peak home-run harvest was an even dozen. He was home-run leader three straight seasons with 9, 10, and 12 and shared it with Sam Crawford the fourth season with 8. At a recent old-timers' game here we asked him how many home runs he thought he might have hit under today's conditions. "I'd say 50 any-

way. The year I hit 12, I also hit the right-field fence in Philly 38 times. All of those would have been home runs with the lively ball."

Baker played his last seven seasons with the Yankees. In '20 and '21 he was to see a teammate hit 54 and 59 home runs, respectively. A guy named Ruth, who in Baker's admiring words "Could hit 50 home runs with a [*sic*] old tin can."

This All-Star team played a benefit game against the Cleveland Indians in 1911 on behalf of the widow of pitcher Addie Joss. *Left to right*: standing, Bobby Wallace, Home Run Baker, Joe Wood, Walter Johnson, Hal Chase, Clyde Milan, Russell Ford, Eddie Collins; seated, Germany Schaefer, Tris Speaker, Sam Crawford, Jimmy McAleer, Ty Cobb (in borrowed uniform), Gabby Street, Paddy Livingston.—*NBL*

Ed Plank and the Fidgets

May 7, 1964. If the Martians don't want to flip their lids they'll stay put. Imagine them trying to puzzle out this sports page headline: "Spahn Needs One More Whitewash to Tie Plank."

Be that as it may, a talk with Ole Case obviously was indicated. If there was anybody still around who had a line on Edward Stewart Plank, it would be the amazin' manager of the amazin' Mets.

"Why certainly I knew Mr. Plank. As a matter of fact, I hit against him. Just once. Which was more than enough. Mr. Plank was what you'd call a miserly pitcher. He'd only give you a piece of the ball, and a very small piece, at that.

"Jack Coombs used to talk about the fella a lot when he joined us [Brooklyn Dodgers] in '15. The year before, the Athletics lost the World Series in four straight,

and for some reason Connie Mack gave Coombs, Chief Bender and Plank, three of his good pitchers, their unconditional release. Remembering what Coombs said, and looking back, I'd hafta say Plank was pretty much like Whitey Ford. About the same size, smart and studious, except that he was hawk-faced and looked even more like an Indian than Bender. It may be that he also introduced the fidgets."

The fidgets?

"That's what I said. You see a lot of them now. Pitchers who act like the last thing they want to do is throw the ball. They tie their shoes, take off their cap to see if it's sewed up right, loosen or tighten their belt, pull their ear, smooth wrinkles out of their socks. They drive you nuts. Coombs told me this was one reason Plank could always handle big hitters. By the time he finally let the ball go they were so mad they would swing at anything, and besides, they was usually off stride to begin with."

How about the time you hit against him?

"Well, it pains me to admit the fella could hardly wait for me to get to the plate. One pitch. Pop-up. I was with the Phillies and this was a spring city series with the Athletics which was a popular thing in those days but which you don't see many anymore."

Why Connie Broke Up the '14 A's

March 19, 1932. ST. PETERSBURG, Fla.— The kingly Athletics were playing the lowly Braves. Mr. Connie Mack sat in a box back of home plate, a long, gaunt figure, and hatless. There was no scorecard in his hand. It is unusual to see Mr. Mack without a scorecard. At all the big-league games he has a scorecard in his hands. The big-league games count in the standings. The spring games don't.

Sitting with him was Mrs. Mack, an elderly, bespectacled woman, apparently as interested in the activities of the players as the veteran strategist himself. She seems to know all the players, all the plays and, as the boys say, all the answers.

The Braves are having batting practice. Hank Gowdy is hitting them out to the infield. Rabbit Maranville, for the first time of the year, is at shortstop, picking up sharp hoppers and tossing the ball around. Dick Rudolph is showing a young pitcher a movement to first base to keep the runner close to the bag.

Mr. Mack looks out upon the scene. "They say time flies, but I am not so sure," he says. "This is my 49th spring trip, and yet there is Gowdy. There is Maranville, still a great shortstop, and there is Rudolph. I don't know whether he can still

pitch, but he doesn't seen to have changed much.

Mr. Mack lapsed into a reflective silence. It was easy to guess that his thoughts rolled back to the 1914 World Series with the Braves, when Gowdy, Maranville and Rudolph created the most spectacular upset in the history of baseball, when the Braves beat the Athletics four straight to win the championship.

Mr. Mack began to reminisce. "I wasn't surprised that we were beaten," he said. "In fact, I don't know whether you know it or not, but I quit on my team in August.

"That was the year of the Federal League war. Practically every man on my team had an inviting offer to jump. Half of them wanted to jump, the other half seemed content. This created a bad situation. The morale of the club was completely broken.

"A number of reasons have been advanced why I broke up that club, the most popular of which was that it lacked color. The fact is that I was very proud of that team. I broke it up solely because the boys had shown me that they could not get along together. In short, the team was broken up by the team itself."

6

Walter Johnson and Clark Griffith

Pitching on Strength

May 29, 1913. Every time the old bug bunch goes into executive session the conversation invariably turns to the spicy subject of slabbing. "The question before the committee," remarks the rabid chairman, "concerns the relative merits of Mathewson, Johnson, Plank and Waddell." Right away the bugs go at it. Each has his own greatest pitcher. If it be a gathering of oldsters, it's a pretty safe bet that Old Hoss Radbourn, Tim O'Keefe and Amos Rusie will come in for quite a few of the fancy befrilled sentences. But there is one notable who has been through the old school and is today still an important figure in the game, who figures that Walter Johnson is the king of them all, barring none. He is Clark Griffith. What he says is worth repeating:

"Believe me," said the Washington leader, "I've seen them all come and go, but Johnson is the greatest of the lot. I don't say this merely because he happens to be a member of my club, I mean that from the bottom of my heart. Radbourn, Rusie,

Matty, all of them were wonders, but none was as good as Johnson. Walter has everything. You hear a lot of talk about his speed, as if that were the only thing he possessed. This is a mistake. He has a splendid curveball, change-of-pace and I wouldn't be surprised a mite if someday he cultivated a spitter.

"And again, he uses his head constantly. There are none of them a bit wiser than Johnson, and none of them who takes better care of himself. He hasn't a single habit that would impair his ability or hurt his usefulness. He is big and strong and I'm certain that he will be pitching just as good 15 years from now.

"Is he better than Matty? I say yes. Matty's pitching is not and never has been pitching on strength. He constantly studies the batters to know their weakness and to learn their groove. Once he has a batter measured then the batter is up against it. But for pitching, as pitching is regarded in baseball, Walter Johnson is the superior."

Walter Johnson and Clark Griffith. — *NBL*

When Washington Went Mad

April 29, 1931. It wasn't so many years ago that Johnson, pitching on his first championship team after many seasons of futile endeavor with motley, misfit outfits, dominated one of the most emotional and dramatic moments any World Series ever saw. This was when he came to the box in the eighth inning of the last game against the Giants and proceeded to pitch the Washingtons to victory in extra innings. Johnson had previously lost a brilliant 12-inning game in which he had fanned a dozen Giants, and practically everybody in the park was pulling for him. Due to the man's great personal charm and immense popularity, the Series had lost the aspect of an intercity competition and had for that murky October afternoon become a senti-mental individual adventure.

I recall that Mr. Billy Evans, the umpire, who was sitting in the press box, became so moved that when it was over and Johnson had won he choked up. I saw him take a handkerchief and dab away at the moisture that had settled around his eyes. You can imagine how the boys out in the bleachers must have felt if the drama of the situation was sufficient to make an umpire cry.

That night downtown Washington went mad. Old Walter had won a World Series game and a championship. Not even the Armistice had brought such wild scenes of riotous insanity to historic Pennsylvania Ave.

"I don't call that pitching"

April 26, 1932.   Walter Johnson is in town with his Senators. They are the only Senators known to public life who know what they want to do. They want to win the American League championship.

When we got away from the routine chatter of the race we shifted to the subject of pitching. I could see no reason why the spitball should not be revived.

"Well, I don't agree with that," protested Johnson. "I think a pitcher ought to be a pitcher and not a trickster." It should be mentioned that Johnson never used a freak delivery of any sort. For years he threw only a fastball, and when he didn't throw a fastball he threw a faster ball. Johnson approaches the subject of pitching with the soul of an artist. To his way of thinking no man on the hill should be permitted to have more than a glove and a ball—and, in deference to public sensitiveness, a uniform.

Johnson pointed out that if the spitter were brought back it would lead to the revival of a number of other mechanical aids, including the mud ball, the shiner and the emery ball.

"Do you remember Russ Ford, of the old Yankees?" asked Johnson.

Do I remember him? Will I ever forget the night when General Grant said: "Ford, you and Williams go out and bring that guy Lee back to me, dead or alive." Do I remember him?

"Well, anyway," persisted Johnson, "he was supposed to be a great spitball pitcher. I doubt that he ever threw a spitball in his life. He had a piece of emery paper attached to a rubber string on his forearm. He would bring his hands up to his mouth as if he were spraying the ball with saliva, but instead he would be rubbing it with the emery paper. This roughened the ball just enough to make it sail and dart like a spitter—maybe more so. I mention this because it goes to show what can happen when you let a pitcher monkey with the ball, and I don't call that pitching."

He Was Unbelievably Gawky

December 16, 1926. I went down to Washington the other day for no good reason and decided to motor out to Germantown, Md., to see Walter Johnson. He's got a fine 500-acre farm there.

Walter was out in the meadows looking after his cattle. Word was sent to him that visitors had called. Through the heavy afternoon haze I could see him making his way toward the house. He must have been about half a mile away, but if you ever saw him walk to the box you could never forget that gangling, awkward stride.

For a man who threw the ball with such an easy, rhythmic motion, he was un-believably gawky. He had a slovenly walk, he was slew-footed and his arms dangled at his side like two cuts of flabby fire hose. But when he swung into action he was a blur of physical poetry.

Walter hasn't changed much except for his costume. He wore heavy, mud-caked boots, blue denim overalls that had been patched more than once, a leather windbreaker and a battered felt hat. . . . "Never expected to see you on a farm," he greeted. "You can't get any stories around here, but if you are interested in a nice 200-pound sow—"

The Big Train Moves Out. — *cartoon by Willard Mullin*

We got to chinning about baseball. Walter thought he was through with the game for all time. "I guess this is where I belong," he said, pointing toward the rolling fields. He saw only three games all last season. . . . "I didn't feel as if I could spare the time from the farm. There's a lot of work to be done around here all the time. You get up at five o'clock in the morning and when sundown comes you are pretty tired."

What became of his boy, Walter Jr.? Baseball's most celebrated farmer picked up a pebble and flung it at two turkeys that were fighting in front of the barn. . . . "Walter's a funny kid. I can't get him to live out here with us. Thinks I'm crazy, and says it's like living in a graveyard. But Wal-ter never saw a farm until I bought this place, and farm life is funny. You've got to be bred to it; either that or you got to have a natural liking for the outdoors. Now Eddie, there—"

Johnson pointed to a tall, sandy-haired youngster who was fiddling around with some barbed wire that was soon to be fashioned into a fence for the chicken enclosure. . . . "Eddie there, he likes the farm. Comes down from college every chance he gets and stays right here. I think he's going to be a real good baseball player, too. He's an infielder, plays with the University of Maryland, hits well and can throw. I guess I'll let him take a fling at the game when he finishes school."

Clark Griffith

April 19, 1940. The Yankees open another season up at the Stadium today, playing the Washingtons, and we suppose Clark Griffith will be among those present, nibbling away at a cigar and glaring fiercely out at the athletes from under his snow-crested eyebrows. He would be the old pitcher who came up the hard way to become owner of the Washingtons and on three occasions to see them win the championship of the American League.

We heard Mr. Griffith on the air the other night. He went anecdotal on his millions of unseen listeners. He told about the time he struck out John McGraw on three pitched balls.

We can remember our pappy—or maybe it was our grandpappy—telling us about seeing Mr. Griffith pitch in the old days. And we remember very distinctly nothing was ever said about Mr. Griffith as a strikeout artist. It seems to us he was described as a little runty guy who couldn't break a pane of glass with his fast one. And here he was going to tell about the time he struck out John McGraw on three straight balls!

We were relieved when he explained how this miracle was performed. It seems that Mr. McGraw had a way of stepping into the pitch and working his way to first base as a "hit batsman." Mr. Griffith knew this, so he stooped to a low, reprehensible deceit. He told the umpire McGraw had uttered some foul things about the official, obviously a gullible person.

McGraw stepped into Mr. Griffith's first pitch, this requiring little daring, considering the feathery nature of Mr. Griffith's most violent delivery, and the umpire called it a strike on the ground the

action had been deliberate on the part of the hitter.

"Well, sir," went on Mr. Griffith in a cackling manner, "McGraw stepped into my second pitch and the umpire said 'Two strikes,' and he stepped into my third pitch and the umpire said, 'You're out!'" So that was the way the Bob Feller of his day struck out John McGraw on three pitched balls, the speed of which was so blinding it was practically impossible to distinguish the ball from a full harvest moon.

Just the same, the old gentleman is one of the richly flavored characters of the game, and we hope he will tarry around for a long time. He's a hustling, articulate, cantankerous remnant of a thinning old guard who has seen the game come over from the other side of the tracks and take its place with the freshly scrubbed aristocrats of sport. Moreover, he was influential in the transformation.

There aren't many like Mr. Griffith left. For the most part, the modern club owner or club director is a product of the business office and the counting room, whose knowledge of the practical mechanics is almost wholly academic. Old Griff has that been-there experience. He's leaped down the startled jowls of perfidious umpires, he's trouped through the bushes and the majors—and don't forget he struck out John McGraw on three pitched balls. Who was that Walter Johnson anyway?

[Walter Johnson's lifetime record was 416 and 279 with a 2.17 ERA. Griffith's was 240 and 140 with an ERA of 3.31. Johnson pitched for 21 years, one year more than Griffith.—P. W.]

7

Assorted Men in Blue, Plus One Executive

Umps in a Tough Era

April 10, 1930. The old type of ballplayer, with his peculiar strut and his badger haircut, practically has disappeared. The few survivors of that school stand out in the majors like so many sore thumbs. And with the old-fashioned player has gone the old school of umpires.

The time was when an umpire was chosen largely for his ability to handle himself. Tim Hurst was the arch exponent of that era. But nowadays the presidents of the majors clothe the arbiters with plenty of authority, and back them to the limit. Men whose failure to impress physically would have barred them from umpiring years ago are now among the most expert of their craft.

Hurst, with his Irish wit and his fistic prowess, no doubt was the most colorful of them all. But Bill Byron, the singing umpire, was quite a card, too. Byron now is in the plumbing business somewhere near Chicago.

All through the years of his service in the National League Byron clashed with John McGraw. In those days McGraw coached at third base. Whenever Lord Bill called what McGraw thought was a bad one Mac would start for the umpire, and Byron would begin to sing "Here Comes McGraw" to the music of Mendelssohn's "Wedding March."

Byron had a peculiarly sweet ditty for such times as he heard the displeasure of the fans. He would sing "The populace is angry, the populace is sore" to the tune of an old Irish ballad. "Strike one!" Byron would bawl; and then he'd sing to the man at the plate, "You can't hit with your bat on your shoulder."

Byron slipped to the Coast League and then out of the game. Hurst is dead. Hank O'Day and Bob Emslie have retired. Bob Hart has quit. Barry McCormick has gone to the International League. The new school is alert, bristling with authority, always serious and sticking to business, and won't let a ballplayer stamp on its toes.

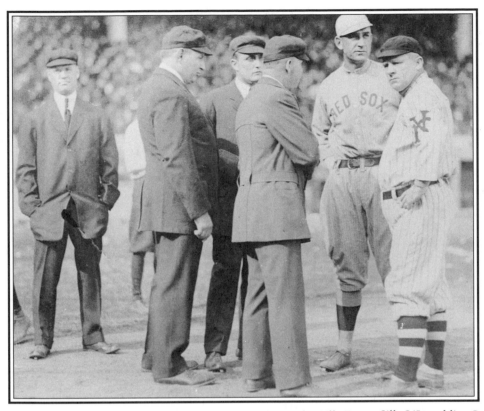

Opening game of the 1912 World Series, Polo Grounds: *Left to right*: Billy Evans, Silk O'Loughlin, Cy Rigler, Bill Klem, Boston Red Sox manager Jake Stahl and New York Giants manager John McGraw. —*NBL*

The Old Arbitrator

October 31, 1918. Umpire Klem has gone to war. Personally we're glad to see the old boy get something soft after what he's been doing all these years.

"I don't read the sports pages"

January 14, 1929. Mr. William Klem is a pretty slick umpire—just about the best in the old league. One of the first to admit this was Mr. Klem himself. For a number of years Mr. Klem has confessed privately and publicly that he is the answer to the league's petition for umpirical perfection. It is Mr. Klem's boast that he has never called a play wrong.

There have been times when the newspaper boys have seen fit to question, in their usual timid, hesitant manner, the man's prodigious infallibility. But this criticism has never worried him.

"I don't read the sports pages," he always says.

I shudder to think that there may be a

number of persons disposed to commend him for his discrimination.

Late last season Mr. Klem gave a decision at the Polo Grounds which provoked a mild furor. The Giants, fighting for the pennant, were playing the Cubs. Hartnett, the visiting catcher, blocked Reese, scoring with a Giants run, between third and home.

In retarding the young man's advance Hartnett did everything but establish a permanent residence on his stomach. From the stands it looked as if Sonnenberg were wrestling Lewis.

After some minutes another Cub player rushed in from Albany, or some other neighboring point, with the ball and the out was recorded under the official auspices of Mr. Klem.

The Giants claimed interference. They are still claiming it. Mr. Klem's attitude is, "Try and get it." He is that type of gentleman, muzzled or unmuzzled.

Advice to mothers: Keep the youngsters away from him.

Pop Bottle Shower

May 18, 1932. A few days ago in Cincinnati Mr. Klem figured in the news as the target for a shower of pop bottles, one of his judicial decisions on a subject of vital interest to the Home Cause having incensed the customers. The Cincinnati customers, like the St. Louis customers, always manifest their more primitive emotions in this manner. It is an old native custom dating back to the nursery or possibly the beer garden days.

Unfortunately (as Mr. McGraw would doubtless view the affair) Mr. Klem was not hit by any of the lethal bottles, so the scientific question, long debated, as to what happens when a thrown missile of weight and substance collides with the skull of an umpire must remain unanswered.

I am surprised that the gentle sport of heaving the 10-ounce bottle hasn't been placed in the Olympic competition under the heading of typical American games. While it is true that the sport is no longer played on a vast scale, this may be said to be due to fanatical restrictions in certain cities where bottles are barred and fluids are served in paper containers. Any old-time bottle heaver will tell you there is practically no mental comfort in heaving a mere paper container at an umpire who has just blown a close play in a pinch. There is no telling how far the boys would have gone in this sport, or how many records they would have set, if the pansy reformers hadn't stepped in.

It probably is true that the country began to come loose at the seams at about the same time the sport of bottle heaving was stripped of its masculine virility. Where is there a Teddy Roosevelt (rah) to lead us out of the chaos of confusion? Or a John L. Sullivan? Or a Pop Anson? Or a Lillian Russell? What does a guy do today at the Stadium or the Polo Grounds or at Ebbets Field when he is moved to display the beast in him? He seizes his scorecard, tears it into little pieces, takes a sissy windup, throws a ball of paper snow at the umps and chirps, "There now, you old dirty-dirty." I ask you, would Lincoln stand for that?

Jack Sheridan

March 21, 1931. There may be some sense in being a judicial officer appointed or elected to preside in courts of law. Particularly in Manhattan. Where it is frequently revealed that such gentlemen by dint of rigorous economy and extreme frugality are able to bank $150,000 out of a handsome $7,000 per annum salary.

But why anybody should crave to be a fight referee, a baseball umpire, a track and field judge or the like is not very clear. At the very best the remuneration is slight, and the social distinction is no better than negligible. There is also the constant possibility of being subjected to public ridicule, personal insult and, in the more extreme cases, physical violence.

Mr. Billy Evans, now general manager of the Cleveland ball club, climbed out of a press box in Youngstown, Ohio, to become a distinguished umpire and noted rules authority. Mr. Evans broke into the game more than 20 years ago. It was pretty tough in those days. President Ban Johnson hadn't yet succeeded in bringing a note

of gentility to the spectacle. Barrooms flourished under the grandstands.

One of Mr. Evans' first appearances was at the White Sox park in Chicago. He umpired behind the bat. His co-worker was Jack Sheridan, a famous official in those days. It was a fairly tight ball game, and along about the fifth inning the customers in the stands began to throw half-pint whiskey bottles at Mr. Sheridan, who had taken up a nonpartisan position of judicial calm in the vicinity of first base.

A shower of glass fell around Mr. Sheridan, but he affected an attitude of complete indifference. This was very mystifying and alarming to the youthful and uninitiated Mr. Evans. In a moment of peace Mr. Evans murmured, "Why don't you move over back of third base where it is safer?" To which considerate suggestion Mr. Sheridan replied: "These fellows never worry me in April. It's in July that I keep my eye on them. By that time they have got their control."

The Nonpareil, Tim Hurst

December 17, 1929. The late Tim Hurst, most colorful of all baseball umpires, was well known to boxing fans 20 years ago. He was an excellent referee and was the third man in the ring at many important fights. Mr. Hurst also officiated at six-day bike races, running races and marathons. He always liked to get these assignments, for the fee was high and he was a gentleman who knew the value of negotiable currency.

But it was not always easy for Mr. Hurst to accept these assignments; in fact, Mr. Ban B. Johnson, president of the

league, had told him he could no longer do the outside work. There was a marathon in New York which Mr. Hurst always refereed. At this particular time he was working a series in Philadelphia. The race was on a Saturday. On Friday afternoon he was still without an alibi that might be acceptable to Mr. Johnson, but he had wired the promoters he would be there.

The game that day was close. When the ninth inning rolled around the Athletics were leading by one run. Kid Elberfeld, of the old Highlanders, was on second, with two out, and the batter hit a single. Elberfeld tore for the plate and easily beat a relayed throw. But all the while Mr. Hurst saw a tie score, an extra-inning game, a missed night train for New York (he would never sleep in Philadelphia) and a missed engagement. He acted quickly.

"You're out," said Mr. Hurst.

Elberfeld rushed at him.

"I said out," repeated Mr. Hurst. "You're out!"

Elberfeld pushed Mr. Hurst, and the gentleman, seeing the catcher's mask on the ground, picked it up, drove it with full force on Elberfeld's head, knocked him unconscious, tossed aside the mask, calmly walked off the field, changed his clothes and caught the train for Broadway.

Mr. Johnson suspended him for a week and fined him $100.

Mr. Hurst collected $500 for refereeing the marathon.

His net profit was $400 and a week's vacation in the big town.

As financiers the Morgans and the Rothschilds were probably more deft, but in his simple, direct way Mr. Hurst was not so bad.

"It's my own ear, isn't it?"

December 11, 1930. "There never was an umpire like old Timothy Hurst," remarked Mr. Billy Evans.

To some of us Johnny-Come-Latelys, Mr. Hurst is little more than a legend. So please stand by for your station announcer. Mr. Evans has the mike:

"Timothy spurned the niceties of office, also its uniform. He never wore shin guards. He never wore a mask, and he never wore a chest protector. All he ever wore for protection was a cap.

"One day while Timothy was umpiring behind the plate he failed to duck a foul tip, and the ball nearly tore his ear off. Timothy went right on calling balls and strikes. He gave no sign that he had been hurt. He prided himself on being a he-man.

"I think the catcher in front of him at the moment was Freddie Payne. Payne turned around and noticed that Timothy was badly hurt and that blood was coursing down one side of his face.

"'Tim, your ear's falling off,' remarked the considerate Payne.

"Tim answered him: 'Well, it's my own ear, isn't it? You mind the pitcher and I'll mind my ear.'

"When he reached the dressing room after the game a doctor had to be called to sew on his ear."

Mr. Evans' comments turned the chin tournament into a Hurst convention. Chief Bender, the great Indian pitcher of another decade, just signed as coach of the Giants, recalled that Timothy never wore spiked shoes. Instead he always appeared on the field in glistening patent leathers.

"One day," relates the Chief, "Timothy bought himself a new pair of patent leathers, and I am told he was very proud of himself when he walked out on the field before his friends in New York. Clark Griffith was managing the New York team at the time. There was a questionable decision which went against the New Yorkers. Griffith and some of his players rushed to the plate. There was a great commotion. Griffith stormed and raved, and he stepped all over Timothy's new shoes.

"Timothy maintained his composure throughout and in due time the game was resumed. An inning or so later Timothy stooped over to dust off the plate. An agonizing spectacle greeted his eyes. Both of his new shoes were cut through where Griffith's spikes had penetrated.

Billy Evans in 1927. — *NBL*

"Timothy raised his hand and called 'Time!' The game stopped. Timothy sauntered over to the water bucket in the New York dugout. Griffith sat next to the water bucket. Timothy took a cupful of water and began drinking. He held the cup in his left hand. Suddenly Timothy's right fist shot out and caught Griffith on the chin. It was a complete knockout.

"Then Timothy strolled back to the plate and yelled, 'Come on, boys, let's go.'"

They say Timothy did not always call them as he saw them. One day he was working behind the plate, and with Jim Delahanty at bat (a great hitter in his day) Timothy called a ball that the catcher insisted was a strike. Ever diplomatic, Timothy agreed to leave the decision to Delahanty.

"Now, me boy, what was it—a ball or a strike?"

Delahanty replied that the pitch was a perfect strike, that it had cut the heart of the plate and that if Hurst weren't blind he would have seen it.

"It did, eh, James me boy? Well, that is very fine to know."

From then on everything the pitcher threw up to Delahanty was a strike—a perfect strike which cut the heart of the plate. At least Timothy said it did.

Apparently it did no good to argue with Timothy. One day Hurst called a strike on George Moriarty, then playing third for the Detroits. He had called the first pitch a ball.

"Why, that strike was worse than the one you called a ball," complained Moriarty.

"What! It was really worse than the other pitch? Then I made a mistake, me boy. The first one should have been a strike, too. Strike TWO." Moriarty turned around to argue the point further and Timothy called him out on the next pitch—a pitch he didn't even see.

Moriarty as Arbiter

June 1 and 16, 1932. Mr. George Moriarty, the umpire, must be slipping. I learn from the news dispatches that it took only four ballplayers to smack him down in Cleveland the other day. There was a time when Mr. Moriarty would have regarded four assailants as nothing more than a preliminary warm-up.

In his day Mr. Moriarty was all man. Nobody wanted any part of him. Once Ty Cobb decided to choose him. This was when they were both playing with the Detroit Tigers. Mr. Moriarty picked up a bat and handed it to Cobb. "A fellow like you needs a bat to even things up fighting an Irishman," said Mr. Moriarty. There was no fight.

You get a faint idea of the kind of bird Mr. Moriarty is, even now, at 47, when you read a detailed account of the Cleveland battle. The four courageous White Sox had flattened Mr. Moriarty; he was on the floor and his hand was broken. Mr. Bill Dinneen, who had helped umpire the game, elbowed his way into the picture.

"You stay out of this, Bill," yelled Mr. Moriarty, "this is *my* fight!"

I am told that he emerged from the Cleveland battle a magnificent figure. Helped to his feet, his hand broken, his mouth bleeding and his head battered, he staggered into a fighting posture and mumbled, "Now who else is there who thinks I'm yellow?"

Using Four Umpires

March 19, 1949. Billy Evans recalls when four umpires were first used in a World Series game. He happened to be one of the four. The three others were Silk O'Loughlin, Bill Klem and Jim Johnstone. The Series was Pittsburgh vs. Detroit, 1909.

"But only two of us were to work any one game at the same time," said Evans. "We were to work in alternate pairs. In the first game O'Loughlin of our league and Johnstone of the National worked. Klem and myself sat in a box, kept score, ate peanuts and had a wonderful time. Next day it was our turn to call 'em while O'Loughlin and Johnstone enjoyed themselves.

"I forget the inning but it was early in the game when the Pirates' Max Carey hit one into the stands. Ground rules were in force. If Carey's hit landed, say a foot to the left, it was a two-bagger. If it landed a foot to the right it was a homer. It made a difference of three runs either way. Neither Klem nor I could tell. Being only 25 at the time, I decided to go out and ask the fans. The rival managers, both squawking, went with me. It's a long story but in the end the fans convinced even the managers that it was a two-bagger, not a homer.

"That night I appeared before Mr. Johnson and argued that if the other two umpires had been on the field instead of sitting in the stands they would have been much more helpful. He agreed and the next day we were all out there. I'll never forget his comment either. . . . 'This is the first time the fans were ever permitted to umpire a World Series game, and I'd say they did a very fine job for you fellows.'"

Plus One Executive

May 22, 1930. Garry Herrmann, the bankrupt Cincinnati baseball magnate, has applied to the Printers' Union for a pension of $8 a week.

At one time he was a tremendous power in baseball. He had plenty of money, a vast energy, nimble mind and never failing spirit of conviviality. He was what is called a good fellow. People used to say he would give you the shirt off his back.

In his rooms at the club and at the hotel when he travelled with the Reds everybody was welcomed. He was baseball's greatest host. There were only two things in which he seemed genuinely interested —the success of the Reds and the comfort of his guests. You don't have to know old Garry to be welcome. Anyone who took the trouble to call on him became a social intimate and a pal. He travelled in a style distinctly peculiar to his personality and philosophy. He was a cross between Bacchus and Falstaff. His baggage consisted largely of assorted hams, sausages and cheese, especially prepared to beguile the gastric juices of the master and his guests. On occasions a consignment of lager went along also.

Old Garry liked his lager. He never could understand why it was a crime for a man to sit down among friends, or people who professed to be friends, and drink a stein of lager on a hot steaming summer night. Or on any other kind of night, for that matter. One day in St. Louis the law walked in on one of his gatherings and confiscated a batch of brew which had been placed in a bathtub to cool. Old Garry was torn between rage and chagrin. "If a fellow can't have a good time in this world he might as well be dead," he said. The hotel manager simulated a pious attitude. "Our bathtubs are to bathe in, not to drink out of, Mr. Herrmann," he admonished. "Nobody can tell me what to use a bathtub for!" Garry stormed.

It is impossible to estimate the amount of money he spent in this way around the National League circuit. Since it was his money and his notion of living, I don't see how anybody can criticize him. Certainly there is something tragically gallant and brave about him in his present predicament. Instead of turning to baseball for help, he turns to an artisans' union of which he is a member in good standing and asks that he be paid the meagre pension to which he is entitled.

A lot of people may say that the climax of his career is that which inevitably follows a loose, slipshod, careless life. I imagine that Mr. F. Scott McBride could go before the congressional committee investigating the problem of prohibition and point to him as a pathetic moral and a convincing object lesson.

I agree, too, that a destitute old age is a terrific penalty to pay for youthful hilarity, and yet I find myself wondering why such things must be. Should the reward of life go only to the frugal, the cloistered and the ambitious? In the league standings of life can't there be a place in the first division, or at least up near the top of the second division, for the whole-souled convivialist whose religion is fellowship? The answer seems to be "no" on all sides.

Possibly the reason I am inclined to a mild sort of emotionalism about the matter is that I realize I will never again sit out a part of the night with Old Garry in a noisy, crowded, smoke-filled room, munching on one of his choice ham sandwiches and drinking from one of his steins. Old Garry came into the game years before it developed into a hard-driving business proposition. It was sport to own a ball club when he bought out John T. Brush back in 1903. By nature and disposition Old Garry qualified as a sportsman.

———

8

Shoeless Joe Jackson and the Black Sox

Editorial Wisdom

December 12, 1951. As a young reporter with dreams I was more interested in the sportswriters who visited the home town in the spring than the players with the big-league clubs. This particular spring was 1911, a Sunday, and the Chicago Cubs, champions of the National League, headed by Frank Chance, "The Peerless Leader," were the visitors—Chance and all the wonderful players I had read about: Three-Fingered Brown (I got to meet him and sure enough a finger was missing from his pitching hand), Joe Tinker, Johnny Evers (The Human Crab), Ed Reulbach, Arthur Hofman, who was known as "Circus Solly" because of his acrobatics in center field, and Johnny Kling, the slender backstop. It was of Kling that Hughey Fullerton had written in a magazine article the previous winter: "He introduced brains to the art of catching."

Hughey himself had introduced a mathematical formula to experting by which he picked winners, had achieved spectacular results and was therefore a man of distinction in press box circles at the time. As he talked to my editor during the game that afternoon, I hung onto his every

word. Presently he made an assertion that shocked me, and no doubt angered me. For at that time nobody could say anything disparaging about Joe Jackson and hope to hold my respect. Not even a writer who had a byline in a great Chicago newspaper, covered the World Series each year, and knew the editor of the *Saturday Evening Post* well enough to call him by his first name.

Mr. Fullerton had written Jackson off as a big-league bust that afternoon, and there was a shattering finality in his words. "A man who can't read or write simply can't expect to meet the requirements of big-league baseball as it is played today," Mr. Fullerton insisted.

Jackson had gone up from our league to join Cleveland the fall before and this was to be the first season as a regular. I don't know when I ever had such a wonderful summer. I had been been taken off space rates and made a member of the staff at a severe reduction in pay, a sacrifice which seemed both proper and trifling in view of the professional recognition and rewards, which included a police badge and free rides on the trolley cars. But that wasn't all: Joe Jackson was tearing the American League apart. Even the great Ty Cobb had to pull back and take his dust. It looked as if he was going to hit .400, a figure Cobb hadn't even threatened.

Well, Jackson went on to hit .408 his first year up, but it wasn't good enough, for Cobb, reacting marvelously to the lash of pressure—one of the things that made him a superlative player—drove himself to .420 to win the batting title for the fifth consecutive time. But Jackson had proved he could play in the big leagues despite his lack of book learning and this was gratifying and reassuring, for if he had made Hughey's gloomy prediction stand up I would have had to devise an entirely new yardstick for big-league success. To my youthful eyes the 6-foot 3-inch, black-haired, 180-pound left-hander, my boyhood idol, could do everything.

Cobb and Shoeless Joe

June 17, 1929. "I have been called a great natural hitter," said Cobb, "but Jackson was a greater one. He hit all kinds of pitching and to all fields. He had a smooth, graceful swing and it was practically impossible to fool him.

"I may be wrong but I always believed he gave little thought to the pitchers he faced or the business of hitting. Most pitchers have certain weaknesses, but I don't believe Jackson ever looked for them in a pitcher; he just seemed to stand up there at the plate and wait for the ball to come, and then he walloped it."

From 1911 to 1915 the battle for the batting championship in the American League was more or less of a two-man race between Cobb and Jackson. They were great friends and great rivals. Cobb remembered with a smile how he was forced to resort to the gentle practice of goat grabbing in order to throw Jackson off his stride and save the batting championship for himself back in 1913.

"Being a couple of crackers," related Cobb, "Jackson and I used to stand behind the cage during batting practice before the game when our clubs met and punch the bag. It was a ritual with us, and we had been doing it for years.

"The time I'm speaking of was in the fall of 1913, in September, and Jackson was giving me an unusually tough tussle. I couldn't pull away from him for more than three or four points, and I began to worry.

"I realized I would have to do something, so when we moved into Cleveland for this particular series I decided to high-hat him. I was pretty vain about that championship and I wasn't going to give it up if I could help it.

"I waited until the batting cage had been wheeled into position and Jackson had walked out there. I knew he was waiting for me to come over and join him. I let him wait a few minutes and then I walked right past him. He stuck out his hand, and I ignored it.

"A little puzzled, he called, 'Hey, Ty, where are you going?' I looked at him coldly, as if he were a total stranger, and walked to our dugout.

"That one of his old Southern buddies should have publicly scorned him got him so angry he lost all interest in the batting fight we were having and—I'm imagining this—spent the next several days determining how to avenge the insult. At any rate, he went through the series without a hit. When the series was over I shook hands with him and he saw through my scheme. This angered him still more, and he went another week without a hit."

[In the 1985 Baseball Research Journal, David Shoebotham shows that this inci-

The Chicago Black Sox, 1919. *Left to right*: front row, Byrd Lynn, Swede Risberg, Nemo Leibold, Dickie Kerr, Hervey McClellan, Lefty Williams, Ed Cicotte; middle, Ray Schalk, Joe Jenkins, Happy Felsch, manager Kid Gleason, Eddie Collins, Shano Collins, Red Faber, Buck Weaver; top row, Joe Jackson, Chick Gandil, Fred McMullin, Grover Lowdermilk, Bill James, Erskine Mayer, Eddie Murphy, John Sullivan, Roy Wilkinson. —*NBL*

dent must have occurred in 1913, and not, as Cobb told Al Stump, in 1911. The above interview, given by Cobb when he was 44 and his memory was probably more reliable, corroborates Shoebotham's version. —P. W.]

He Was Pure Country

February 9, 1946. Shoeless Joe should rank in conversation with any man who ever played baseball. But it's only with the old-timers who saw him and knew him that he is remembered today. One reason (the whole reason, no doubt) is that he was identified with the Black Sox scandal of 1919 and expelled from the sport. Apparently this makes him an untouchable.

Perhaps this is as it should be. But it is only fair to point out that many another man has drifted from the path of strict morality, paid his dues to society and been reaccepted. And Shoeless Joe always claimed he was innocent of the rap. I, for one, certainly wouldn't know. In any case it is interesting to note that he was practically the standout star of the fraudulent Series. Among other things he banged out 12 hits to set a Series record.

I knew Jackson, the ballplayer, well. I saw him play in the Southern League, and later, as a Cleveland reporter, I travelled with him. He was pure country, a wide-eyed, gullible yokel. It would not have surprised me in those days to learn he had made a down payment on the Brooklyn Bridge.

In keeping with his eminence he demanded and got a drawing room for road trips. He was a drinker but not a heavy one. He carried his own tonic: triple-distilled corn. And on occasions he carried a parrot, a multicolored pest whose vocabulary was limited to screeching "You're out!"

"That kid's got more brains than the old man," Jackson would beam in the privacy of the drawing room as he poured crystal-clear corn for his few selected guests. This was his painfully brave way of laughing at his own ignorance; he couldn't read or write, and, down deep, this saddened and humiliated him.

But taking him by and large, Jackson was as nice a fellow as I ever knew in sports, and the disclosure that he had sold out to the Rothstein-Attell combination came to me as a small personal tragedy. I didn't believe it then, and there are times, even now, I don't like to believe it.

Off the Record with Abe Attell

April 10, 1934. We were sitting in a café drawing moist circles on the bare tabletop with the bottom of our glasses.

"The real story of the framed World Series would make interesting telling," said the little middle-aged man, "but I wouldn't tell it now even off the record. It's too long in the past, and, besides, I am doing all right for myself."

The little middle-aged man had a lot to do with framing that 1919 World Series in which the Chicago White Sox sold out to the gamblers and, in accordance with their contract, clumsied enough games to lose to the Cincinnati Reds.

"Still, it's funny some of the stuff you hear and read about what happened and what was to happen, about who did this and who did that," smiled the little middle-aged man. "Yes, it certainly is."

The waiter brought another round of legal tonic.

"I suppose you read Ban Johnson's account of the frame?"

If I had, it had escaped my memory, though, of course, I recalled that Johnson had led the fight which brought the matter into court.

"Well, among other things," continued the little middle-aged man, "Johnson wrote the gamblers had certain unanticipated difficulties in getting the fix money up early enough, and, as a consequence, the first game of the Series was played on the level. The fact is that was the one game above all others we just had to have in the bag."

A couple of gentlemen moved up to the table to say hello to the little middle-aged man, and for the next several minutes the talk turned to other sporting subjects. Presently they moved on.

"As I was saying, that game was vital to the success of our business transaction. There is always more money bet on the first game of a World Series than on any other game. I don't know why that is, but it is a fact, just the same. Johnson was partly right about our having difficulty in getting the money up. We got it up in plenty of time to convince the White Sox players we were dealing with that they had no fear of a double cross, but we didn't have it up in time to get the final word around the country to all our agents."

The little middle-aged man paused to apply a light to a cigar that was grotesquely large. "This whole thing is really a

Ray Schalk, as White Sox manager in 1927.—*NBL*

hell of a story, Williams. I wish you weren't a newspaperman. I feel like talking tonight." And then he went on talking.

"So what did we do? We sensed far enough in advance that we might have difficulties, so we settled on a signal that in no way involved us personally in the use of the telephone or the telegraph wire. It was a signal that all our agents would recognize as they sat in the betting rooms around the country listening to the play by play.

"As you know, Eddie Cicotte was the White Sox pitcher in the first game. And since he was the team's star pitcher, the odds naturally were heavy on the American Leaguers, generally conceded to be much the stronger team, anyway. That was another reason—those heavy odds—that

it was important we have the first game won before it started. We recognized, of course, that Cicotte was our key man in this game, so we took very good care of him before he went out on the field. We gave him $10,000. He had insisted all along he must win one game in the Series to avoid suspicion. That was all right with us, but we wanted to be positive he didn't win this first game. We gave the other six players $5,000 apiece—"

"The other six players?" I interrupted. "You mean the other seven, don't you? There were eight all told."

"No, I mean the other six. One of those players they barred from baseball for life didn't have any more to do with throwing that series than Greta Garbo. One of these days I'll tell you about that. Anyway, we had to have a signal to start action from coast to coast. Know what it was?

"Well, it was this. We got hold of Cicotte and told him it was absolutely necessary that he either pass the first batter or hit the first batter. The instant that came over the wire our agents would go into action. Look up your records and see what happened."

(The records show that Rath, the Reds' second baseman, was the first batter against Cicotte. The first ball was off the line but was called a strike. The next pitch hit Rath in the back, and he went to first.)

The little middle-aged man sent a plume of blue-gray smoke spiraling toward the ceiling and laughed.

"Can you imagine all those sharp-shooters sitting around with a lot of dough in their kick itching to get it down on a sure thing and waiting for that flash, wondering whether it will be a pass, a hit bats-man or some other turn that could do them no good. Boy, that must have been funny!"

Johnson accused Arnold Rothstein of financing the swindle. The gambler always denied he had anything to do with it. Some of his closest associates concurred. Who, then, was the master man?

"Rothstein, of course," said the little middle-aged man. "Wouldn't he have been a sucker to admit it? That would have meant an indictment and a prison sentence. It cost him in the end $125,000—not the even hundred grand that is always mentioned."

"Of this amount $110,000 went to the players—or was supposed to, anyway. I heard later Chick Gandil, the White Sox first baseman, double-crossed his team-mates and kept most of it. The other $15,000 went to some gentleman who was familiar enough with the operation of the District Attorney's office in Chicago to lift and destroy certain Grand Jury records which implicated Rothstein."

The little middle-aged man got up to go. "The whole thing was pretty dirty, and I'm sorry now I had anything to do with it. I'm particularly sorry because they kicked Buck Weaver out of the game. I even went to Landis and made a personal plea for him. The kid didn't get a dime out of it, and he didn't know what was going on, either."

Weaver at the time was the star third baseman of the American League, just coming into the greatness of a career that promised to establish him as one of the all-time standouts of baseball. The last I heard of him he was a day laborer in Chicago.

[I met Abe Attell in Shor's one night. I was about 18. I didn't know him as a great fighter at all—I may not have even known he was a fighter. Before I was introduced my father made me promise to say nothing whatsoever about 1919, and I remember worrying about making a slip. Evidently this was a subject only Attell could bring up.—P. W.]

"Quit trying to alibi"

July 10, 1943.   Eddie Collins was captain and second baseman of the Sox. He was hard to convince, but looking back he says he should have recognized the tip-off in the very first game.

"I was on first base. I gave Weaver the hit-and-run sign. He ignored it and I was out a yard at second. Coming back to the bench I said to him, 'You took that sign and did nothing about it. Were you asleep?' Weaver snapped back: 'Quit trying to alibi and play ball.'"

Eddie Collins and Kid Gleason.—*NBL*

More Than Their Suspicions

July 12, 1943. The Black Sox still were throwing games in 1920. Collins recalls one they threw for the Boston gamblers late in the season. In a critical spot Kerr fielded a bunt to Weaver at third on a force play. Weaver put on an ornate juggling act and lost the runner. The inning over, Kerr came back to the bench and screamed: "If you fellows are throwing this one let me in on it." That same day Schalk beat up Risberg in the dugout. By this time the honest players had more than their suspicions. They had their convictions. Unhappily they had no proof. "It was really a great team," Collins says. "It even had a tough time losing on purpose."

"He'll tell the world"

March 27, 1951. Perhaps the finest tribute ever paid to Eddie Collins, dead at 63, came from an evil ballplayer, a crook who happened to be a teammate. It was tribute to his stanch incorruptibility.

Over the years, piece by piece, I believe I have heard most of the details of the infamous World Series fix of 1919. Chick Gandil, the first baseman, was the contact man. It was his job to deliver players who would go along. Collins was captain and key man of the White Sox and as such loomed importantly in the conspirators' plans. There was doubt that the plot could succeed without him. "That's one guy we can't get," Gandil told the gamblers' agent.

"And if he ever gets wise we are sunk. He'll tell the world."

You read that Collins was reluctant to discuss the sellout or any of the crooks involved. I discussed the matter with him several times. He seemed to have no sympathy for any of them, not even Jackson who was practically an illiterate, or young Buck Weaver who had been caught up in the polluted swirl of bad company, nor did he have any patience with the explanation that a penurious owner had shabbily underpaid hired hands.

"They were old enough to know the difference between right and wrong," he would say with cold level finality.

9

Ray Chapman, Tris Speaker and Co.

It Bounded Clear Over Wally Pipp's Head

August 14, 1941. There is an unwritten law in the press box that no piece having to do with the beanball shall be written without reference to the death of Ray Chapman. A ball thrown by Carl Mays of the Yankees hit him in the head at the Polo Grounds and some hours later he was dead.

Chapman was a crowder and as such he courted danger every time he went to bat. Mays wasn't the only one who threw in such a way as to make him back off. The difference in Mays' case was that he made a practice of throwing at the hitters, whether they were crowders or not.

There have been several versions of the Chapman affair. A popular one is that the little Cleveland gamester, still dazed but knowing he was entitled to his base, went all the way to second before he collapsed. What actually happened was this: the ball hit Chapman with such force it bounded clear over Wally Pipp's head at first base. Pipp fielded the ball and threw to Mays who covered. Meanwhile, Chapman spun around twice and fell into the arms of Schang, the Yankee catcher, and some minutes later was carried off the field on a stretcher. The crowd gave him a sympathetic cheer and he waved feebly back from the stretcher. That was his exit from baseball.

"Mays the Murderer"

January 20, 1945. Jack McAllister, scout for the Boston Braves, recalled the circumstances under which the Cleveland shortstop was killed by Carl Mays. McAllister was assisting Tris Speaker in managing the Clevelands in those days.

"A finer fellow never played the game," said McAllister. "Naturally, I was with the club in New York when he was killed. The instant the ball struck his head I had the

Carl Mays. —*NBL*

awful conviction he would be dead within seconds. As it turned out he lived until four o'clock the next morning, never regaining consciousness.

"Mays was lucky he was not torn apart by our players, particularly Jack Graney and Steve O'Neill. When the ball struck Chapman it made an explosive sound. Mays protested to Tommy Connelly, umpire at the plate, that the ball had struck the wrist of Chapman's bat and that he was feigning distress. One look at Chapman

was enough to prove to anyone he wasn't. I think it was Pipp who finally made Mays pipe down and led him away, while I did what I could to hold Graney and O'Neill, Chapman's greatest pals, in check.

"We refused to play the next day, though a game was scheduled and advertised. The day following we did play, and, with Lunte replacing Chapman at short, we lost a close one to the Yankees. Then we moved on to Washington, and when we went out to the park to dress, there on the lockers, scribbled in foot-high chalk lettering, were these words: Mays the Murderer. Before the game started Clark Griffith heard about the sign and had it erased. But the next day there it was again. I didn't learn until months later who was the author. It was Griff's clubhouse boy."

Indians 4, Yankees 3

February 8, 1964. Chapman's body was shipped back to Cleveland the following day. Thousands, literally, were turned away from the funeral services held in downtown St. John's Cathedral, services which I attended both as a saddened friend and reporter.

Manager Tris Speaker was still too emotionally distressed to be present. All the other players, though, were on hand. In such an atmosphere reportorial probings no doubt were irreverent, but I had a deadline to meet. The players' verdict was unanimous: Mays had deliberately fired at Chapman's head.

If Mays was haunted by brooding memories the record book doesn't show it. In his very next start, he low-hit the Tigers in a 10-0 shutout. His season's log was 26-11. Nine years later he retired, having won 204, lost 127. One of the losses, ironically, had come on the day his submarine ball shattered Chapman's skull. Final score: Indians 4, Yankees 3.

The Gray Eagle's Version

September 23, 1941. From time to time we have occasion to refer to the game in which Ray Chapman of the Cleveland Indians was killed by a pitched ball thrown by Carl Mays of the Yankees. Any such reference never fails to bring a number of letters from the customers, describing just how the accident happened.

Since there seemed to be so much interest in what actually happened we decided to find out for sure. It was our thought that the one man who would know above all others was Tris Speaker. He was managing the Indians at the time and Chapman was his closest friend in baseball. So we wrote to the old Gray Eagle and here is his reply:

"Dear Joe: Here's what happened. The ball hit Chappie, bounded back about halfway to the pitcher's box and a little to the first-base side. Mays rushed over, fielded the ball and threw to Pipp at first base, claiming the ball had been hit. I followed Chappie in the batting order and naturally was not very far from the plate at the time he was struck. I immediately made a rush to catch him, since he started to fall almost instantly, but before I could get there he had dropped to the ground. He wasn't unconscious at the moment. In fact, he made an effort to get up and to charge at Mays but it appeared his body was paralyzed. We fetched a stretcher, carried him out of the park, put him in an ambulance which had been called, took him to a hospital and he died at 4:50 the following morning. I trust this will straighten you and the fans out as to just what happened that awful day."

Mr. Speaker had some other remarks which may be of interest. . . . "Chappie wasn't hit very often. As you will recall, he was very active at the plate and most always was able to get out of the way of pitches thrown close to his head. But on this occasion he seemed to be in a strange daze. He just stood still at the plate as if in a trance and made no effort to pull away from the pitch."

[Mays was so flustered by Chapman's death that the following year he led the league with 29 wins and a .750 percentage. He pitched for a total of nine years after 1920, winding up a 15-year career with 208 wins, 126 losses and a 2.92 ERA.—P. W.]

Speaker's Injured Ankle

February 11, 1939. The Clevelands trained at Dallas in 1922. Thirty miles away, at Ft. Worth, there was a rodeo in progress. Tris Speaker, a product of the wide open spaces and an excellent horseman, slipped away and entered the competition with the professional ropers and bull-doggers. He was pretty gifted in this sort of stuff. He had been known to rope and tie a steer in close to record time.

On this occasion Speaker had tough luck. He slipped and fell from the saddle and twisted his ankle badly. Roping steers was extremely foolhardy business for the manager and star of a big-league ball club in training. Speaker felt mighty sheepish about it and went to painful lengths to conceal the true circumstances of his injury.

There was a spring game with the Detroits the next afternoon. Masking his injury as best he could, Speaker took up his position in center field. The game wasn't two minutes old before he came limping back to the bench demanding in pictur-

esque phrases the immediate presence of the groundskeeper.

"What kind of a park is this?" he exploded. "There's a hole out there as deep as a well and I just stepped in it!" We still blush in shame when we recall how we panned the Dallas park and the Dallas groundskeeper for the mishap that had befallen our sterling leader. We were younger in those days and we believed everything the manager told us.

As a matter of fact, we didn't learn the true story until Speaker laughingly told us just before the All-Star game several years ago at Cleveland. He admitted, too, he never had thoroughly recovered from the injury and that it handicapped him the rest of his playing days. We always regretted not asking him at the time who dug the hole. It was anything but a myth. We went out to see for ourselves after the game that afternoon. You could have hidden Judge Crater in it.

"There's only one thing wrong with you, Lutzke"

January 21, 1941. Cleveland used to have an infielder, a Dutchman named Lutzke. He could palm the state of Texas in his hands, but he was always on short rations in the matter of base hits. Once in a while he'd get hold of a ball and drive it to hell and gone and this kept the management's

hopes alive.

Mr. Lutzke helped manfully in this connection. There was always something the matter with him, and he'd make the discovery along about August and start planning for treatments. First, it was his appendix. He'd have an operation after the

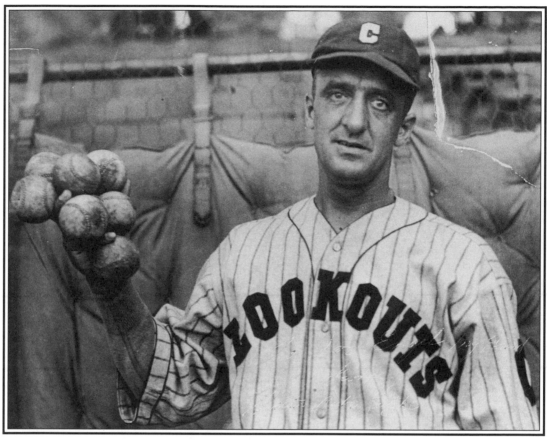

Walter (Rube) Lutzke demonstrating his grasp as a member of the Chattanooga Lookouts.—*NBL*

season and that would make him a hitter. Next, it was his teeth. He'd have them taken out and that surely would be the answer. Finally, it was his eyes. Funny he hadn't thought of that before. He'd been seeing too many movies and doing too much reading. That's what had weakened his eyes and made it hard to follow the twists and turns of those curveballs. Rogers Hornsby had the right idea. You couldn't drag him into a movie theater and he wouldn't even read the box scores, and look what a great hitter he was. So Mr. Lutzke had his eyes examined and got himself some glasses and abandoned all his simple pleasures, and the next season, his

last with Cleveland, he hit worse than ever.

This took all the bounce out of the ebullient Mr. Lutzke. He went to Tris Speaker, the manager, and took down his hair. "I've tried everything," said Mr. Lutzke in mournful Jack Pearl gutterals. "I've had my appendix out. I've got rid of my bad teeth, I won't even read a menu without glasses and still I can't hit. What's wrong with me?"

"There's only one thing wrong with you, Lutzke," replied Speaker. "You can't hit."

[In five seasons Lutzke averaged a little less than one hit in four trips.—P. W.]

Joe Wood
(Red Sox)

Jeff Tesreau
(Giants)

Pitchers before 1st game 1912 World's Series

NBL

Smoky Joe Wood

March 7, 1922. There will be nobody out there in right field for the Indians next summer but Joe Wood. And every indication points to the confident presumption that the Parkers Glen Adonis will be quite sufficient. Wood was on the ground here [Dallas] early this spring for two reasons: One was to lend a subtle hand in the coaching of some of the young hurling recruits, and the other was to get in as much batting and fielding practice as possible before the race began. If he has his way in the games to come he will be in there every inning, and when the season gets under way the reformed pitcher will be ready to strut his stuff before the best of them.

Col. Speaker does not regard Wood as an experiment in right field. He is reasonably fast, a sure fielder and a hard hitter. His batting skill against left-handed pitching has been thoroughly established. Perhaps the only reason any doubt at all exists as to his ability to hit right-handed pitching equally as well is because he hasn't been given the opportunity.

As a matter of fact it should be stated that Wood did not start as a pitcher but as a shortstop, and as such was listed as a phenom. This was when he played with the Hutchinson, Kansas, club in the old Western League.

You may recall how he happened to take up pitching. An epidemic of sore arms on the Hutchinson outfit caused Jay Andrews, the manager, to send Wood to the box. Independence, Kan., was the opposing team on that day. Wood scored a shutout, letting the enemy down with two hits, and fanned eighteen. From then on he was a pitcher.

There should be nothing astonishing connected with the transformation of a player of the Wood type from pitcher to outfielder. And there is not. Being a natural-born ballplayer, this simply comes natural with him. Even when he was the pitching sensation of the Red Sox, Wood always practiced in the outfield. That's how he acquired the consummate grace and skill he imparts to the assignment. No player in either league fields a ball with greater ease, finish and poise than Wood.

Only one concern presents itself in the case of Wood as the regular outfielder, and that is: will he be fortunate enough to stand up under the wear and tear of a steady 154-game grind? Wood is in the veteran class, and the old boys are a bit more brittle and tender than the youngsters.

What the Boys Call an Epic

May 25, 1932. Perhaps some of the newcomers have forgotten a pitcher named Joe Wood. Well, he's down at New Haven coaching the Yale baseball team. Of recent years he has turned out some pretty fair ballplayers, among them Bruce Caldwell.

As a member of the Boston Red Sox, when the Red Sox were a real team, Wood was one of the greatest pitchers of the game. It is still a question whether Walter Johnson had any more speed than Wood. I mean on certain days.

I think one of Wood's finest performances was in the 1912 series against the Giants. He went into the ninth inning leading, 4 to 3. The Giants put on the pressure and pretty soon there were men on second and third with only one man out. Obviously a base hit meant two runs and the game for the Giants.

The next hitter was Fletcher, particularly dangerous in a pinch. Wood struck him out. McGraw then sent up Otis Crandall, one of the best pinch hitters baseball has ever known, a man with little imagination and consequently no nerves. Wood, then a youngster, with sleek black hair and a strong arm, looked at him. So this was the man who could hit anything! There were a couple of foul tips. In between there were three curveballs. Crandall missed all of them.

Remember, it was the ninth inning, a World Series game, a young pitcher pitching, men on second and third and the present-day Yale coach fanned the next two batters. When anybody asks you about guys coming through in a pinch, remind them of Joe Wood and his pitching in the 1912 Series. It comes close to being what the boys call an epic.

[Wood's record in the regular season in 1912 was a passable 34 and 5.—P. W.]

10
Judge Landis

Essentially a Dramatist

April 17, 1929.   There are men who will talk a leg off you. Judge Kenesaw Mountain Landis isn't like that. But if you sit around in his room long enough he is likely to knock a leg off you. It takes courage to interview the Judge. He drives his points home with a swishing hand and a roughhouse windup.

Whack! That is the Judge telling you tricky baseball deals must end.

Whack! That is the Judge telling you the chain-store system of baseball ownership is an evil.

Whack! That is the Judge telling you that his cold is worse, that the weather is bad, that you can't get good tarpon steaks in the East; in short, that is the Judge telling you 'most anything.

I am not much of a boxer. I suppose you would call me a Dempsey type. I am all offense. I either knock 'em squirming or they scrape me off the canvas. But the Judge is an old man. He is 63. He has white hair.

I have no doubt that if I cared to use what I call my Iron Mike on him baseball would have to get a new czar. The blood of proud Southern ancestors races through my veins; I am one of the old school. The old Bourbon school, to be specific. I venerate my elders. Just the same it is a good thing that the Judge got tired. I think if he had taken another whack at me I would have let go.

I'm not so sure yet that he wasn't getting even with me for some of the things I had written about his coiffure. At least two of the whacks with which he whacked me carried entirely too much violence to be meaningless. And, besides, I'm not so dense that a man has to knock me clear out of my chair to stress a point. The next time I interview the Judge I shall borrow Ray Schalk's shin guards, chest protector and mask. And then I'll use the phone.

The Judge is essentially a dramatist. He is intense, vibrant and emotional. He puts on a good show for you, and it's a pretty sincere show, too. He was nourished in the tradition that oratory and gestures are essential. He likes to talk about the old days in Washington, when he was in the State Department during the Cleveland

Left to right: American League President William Harridge, Commissioner Kenesaw M. Landis, Clark Griffith. —*NBL*

administration—the days of the panic when free silver was an issue and the financial stability of the nation trembled in the balance. Cleveland is probably his idol, as well as his ideal. He talks of him almost with reverence—a man with a "stubborn, unyielding integrity."

I suspect the Judge regrets he didn't go higher in politics. Baseball was never his first love.

11

George Sisler

"It's my eye, and my affair"

May 26, 1923. Both the heavens and the Browns' management were disagreeable yesterday and when a few scattered drops of rain [fell] 30 minutes before game time for the second skirmish of the series, the fray was called off. At three o'clock the rain had stopped, and a game could easily have been played, but it would have been an unprofitable investment. No more than 300 fans were in the stands. On Thursday, the opening day of the series, the paid admission was approximately 2,400 fans. True, it was threatening then just as it was yesterday, yet even if the weather had been perfect the attendance would hardly have measured up to normal. The American League fans here are holding back for some reason or other. The fact that Sisler isn't in the game is one reason. So much mystery has been made of the star first baseman's ailment that the fans have grown suspicious.

Actually in some quarters the belief exists that Sisler is not only through for all time, but that the Browns' management realizes it and is withholding the information in order to keep the interest of the fans buoyed up. The reasoning in the case is that

if it were definitely known that Sisler can never play again the fans immediately would lose all interest in the local flag race, recognizing that without the great star all hope would be lost.

We happen to know that this is unfair to the Browns' management and untrue as well, but that doesn't keep a certain element of fans from thinking otherwise. We happen to know that Sisler was called into the president's office in the early days of his trouble, and was asked to give a written statement to the papers detailing the nature of his difficulty in order to put a stop to a flow of rumors that already were swelling up on all sides.

Sisler refused emphatically. "It's my eye and my affair," answered Sisler. "When I get well I will be ready to play again. If I fail to get well, of course I will never play again."

It would have been much better, of course, if Sisler had not permitted his trouble to be cloaked in so much secrecy. A clear, frank, understandable explanation of the malady would have silenced the rumor-

George Sisler and a still slim Babe Ruth, at Sportman's Park, St. Louis. —*NBL*

mongers in the very beginning, and would have made matters more endurable for everybody concerned.

All sorts of rumors still fill the air about Sisler here. The more popular one describes a morning trip to the ballpark by the disabled star in the company of the groundskeeper. Sisler is supposed to have gone to his old position at first base. The groundskeeper took up a position at another part of the field, so the legend runneth, and began throwing balls to Sisler. At the end of 15 minutes Sisler is reported to have broken down and sobbed, having failed to stop any of the numerous balls thrown to him.

The narrative interested us and we carried it to Bob Quinn, business manager of the Browns.

"It's a damn lie," shrieked Quinn. "Sisler has not had a glove on all spring and he has not been on the diamond, and who in the hell ever concocted that fairy tale anyway."

This may strike our more timid readers as being horribly profane, but they should have heard what Bob Quinn actually said.

Sisler Played It Big League

March 6, 1956. One of the hardier perennials of spring-camp journalism concerns itself with the dearth of big-league first basemen. There aren't enough around to start a game of jacks. Morbidly, the question is insistently asked: Are first basemen a doomed race?

It's true that more than half the clubs have either a problem or an absurdity at first base, but to say a dearth exists is to imply there once was an abundance, and that would not be correct.

Practically from the beginning of organized baseball we have had fewer genuine big leaguers at first base than at any other position. For example, once the All Time All-Star selector gets past Hal Chase and George Sisler he's through. That's not true of any other position.

Sisler's views on the subject were solicited. He's down here with the Pittsburgh Pirates; in fact, he's their Secretary of Agriculture, or farm director. He agrees that much of the current mediocrity is attributable to baseball's laissez-faire attitude toward the position.

"I'm not of the school that believes anybody can play first base," the Hall of Famer said. "Actually, there is nothing funnier, or more pathetic, than watching a man try to play it who can't."

Sisler explained why managers don't hesitate to play an ill-equipped man at first, provided he can hit, and also why, in many cases, the man makes an acceptable appearance.

"If a fellow can't move in the outfield, or the infield," he said, "it's noticeable, but put him on first base and it isn't. Mistakes are not easily seen there, though, of course, they are just as damaging as mistakes made in any other position.

"Most present-day first basemen know nothing about shifting their feet on thrown balls, and few are capable of making the throw to second (on the first-to-second-to-first double play) properly."

Sisler names Gil Hodges of the Brooks as the best first baseman in the game today, an excellent example of a young player who recognized the possibilities of the position and obviously worked hard to exploit them.

"I've always maintained first base is what you make it," he added. "You can either play it big league, or use it to get by."

Sisler played it big league. With due deference to the judgment of others who make Chase their choice, I nevertheless wonder how anyone could possibly have surpassed Sisler.

I saw him all during his peak years, when he hit .353, .341, .352, .407, .371, and .420 successively. Only Ty Cobb ranked with him as a hitter then, nobody with a glove at first base. He stood 5 feet 10½, weighed only 170, but, of course, he was lucky . . . nobody told him first base was easy.

[Sisler's peak was the 10-year period from 1916 through 1925. It's worth noting that he hit .305 and .345 in the two years immediately after the illness that almost made him blind. — P. W.]

12

Rogers Hornsby

The Rajah

March 3, 1925. Mr. Rogers Hornsby has signed a three-year contract to remain in St. Louis. Mr. Hornsby is the greatest right-handed hitter in baseball.

If consistency is a jewel, then Mr. Hornsby is a whole rope of pearls. He has led the National League hitters for so many years that the name of the man he suc-ceeded is lost to the memory of the oldest inhabitant.

Mr. Hornsby has no weakness at the plate unless it is for fresh Mobile shrimps. His record for shrimp-eating from a sitting position, form and distance considered, is 4,523.

"Pick out something funny"

August 4, 1932. In the day's news— Hornsby, released as manager of the Cubs.

It seems to have been the fate of Hornsby to play a dark, sinister role on the big-league stage, a cross between a character in Ibsen and one in Conan Doyle. For years his steps have been dogged by mystery and mutiny.

He has been the manager nobody knows. He brought St. Louis its first pennant in more than 30 years and was fired. He joined the Giants, long interested in his acquisition, lasted one season and was summarily dismissed. From the Giants he went to Boston and replaced his manager in mid-season. Moving on to Chicago, he had a similar experience; a hired hand at the start, he ultimately took over the club.

No other man in baseball has ever had such a turbulent career. No other man has ever been the pivotal figure in so many un-explained revolts. No other man has ever been such a consistent success and yet the man cannot hold a job. Eagerly club owners reach for him, enthusiastically they drop him.

What is the answer?

"The trouble with Hornsby," a club owner told me yesterday, "is that he refuses

At the 1929 World Series, Shibe Park, Philadelphia: Rogers Hornsby and Hack Wilson, Chicago Cubs, and Al Simmons and Jimmy Foxx, Athletics.—*NBL*

to admit that the man who pays his salary is entitled to any voice in the conduct of the business he controls. I think Hornsby would be a success if he had his own club. Then he could dominate both the diamond and the front office."

This seems to be the real indictment against the man. I'm not sure that it is a serious one. There are some club owners who probably would make greater progress if they turned over their interests to the manager—or the bat boy.

Hornsby's credo is: "Take care of your affairs and I will take care of mine." He is impatient of advice, intolerant of suggestions, a lone wolf in thought and action. His intense passion for the game developed in him a sense of infallibility; he was so close to the mechanics of the game that he felt every move he made was instinctively right. It was probably this more than anything else that provoked his sudden dis-

missal from the Cubs, since it develops that Hornsby and the club president were at odds over the relative abilities of some of the players who were in the lineup and some who were not. It is easy to picture the outspoken Hornsby saying: "I'm running this team. Stay out of it."

The Cubs' action must have been as big a shock to Hornsby as it was to the public. I had talked with him at noon and he had no inkling of the impending stroke. He was going to start Warneke in the last game of the Brooklyn series. "We'll win with the kid today and then watch us go. This race isn't over by any means. The Pirates haven't got the class to stay up there much longer."

Hornsby got ready to catch a subway for Ebbets Field. "Give me a ring Saturday night and we'll go to a show." Then as an afterthought: "Pick out something funny.

I want to forget these ball games we've been booting away.'' The blowoff must have come a few hours later. The next day Hornsby, deposed as manager and released as player, was heading back for his Missouri farm.

[Hornsby signed on to manage the Browns in mid-season, 1933, and stayed in St. Louis until halfway through 1937. He never finished higher than sixth. He started managing them again in 1952, but took over the Reds halfway through that season; and he stayed in Cincinnati, where he never did better than sixth, through 1953. In 1962, the summer before he died, he coached for the Mets and ended up in the cellar. You've got to figure he felt a certain amount of nostalgia for the '20s, when he led the league in hitting seven out of nine years, topped .400 twice and came within less than 20 percentage points three more times.—P. W.]

"It's all I've got to sell"

June 22, 1931. It occurred to me that I had written about all there is to be written about Hornsby, with this possible exception:

Of all the stars baseball has produced the young Texan has attracted more traducers than anyone else I ever heard of. For every worshipper he has a defamer. His worshippers will go from here to Little America to sing his virtues; his defamers will go equally as far and manifest just as much heat.

This is unusual in baseball, where the headliners generally are universally and boisterously acclaimed. With the public the Ruths, the Cochranes and the Johnsons are clear-cut, blue-white, perfect idols. There is never any doubt as to their popular status. Even in failure they are sure of a sympathetic support. Not so with Hornsby.

Of course, there is nothing strange about a man having enemies. Only in sports is the emotional situation different, and this is due, I suppose, to the indiscriminate eagerness of the sports follower to make gods of anyone that can hit a ball or land a knockout.

Now consider Hornsby. Baseball is his business. It has made him a wealthy man. I know of nobody who is more intensely interested in baseball. To him it is something more than a business. It comes close to being a religion. It may not be fantastic to say that no scientist makes a greater sacrifice at the altar of labor, research and hope.

With Hornsby baseball is life. Nothing else interests him. He has never tried to become interested in anything else. He will not talk with you unless you talk baseball. He is intolerant of other ballplayers who play golf, and particularly such players as bring their golf back to the dressing room or hotel lobby.

He is always the first to report to the ball field. If there is no one else around he will talk baseball with the groundskeeper, the caterers, the ushers and the taxicab drivers. He has mid-Victorian ideas about physical fitness. If he had his way a pitcher would unhinge his arm and hang it up in the locker until he was due to pitch again. A pitcher who bowls, for instance, is abusing his arm. Being a hitter himself he has similar ideas about vision, which, in his mind, is the most important part of hitting. Hornsby won't go to a show or a movie during the playing season. He thinks this is a strain on his eyes. If there is a movie he wants to see he will wait until the season is finished and trail it to some obscure theater. All players read the sports pages with avidity. Hornsby reads them only in

ROGERS HORNSBY... THE GREATEST RIGHT-HANDED HITTER OF ALL-TIME WAS THE ONLY MAN TO CRASH THE HALL OF FAME IN THE FIRST ELECTION IN 3 YEARS —

COOPERSTOWN HALL of FAME

.358 LIFE TIME AVERAGE

B.B. WRITERS

Hornsby's Bat. — *cartoon by Willard Mullin*

the off season. To some ballplayers reading is a strain on the mind; to Hornsby, it weakens the eyes.

Here, then, is a made-to-order sports hero. A tremendous hitter, a devout apostle of the game he is in, a man who would rather win a ball game than rule, and yet for every Hornsby booster you will meet a Hornsby knocker. There is no middle ground, either. The boosters boost with enthusiasm and the knockers knock with venom.

I had breakfast with the young man yesterday. I asked him if he was aware of the situation, how he felt about it and what was his explanation.

"Sure, I know there are a lot of people that dislike me," he answered. "But then there are a lot of people I don't care for. I don't go around trying to make enemies. There's nothing I can, nothing I intend to do about it.

"All my life I've been outspoken. I figure if you can't be honest with yourself, which means saying what you think, then you might as well crawl into a hole.

"I'm a ballplayer, and my only interest is baseball. It's all I've got to sell. I always try to make the best deal possible for myself. I don't believe I can be blamed for that."

13

Nick Altrock

Ballplayer and Buffoon

January 7, 1922.   A little wisdom may be a dangerous thing but a little nonsense is an important asset. An abundance of nonsense is even more important. Consider the case of Nicholas Altrock, Washington ballplayer and buffoon, who is now in our misty midst [Cleveland], demonstrating the amazing powers of Martin's celebrated liniments at 411 Euclid Ave. Altrock in his day was one of baseball's greatest left-handers. His slab achievements stood out in cameo clarity even in a period when crack southpaws abounded, southpaws like Waddell, Plank and White.

Altrock made as much money in those times as most of the topnotchers. Stampeding along with the rest of the crowd Nick finally arrived at the end of his string and dropped to the minors. One by one the others drifted out of the headlines. Now they are but memories of an eventful past. But Altrock is back in the majors, and as celebrated as ever.

"I've never forgotten to laugh," Nick tells you when you ask him to talk about his unique career. "If it's silly to enjoy yourself, then I'm a half-wit. I went in for baseball when I was kid on the Cincinnati sandlots because I found it fun. I have as much fun on the diamond today as I did in the old days. When the time comes that I don't get fun out of the game nobody can hire me to go near a baseball park."

That time, obviously, is not near. Altrock makes about twice as much for clowning on the coaching lines in major-league ballparks now as he did when he was one of baseball's most effective pitchers. The art of "being silly" keeps him in the majors years after Plank, Matty, Walsh, Donovan and other pitching greats, noted for their sagacity, have hurled their last ball.

The younger generation has about forgotten that Nick, the farceur known as "Torn Pockets," in earlier days was a genuine slab genius. Few left-handers, then or now, had better control. And he was one of the best fielding pitchers the game has ever known. Traces of his great fielding ability are yet to be seen in the astonishing manner in which he handles a baseball at first during fielding practice.

Nick said Saturday the greatest game he ever pitched was one he lost to Addie Joss of Cleveland. That was back in 1905. It was a 16-inning affair. Nick had held the old Naps to five hits and no runs for

Nick Altrock and Al Schacht as baseball clowns. — *NBL*

nine innings. In the ninth the Naps got two runners on and Eddie Hahn lost a fly ball in the sun. This would have been the third out. Both runners scored, tying the count. Scoreless baseball ensued until the 16th, when Nick weakened and the Naps slugged two runs over, winning 4-2.

Another notable game Nick pitched helped bring the 1906 championship to the White Sox. Sox, Naps and Yanks were battling for the title, which was still in doubt when the final week of the race appeared. Altrock opposed Barney Peltey, a star 15 years ago, and blanked the Browns, 1-0, in a game that decided the pennant for the Chicagoans.

Nick disagrees with his famous co-worker, Ed Walsh, that Nap Lajoie was the greatest batsman of his time. Nick is in-clined to hand the palm to Ty Cobb. "It made no difference where I put the ball, Ty Cobb would kill it. When he failed to get three or four hits off me I figured I was pitching invincible ball. Larry, the records will show, was not tough for me to handle. Of course he smacked my delivery hard at times, but as a general proposition I think I had it on him.

"A tougher bird to handle than the Frenchman was Lave Cross. Lave had a habit of coming over to the bench on days I was due to pitch and telling me how many hits he planned to make. 'I'll let you down easy today, Nick,' he'd say. 'I won't get but three.' Generally he was right. When he was wrong he would get four or five. I actually believe he's the guy who drove me crazy."

14

Gabby Street

A Catcher

July 21, 1930. When Walter Johnson broke into the majors Gabby Street, now managing the Cards, caught him. He continued to catch him for several years. Johnson's blinding speed gave Street a distinctive reputation. Since he was always behind the bat when Johnson pitched the belief grew that no one else could catch him. Thus Street became an awesome personage among the catchers in the league. Legends grew up around his terrific task, and Street supported them in various ways. He used to bring a piece of raw beef to the park and insert it in his glove. The beef presumably made it possible for the brave man to catch Johnson.

Street was a much-interviewed man in those days. The papers presented closeups of his hands, of his glove and of the piece of beef he always used. He added to his reputation by catching a ball thrown from the top of the Washington Monument. No other player had ever done that. This was the final touch. Mr. Gabby Street must be a great citizen indeed!

Everything went well for the Washington catcher until one Eddie Ainsmith joined the club. Ainsmith was also a catcher. One day he warmed up Johnson in front of the press box wearing a fielder's glove. This was news. "Rookie Backstop Smothers Fire Ball King's Slants with Third Baseman's Mitt."

That wrecked Street. He left the club soon after, and Ainsmith went on to catch Johnson for a number of years. And without the raw beef.

"Didn't we win the war?"

June 14, 1932. The game with Brooklyn had been washed out, and Sergeant Charles Gabby Street sat in his room in the hotel sucking away at a large black utensil that looked like a soup kettle.

It proved to be a pipe. The manager of the world champions likes his pipes big and black and apparently smelly. So

Gabby Street and Connie Mack as rival managers, exhibition game, Miami, Florida, 1931.—*Wide World*

did Miller Huggins. Maybe all managers should smoke pipes. Most of them seem to, at that.

Right now the sergeant's ball team isn't doing so well. "This is a topsy-turvy year," he says. "Anything is liable to happen. It wouldn't even surprise me to see us get beer back, and I hope we do. Personally, I haven't had a drink in 10 years, but I can't see where beer hurts a ballplayer. It's certainly better than some of the stuff they drink now."

A couple of years ago one of the sergeant's pitchers—Mr. Flint Rhem—went out and got himself all tangled up in some speakeasy hogwash with a fancy label on it and came back to the hotel with a lurid story of how two uncouth New Yorkers took him for a ride and made him guzzle at the point of a gun.

The sergeant remarked as how he was sorry that ever got out. "I don't know where he cooked up that story, but I always tried to believe it. I mean even Flint wouldn't drink that kind of stuff unless somebody threatened to shoot him.

"I never even fined him or anything," said the sergeant. "I remembered one night in the Argonne when my captain had me arrested. We had just come back from the front. I got leave for most of our men. About 30 of them were late coming back, but I checked 'em in, anyway. I knew they'd be back by morning, and they were. But this captain didn't like it, and I caught hell."

The sergeant took a prodigious pull at the black boiler. "What difference did it make? The men were back in time for duty —and, well, didn't we win the war?"

15
Murderers' Row

Colonel Ruppert

December 18, 1931. I dropped in the brewery to see Colonel Jacob Ruppert yesterday. It was my first visit to a brewery other than by proxy.

I suppose I had expected to find a lot of florid-faced burgomasters with uplifted steins singing "Old Heidelburg." I certainly expected to see some beer, or what passes for beer these days.

But there was none on display. The place didn't even look like a brewery. There were large mahogany desks, white-marbled walls and obsequious clerks. Any moment I feared some junior vice president was going to pop out and remind me that my bank balance had taken another nosedive.

On one of the walls hung a picture of the two Rupperts, father and son. It showed the Colonel as he looked back in the Waltz-Me-Around-Again-Maggie '90s. In those days the Colonel was known as the Prince of Beer, was a member of Congress and was written up in the social gazettes as New York's most eligible bachelor. He is still a bachelor, with a fine home up in Garrison-on-the-Hudson. Instead of a family, he maintains a collection of assorted monkeys—a circumstance which may or may not reflect his viewpoint on matrimony. Back of the Colonel's desk is a Talburt cartoon depicting a tall-hatted bluenose climbing aboard a camel and preparing a hasty exit in the face of approaching storm-clouds labelled WETS. The Colonel is an optimist. He even believes the Yanks are a sure thing to beat the Athletics and win the American League championship next season.

The Colonel denies that he told newspapermen on the West Coast that he was going to cut Ruth's salary. "All I said was that no ballplayer ever will be worth $80,000 again." . . . "Well, does that mean —?" . . . The Colonel threw up both hands. . . . "Don't ask me. I don't want to talk about it."

Always eager to be of charitable service, I have never hesitated to help spend the Colonel's money for him on baseball salaries, and I suggested that it might be a sporting gesture to renew Ruth's contract at the old figure, in spite of his waning ability, this as a sort of public recognition of the slugger's tremendous achievements of the past.

The Colonel answered me by peering out of the window and twiddling his thumbs. It may be that he is hard of hearing.

Yankee manager Miller Huggins and owner Jacob Ruppert.—*NBL*

"That's his favorite team"

October 26, 1937. Jumping Joe Dugan, the old Yankee third baser, operates a tavern in uptown Manhattan. The other day Colonel Ruppert sent for him. . . . "You don't sell my beer," complained the Colonel. "Why not?" It seemed Jumping Joe just hadn't got around to putting it in. . . .

"You know, the Colonel is a remarkable fellow," said Jumping Joe. "Imagine a busy man like him knowing I didn't carry his product—and getting disturbed about it! I guess I talked with him for an hour,

and the longer I sat in his office the more amazed I became.

"Do you know, he keeps intimate tabs on most of his players— not only the current ones but the old-timers? For instance, he knows the whereabouts of all the 1927 team and just what they are doing. That's his favorite team—the 1927ers. He said to me the other day: 'They were a great bunch, Dugan, really great. They would have beaten even my 1937 team. That's how great they were.'"

The pitching staff of the 1927 New York Yankees. *Left to right*: Bob Shawkey,
Joe Giard, Myles Thomas, Urban Shocker, Waite Hoyt, Herb Pennock, Wilcy Moore,
Walter Beall, Dutch Reuther, George Pipgras.—*NBL*

Huggins and Ruth

February 1, 1928. Miller Huggins, of those Yanks, has succumbed to the saxophone. For days the sports pages have been cluttered with pictures of the mite manager grappling futilely but none the less gallantly with the monstrous instrument. Conceding reach, height and much poundage, he has been shown trying every known hold in his effort to master the mechanism of the thing.

Beyond all this is a deep and hitherto unsuspected significance. He is going after Babe Ruth. A year ago Ruth took up the business of saxophoning in a serious way. This followed, as everybody knows, a crack in the clubhouse one day when it was insinuated that Ruth lacked sex appeal. Quick as always on the trigger, the home run genius snorted: "Is that so? Well, I'll have one of those things tomorrow." And 24 hours later he appeared with a saxophone.

It is a matter of common gossip that Huggins seldom wins a decision, verbal or otherwise, over Ruth. The standing at present is 53 disputes, with Ruth winning them all. But now the saxophone may make a difference. The disputes may take a new turn, with Huggins offering to out-toot Ruth. Even here the odds would seem to be against him. Nobody has ever been able to out-toot that young man when he felt in the mood for earnest and conscientious tooting.

Huggins and Gehrig

December 27, 1938. Did you ever hear about the time Miller Huggins socked Lou Gehrig in the jaw? . . . Gehrig was telling me the story the other day. . . . "It was the second or third year I was with the Yankees. One day I came into the dressing room and Huggins walked up to me and said, 'You big, stupid clown'; and with that he bounced a right hand off my kisser. . . .

"I didn't know what it was all about, except it was funny. Huggins was such a little guy he practically had to leap into the air to reach my chin with his fist. I stood there laughing and he glared at me. 'Here I've been trying to teach you some sense and you go out and spend a year's salary on an automobile!' . . .

"Then it came out. I was making about $6,000 at the time and someone told Huggins I had just spent $5,000 for a new car. Which didn't happen to be the truth. I had spent $700 for a secondhand Peerless. When I explained the facts, Huggins said, 'Well, let that punch be a lesson to you; that's what will happen to you if I ever hear you are throwing your money away.'"

Ed Barrow

January 30, 1933. A swivel chair general can be of vast assistance to a ball club, provided he knows his swivels. Mr. Edward Grant Barrow is the swivel chair general of the Yankee field force—the business manager, if you insist on being precise —and in this sphere he is supreme. You get some idea of how Mr. Barrow stands as a swivel chair general when you are told that next to Ruth he is the highest-paid man in baseball—and the gentleman never played a big-league game of ball in his life.

Mr. Barrow is a stocky, square-jawed, clean-shaven man of some 250 pounds, genial enough, but sheer granite in temperament when there is a battle to be fought. Those who know him longest like him best. He wears well.

To him the world is made up largely of baseball people and baseball problems. Little else interests him. He has no recreations. "A fellow with work to do doesn't need any." Once he played golf. Once, it developed, was enough. He never goes South or travels with the team. Away from his swivels he is jumpy and ill at ease.

Mr. Barrow, born in a covered wagon out on the Illinois wastelands, will be 65 in May. The flight of time has done nothing to dampen his ardor for baseball. He still reads everything there is to be read about the game. He is probably the best-informed baseball man in the country.

At various times Mr. Barrow has been a newspaper reporter, soap salesman, theatrical manager, hotel keeper, club manager and league president. For a brief spell he ran a fight club and presented some memorable battles. But his chief interest was always baseball. His judgment in picking players has always been remarkable. He has made few mistakes.

Mr. Barrow picked Hans Wagner off a slag heap in Pennsylvania, developed him and sold the bow-legged German to Barney Dreyfuss, then owner of the Louisville club, for $2,100, the first big sale the swivel

Waite Hoyt and Benny Bengough. — *NBL*

chair general ever made, and I think he is still very proud of it. At that time Mr. Barrow was running the Paterson club, defeated for the pennant by one game on the final day of the season. A picture of the club still hangs in his office. Mr. Barrow is seated in the middle, in his stand-up collar, ascot tie, high-buttoned frock coat and silver-headed cane—not to mention his moustaches with the sweep of the horns of a Texas steer.

Before coming to the Yankees Mr. Barrow managed two big-league clubs

—Detroit, in the pre-Jennings era, and the Boston Red Sox. It was Mr. Barrow who took one look at Ruth, at that time potentially the greatest southpaw pitcher in baseball, and decided to make an outfielder of him. "You are too valuable as a hitter not to be in the game every day," he told Ruth. But not even Mr. Barrow could foresee, on that mildly historic afternoon, that the day would come when he would be sending out $80,000 contracts to the round-faced youngster from Baltimore.

Waite Hoyt

January 15, 1952. Out in Cincinnati last week Charles Waite Hoyt, the old Boy Wonder, was talking of the old Yankees and, of all things, the virtues of team

spirit. . . . "Don't laugh," he warned, "but we had it. In fact, I think we set the pattern for the Yankee teams that followed.

Let's say we had our own conception of team spirit," he smiled.

This modification is necessary. The Yankees of Hoyt's day were quite different in character from the Yankees of today. They paid little attention to the training rules. They had no stern respect for their manager. There were not always one big happy family. They fought among themselves, even in the dugout where all could see. The old Boy Wonder nodded.

"But when we were challenged, when we had to win, we stuck together and fought with a fury and determination that could only come from team spirit. We had a pride in performance that was a form of snobbery. We felt we were superior people. And I do believe we left a heritage that has become a Yankee tradition."

The old Boy Wonder need not have apologized, as he seemed to, for saying the old Yankees felt like superior people. By the standards of any baseball generation that's what they were. Just for the record, the '27 Yankees won 110 games, finished 19 lengths ahead of the second-place AAA's, had five .300 hitters, four who drove in 100 or more runs; Ruth set his home run record of 60, Lou Gehrig was not too

far back with 47 and they furnished three of the league's first four pitchers in earned runs, Wilcy Moore, Urban Shocker and the old Boy Wonder himself.

What the records didn't show is how the Yankees of those days approached their responsibilities. They were, for the most part, men of light hearts and high spirits, happy warriors, indeed. Only on the field were they deadly serious. It was then that they got down to business, closed ranks and carried the fight to the common enemy.

The old Boy Wonder recalled Washington came into the Stadium in mid-season in '27 riding high and Bucky Harris, the manager, was talking pennant.

"It was a double-header. We won the first game, 12-1, and the second, 21-1."

Another time Miller Huggins put the Yankees on a slow train out of St. Louis for Chicago. It left at nine o'clock. . . . "We had been taking the midnight express," the old Boy Wonder said. "Hug figured that gave us too much time to visit our speak-easy friends. What happened was that we just drank that much faster. We stayed up most of the next night fighting, believe it or not, with pillows. Next day we beat the Sox 19-2, or something like that."

Benny Bengough

March 1, 1939. It cannot be said that Mr. Benny Bengough, the old big-league catcher, is a fellow who takes the brutal buffetings of Fate sitting down.

Some time ago we told you of the heroic measures he took to restore life to his deceased throwing arm. He never did effect complete resurrection, but it wasn't for lack of trying. Right up to the end of his catching days Mr. Bengough was a bright-eyed optimist and an enthusiastic patient. When he wasn't on the ball field he was Exhibit A in a clinic. In due time he became the All-America guinea pig.

When the routine and approved treatments were exhausted, Mr. Bengough embraced the mystical and esoteric. Once he had his arm painted with a mysterious fluid which had the qualities of liquid fire. The results were not altogether surprising.

"It burnt like hell," commented Mr. Bengough.

Another time when his club was playing the Browns in St. Louis a gentleman approached Mr. Bengough at the park. By now the state of Mr. Bengough's arm had become a matter of national interest, if not concern.

"Come to this address after the game," commanded the gentleman. "I can fix that arm." He handed him a printed card.

The game over, Mr. Bengough appeared at the indicated address and presently was ushered into a small, square room bathed in sinister green light. In the center of the room was a chair equipped with coils, wires and lengths of exposed plumbing. It looked very much like an electric chair.

"It isn't exactly an electric chair," explained the gentleman, "but it works on the same principle. Now sit down, if you please."

A man with less courage might have demurred on the grounds that life with a dead arm was to be preferred to no life at all, but Mr. Bengough belongs to the Spartan family. The gentleman pulled the switches, the coils and wires and plumbing danced to a sizzling, fire-spitting tune, and Mr. Bengough set a new world record for the high jump, his head barely missing the ceiling.

"If that doesn't help you nothing will," said the gentleman, comfortingly.

But Mr. Bengough's dead arm and the valiant fight he made to bring the cadaver back to life belongs to the past. There is another problem which concerns him at the moment. It has to do with the distressing fact that he has developed an entirely nude skull. Except this isn't distressing to Mr. Bengough. On the contrary, it is a happy circumstance, since it brings him back in contact with the scientific world.

Where once Mr. Bengough's dead arm was a wide-open, free-for-all laboratory for surgeons, muscle kneaders and experimental electricians, now his skull offers a boundless clinical field. And it is a pleasure to report that Mr. Bengough's lofty optimism remains unshaken in spite of previous discouragements. Sooner or later this sort of faith must be rewarded.

Just how Mr. Bengough lost his hair he isn't sure. One day he awakened and he was bald. "I thought I had been scalped," he says.

Not long ago a party with a long white mane approached him in the lobby of a hotel. He was carrying two green bottles under his arms.

"See this hair of mine?" said the party. Mr. Bengough cast a set of envious eyes over the rolling contours of the hirsute meadows. "This did it," he added, holding out the two green bottles. "I'm still using the stuff," said Mr. Bengough, "and I think it's going to work. Every time I use it I have a headache. I think that means the hair is trying to break through."

Until recently Mr. Bengough placed his faith in a suction cup. The is a round rubber gadget which fits the skull tightly and pulls desperately on the barren skull.

"That probably would have worked, too," said Mr. Bengough, "only the wife objected to my wearing the thing around the house. She said it frightened the children."

16
The Babe

Babe's First Game

August 16, 1951. There is in the mail a thoughtful gift from a member of the WOTC (Williams Old Timers Club). A box score of the first big-league game in which George Herman Ruth appeared. The box score shows Larry Gardner was at third the day Ruth broke in.

This was July 11, 1914. The Cleveland Naps, as they were then called, were in the other corner. Nap Lajoie was still in the lineup, playing second, hitting cleanup and following a young fellow whose bat was beginning to attract wide attention. Fellow named Joe Jackson. He hit .500 against Ruth that day.

The Red Sox won a close one, 4-3, but the Babe didn't go all the way. The Naps started to get to him in the seventh, tied it up and Dutch Leonard was rushed to the rescue. The box score shows Ruth walked none, fanned one and gave up eight hits, all singles. A very creditable performance for a first time out, especially if the old box score is correct that he walked none.

As Ruth went along, his remarkable ability became evident. "There were times when he looked to be the best pitcher you ever saw," Gardner told me. I saw him pitch often myself and I thought so too. It was not surprising to learn the Babe seldom pitched from "the book."

"He'd seem to listen when he went over the hitters in the clubhouse before the game," Gardner remembered. "But either he viewed the business as a sheer waste of time or wasn't able to retain it. Anyway, he seldom put into practice what he had decided was the smart way to pitch to the various hitters. Often, in fact, he'd pitch just the opposite."

It isn't necessary to deal in speculation as to how good Ruth was as a pitcher. He pitched long enough to establish himself. The records bespeak his lofty skills. He won 92, lost 44 and had an earned-run average of 2.24.

[Creamer prints a detailed account of Ruth's first big-league game in Babe, *adding some interesting details, such as the fact that Ruth picked Joe Jackson off first in his first inning in the majors, and the fact that Ruth (Ruth!)* was lifted for pinch hitter Duffy Lewis in the seventh.—P. W.]

"I was a great pitcher"

January 27, 1931. Ask Babe Ruth what he considers his greatest feat in baseball and he will tell you this: "It didn't come as a batter. It came as a pitcher during my days with the Boston Red Sox. Detroit was the opposing team. In those days the Tigers were the hardest hitters in baseball. In this particular game I had them whipped 1 to 0 when they came to bat in the last half of the ninth. The first three men up got on. It was a swell situation. Three on. Nobody out. And nobody coming up but Veach, Cobb and Crawford! I suppose a gambler would lay you at least 100 to 1 on a sure score in such circumstances. But there was no score. I put all I had on the ball and struck out Veach, Cobb and Crawford in succession. And, what's more, I struck them out on ten pitched balls. Nobody ever accused me of being modest. I was a great pitcher."

"The lucky stiff"

June 7, 1926. CLEVELAND—Whenever Babe Ruth lifts one out of the park and ruins a ball game for the home side the manager storms: "What did you throw him that one for?"

The second-guessing expert in the press box speeds his rheumatic fingers across the keyboard of a clanking typewriter . . . "Manager Speaker made a grave blunder when he permitted pitcher Whoozit to pitch to the Bambino, as I have nicknamed him, in the fourth inning of today's game. Anybody with the brains of a half-wit would have known—" . . . etc., etc.

Pitcher Whoozit swallows his wad of Mail Pouch as he watches the white streak turn to a gray haze in the distant clouds, and grumbles, "The lucky stiff!"

'Tis said the valiant taste of death but once. Perhaps this is the impulse that prompts the pitcher to try to throw one past the Bam. Or it may be vanity. Sometimes the difference between sheer foolishness and cold courage is very slight.

Ruth and the Arts

December 27, 1926. This year Ruth is an actor. He is uplifting the drama over a vaudeville circuit, playing four shows a day. His act consists in standing upon an elevated home plate in uniform and smacking a baseball that is suspended on a string from upstage, the while keeping up an animated line of chatter.

Mr. Harry Heilmann, another apple-knocker of some distinction in the American League, was present on the occasion of Ruth's initial appearance several weeks ago in Minneapolis. Mr. Heilmann assures me that Ruth, on this particular occasion at least, was a riot.

It seems that Ruth himself in person does not appear until a movie showing him

Babe Ruth on sax, with Lou Gehrig. — *NBL*

smacking the apple at the Yankee Stadium before a World Series crowd is screened. There is a moment of total darkness followed by light and a swishing crash as the great man batters his way through a paper background. Ruth, as I gather the details, must have imagined on this day he was swinging against Uhle with the bases filled. At any rate, he swung with such violence and histrionic savagery that he fell from the elevated home plate and went skidding downstage center, not coming to a pause until his spikes had beheaded a bass viol.

The members of the orchestra began to scramble therefrom with precipitate dis-order, leaving in their wake pianos, tuba horns, kettle drums and such implements of musical art as are habitually identified with vaudeville orchestras. The effect was most realistic, as Mr. Heilmann reports it, and went over very big with the esthetic patrons of the drama who had gathered for Ruth's first performance.

Only the manager of the theater was disappointed and his disappointment was not registered until he learned the slide into the orchestra pit was not a regular part of the act but merely an impromptu gesture somewhat characteristic of the great man.

Ruth Reformed

December 7, 1927. I am living in desperate hope that the report proclaiming the complete reformation of my friend and fellow wastrel Mr. George Herman Ruth is, if not a base canard, at least a vicious exaggeration.

Mr. Ruth, frankly, has no business reforming. I have a notion that he owes much of his present eminence as a worldwide figure to the simple fact that he has gone along all these years just being himself. It is not going to be easy to accept Mr. Ruth on any other basis. That heroic knob of his was never fashioned for a halo. He needs no skillful makeup to play "The Playboy of Baseball." But as a Great Shining Example or a Mighty Moral Force he would be as artificial and unconvincing as Bozo Snyder in a Walter Hampden cast.

Mr. Gene Tunney can go before the Boys' Clubs of New Jersey and speak with great earnestness on the value of Clean Living, and it sounds very natural and sincere and you didn't mind particularly listening to him. But I am afraid if Mr. Ruth, touched by the immaculate fingers of chastity, tried the same thing he would have a hard time keeping the boys in the back rows from laughing out loud, and I have a notion he would spend several embarrassing moments ducking a vegetable barrage.

I prefer to remember Mr. Ruth as he used to be—when he would bet you $1,000 on Tanglefoot in the fourth at Empire City, or $500 on a two-way point at craps or, if you tired of the routine of the play, $20 on the high spade. The Mr. Ruth of those days didn't care much whether he won or lost. What held him was the gaiety of the hour and the conviviality of the crowd. Even royalty moved him not.

There was that lovely afternoon in St. Paul one year when Mr. Ruth was playing vaudeville and arrangements had been made for the King of Swat to meet the Queen of Romania, a visitor in the city at the same time. The Queen, for all Mr. Ruth knows, may still be waiting to meet him. It developed that the hour of appointment conflicted with a previously arranged pinochle game with a couple of old friends, and to the extreme regret of Mr. Ruth he was compelled to ignore the Queen. This was the old Mr. Ruth. I have no way of knowing how sharply he has been changed by his reformation.

The truth is he cannot afford to change too much, if at all. The customers, sadly, aren't wild about perfect people. Mr. Ruth has always been looked on as something of a "character." This has added to his appeal at the box office. When he loses this he will become just a ballplayer who can swing a big bat harder and knock a leather pill farther than anybody the game has ever known. This is something, but is isn't enough to ensure immortality.

Even the Babe Isn't Immune to the Cabbages of Time

January 29, 1929. Some time today Mr. George Herman Ruth is supposed to start for the Southland. A large amount of fashionable secrecy surrounds the operation. The great man will not say where he is going nor precisely what time he intends to leave. There is a report that he will travel incognito. This is a good trick if it can be done. Trying to make Mr. Ruth look like

Ruth crosses the plate after hitting his third homer in the fourth game of the 1928 World Series.
Note the straw hats.—*NBL*

anything else but Mr. Ruth is no easy assignment. Mr. Barnum, in all the years he was in the show business, had only one Jumbo, and baseball has known only one Babe.

Mr. Ruth has arrived at a critical stage in his career. Early next month he will be 35 years old. He has been in the big leagues since 1914. For years he has been the most dominant and dazzling figure in the sport. He has lasted a great deal longer than anybody figured he would.

With a top-heavy body perched perilously on pipe-stem legs the Babe, flaunting training rules, scoffing at accepted standards of health preservation and burlesquing all the quaint laws of the game, has thundered on from one epochal baseball accomplishment to another—a human Niagara charting its own course. But the time will come when even the roar of Niagara will drop to a thin whisper. So it seems reasonable to suppose that the Babe cannot last forever. Indeed, even now the boys

are beginning to look askance at him and nod their critical heads in a significant manner, as if to say, "This is the year."

It is always dangerous to prepare an obituary to the memory of the Babe. He has a way of kicking off the casket lid and walking out on the wake, leaving his mourners in a state of consternation and astonishment. Three years ago he began to show what some of the boys imagined to be symptoms of decay, and long, lugubrious pieces appeared in the daily gazettes forecasting the inevitable. Twelve months later the Babe was boisterously clinking steins in his favorite tavern in celebration of a new home run record.

Maybe this will be another great season for him, and maybe it won't. Personally I'd say the odds are quite against him. Even the Babe isn't immune to the cabbages of time, as my friend Mr. Tammany Young would say. And when you are 35 in baseball, you are pretty old.

The "Called" Shot

It is now generally agreed that Ruth did not predict his center-field homer off Charlie Root in the '32 series. The best summary of how the myth got started is Robert Creamer's in his biography of Ruth, where it is pointed out that the only journalist to say Ruth had "called" his shot was Williams. Creamer suggests that "Williams' strong personality and the wide circulation given his original story in Scripps-Howard newspapers got the legend started and kept it going." The birth, amplification and finally the abandonment of the legend can be traced in Williams' columns. It should also be noted that as Williams and many of the other writers became more convinced that no shot had ever been called, Ruth seemed to become more convinced that the story was true, or at least less willing to deny it. —P.W.

Ruth Calls Shot as He Puts Homer No. 2 in Side Pocket

October 1, 1932. WRIGLEY FIELD, CHICAGO—George Herman Ruth, who gets as much dough as Herbert Clark Hoover, seems to be worth it. He certainly gives you more thrills.

The bambino hit two homers during the day, each of them a record-breaker, and on the occasion of his second round-tripper even went so far as to call his shot. He also cross-fired gags with hecklers on the Cub bench to draw rounds of laughs, and almost moved a most unsympathetic gallery to tears when he stretched pathetically on his broad tummy in a vain effort to field a line drive.

The Babe's first homer came in the first inning with two out, a zooming drive that landed high in right center, the longest ball ever hit to that section in this park. In the fifth, with the Cubs riding him unmercifully from the bench, Ruth pointed to the center field and punched a screaming liner to a spot where no ball ever had been hit before.

When Ruth came to bat in the fifth Bush and Grimes gave him a verbal roasting from the Cub bench. The first strike was called and the razzing from the Cub bench increased. Ruth laughed and held up one finger. Two balls were pitched and Babe jeered the Cub bench, the fans and Root, grinning broadly all the time. Another strike was called, and Bush ran part way out of the dugout to tell the Babe that he was just a tramp. Ruth hit the next pitch farther than any other ball ever was hit in this park.

On the Radio, Ruth Says He Called Two

October 24, 1932. Earlier in his career Mr. Ruth used to say his greatest feat in baseball was performed as a left-handed pitcher against the Tigers when they were the hardest-hitting team in captivity. He had them shut out, 1 to 0, going into the last half of the ninth when they filled the bases with none out. The next three batters were Veach, Cobb and Crawford. Mr. Ruth struck them out on 10 pitched balls. But now he has made a revision in estimating his greatest contribution to baseball. Those two home runs he made against the Cubs in the third game of the World Series this year.

This was the game in which the Cubs ragged him boisterously before their home supporters. The great man replied by stepping to the plate on two different occasions and announcing to one and all that he intended to show how bush-leaguish the Chicago pitching was by driving the ball out of the park, which in each instance he promptly proceeded to do.

Four Hall of Famers: Eddie Collins, Ty Cobb, Babe Ruth and Tris Speaker.—*Wide World*

Mr. Ruth was asked if he really believed he was going to hit those home runs when he came to the plate.

"I knew I wanted to hit them, but of course I wasn't sure. That's what gave me such a big kick—hitting 'em after saying I was going to. I've hit more than 650 home runs, but those two I hit off Charlie Root will always stand out above them all."

As an afterthought Mr. Ruth roared into the mike:

"Can you imagine what a mug I would have been if I had missed them? Say, those people in Chicago would be laughing at me yet—and I wouldn't blame them, either."

Gabby Hartnett's Version

February 7, 1950. From now on it's going to take some mighty powerful persuasion to convince Virginia there's a Santa Claus. Particularly after what Gabby Hartnett's done to the most fantastic of all the Babe Ruth legends—you know, the one about him calling his shot in the '32 World Series.

It came in the fifth inning. One was down when Ruth came up. Earlier, in the first inning, he had rocketed a homer into the stands with a runner on. In the second he had missed another by no more than the width of a small boy's hand. Presently, in this situation, Root had two called strikes on him.

All the while Ruth was at bat the Cubs, led by Guy Bush, a pitcher, had been trying to heckle the big fellow. Ruth was more amused than annoyed. From time to time he'd look toward the enemy dugout back of third, jabber something and laugh like crazy. He made several gestures. I have a distinct memory that once he pointed the bat at Bush who stood on the top step in the dugout. And just before he hit the home run from which Hartnett would now divest of the grand, matchless theater which has been associated with it for so many years, he did motion in the general direction of the stands in right center. I can still see him doing it. Whatever actually was his thought at that precise moment, there seemed only one way to interpret the sweep of his arm . . . "I'm going to slam the next one into the stands."

But Hartnett says, no, that's not the way it was. Hartnett was catching for the Cubs that day. . . . "Ruth waved his hand across the plate toward the Cub bench. At the same time he said—and I think only the umpire and myself heard him—"it only takes one to hit it."

Mickey Walker's Deposition
June 24, 1953. The most fascinating stories, unhappily, are not always true. Biographers assure us George Washington felled no cherry tree, the she-wolf did not wet-nurse Romulus and Will Tell wasted no arrows shooting apples off junior's noggin. And now comes reliable testimony that Babe Ruth didn't call that celebrated home run.

It comes, singularly, from a prize-fighter, yet not so singularly when it is pointed out that Mickey Walker and the Babe were the best of pals.

There came a night when the Babe and Walker and a kindred soul, Jack Schafer, a hotel man and ardent sports follower, were sitting around nibbling on nutritious, body-building scotch, and the fighter put the question flatly to the old King of Swat, then

retired: Did he or did he not call the home run he hit off Charlie Root in the 1932 World Series?

He didn't.

"I had two strikes on me and the pitcher was levelling with speed curves," the fighter quotes Ruth. "We were kiddin' one another and I swept my arm, motioning to the outfield, trying to rib him into a fastball. I was waiting for the pitch and when it came I belted the ball over the center-field fence."

The ball went into the center-field bleachers, not out of the park, but this does represent the first trustworthy deposition relating to the historic incident. There *was* an immense amount of "kiddin'" (except it was razzing) and the ringleader was Guy Bush, another Cub pitcher, who, propped against a dugout, was directing a flow of invective at Ruth through cupped hands. And Ruth did make the gesture: in fact, he made several gestures, some even before the second strike.

It was just as easy to believe Ruth had actually called the shot as not and it made a wonderful story, so the press box went along with it. First intimation I got that not everybody in baseball concurred was at dinner in Newark one night. I happened to be seated between Lou Gehrig and Joe McCarthy. I disremember how the subject came up, but Gehrig laughed: "The gestures were meant for Bush. Ruth was going to foul one into the dugout, but when the pitch came up, big and fat, he belted it." McCarthy only smiled quizzically.

Some years later I was in Hollywood and the Babe's life story (or what passed for it) was in production, and I was having lunch with Bill Bendix, who was playing the lead and Joe E. Brown's son, who was doing the ballyhoo. A problem in casting had developed that day. To give the picture a touch of authenticity—and no sports biography ever needed one more—Root had been asked to play himself in the film, for which contribution to realism and the higher arts he would be suitably rewarded.

"But Root wouldn't do it," said young Brown. "Says it's a damn lie and never happened."

This was realistic evidence that there was more fable than fact in the called shot, for Root was known to have no small respect for the dollar, and the opportunity to appear in a Hollywood epic must have been tempting.

Gehrig "Read About It in the Papers," Too

July 14, 1965. Old myths didn't die either. Nor do they fade away. Another Babe Ruth memorial has come and gone. Predictably, THAT home run was taken down from the shelf and dusted off for the occasion.

The details are too familiar to require recounting. Apparently the story is too good to die, so it lives on, true or untrue depending on the version you wish to accept.

I think I was as close to the Babe as any sportswriter of the era. Possibly closer. I was often a houseguest. I sensed early it was fruitless to try to draw him out on matters of controversy or personal conflict.

I've always thought it significant that he never once stated in my presence that he had called THAT home run off Charlie Root of the Cubs in the 1932 World Series —except possibly by inference.

Casually I remarked: "I guess you'd have to say the home run you hit after pointing to the center-field stands in Chicago was your biggest thrill?"

"Hell, no," the Babe roared. "It was the time I struck out Cobb, Crawford and Veach with the bases full. That was some pitching, you gotta admit."

Did the Babe deliberately evade the baited question? It was my surmise that he did. In interviews he could be surprisingly adroit.

McCarthy never agreed with the legend. Neither did Lou Gehrig or Art Fletcher.

"There was no talk about it in the dugout at the time," recalled Fletcher. Gehrig said he read about it in the papers the next day. "And that was the first I'd heard about the Babe 'calling' the shot."

Through the years Root consistently dismissed THAT home run as sheer fantasy. "The Babe didn't point to center field; he pointed to our dugout, specifically to Claude Passeau. We were giving him a rough time from the bench and Claude was the jeer-leader."

The Big Scoop—Ruth Quits Yanks

After the fifth game in St. Louis, [Ruth] was walking along the platform at the railroad station with Joe Williams, Dan Daniel and Tom Meany. The conversation was general for a while and then Williams, always probing, asked, "What are your plans, Babe. . . . Are you going to play again?"

"Hell, no," Ruth said. "I'm through with the Yanks. I won't play with them unless I can manage. But they're sticking with McCarthy, and that lets me out."

Williams wrote the story, which created something of a sensation because it *stressed the McCarthy-or-me angle. Newspapermen were amused that Ruth had scooped Bill Slocum, his own ghost. . . ." (Robert Creamer, Babe)*

Ruth wanted to take a look at the engine before the train pulled out for Detroit. It was the engineer, not Williams, who asked Babe whether he would play for the Yanks next year, and what Ruth actually said was "Fuck, no." Williams simply asked Ruth if he meant it. Ruth said yes, and Wil-

*liams took him into his drawing room, or-
dered two steaks and a bottle of scotch
(Haig & Haig Pinch) and pulled out his
typewriter. The next time the train stopped
for any length of time, probably in Chicago, Dan Daniel dropped Williams' story
off at the Western Union office. Another
reason it created "something of a sensation" was that this was a train full of writers, all of whom presumably picked up the
paper containing the following column
when they got off at Detroit.—P. W.*

October 28, 1934. DETROIT—Colonel
Jacob Ruppert will pay off Joe McCarthy
and appoint Babe Ruth as manager of the
Yankees for the next year or the Babe's career with the New York club has come to
an end. You may accept that from Ruth
himself.

"I will not sit on the bench as a Saturday and Sunday player or pinch hitter with
the Yankees or any other club next season,"
said Ruth to me as we walked up and down
the platform in the St. Louis railroad station at dusk yesterday.

I had stepped out to gather my im-
pressions about the game in which the Tigers had got the upper hand in the World
Series with the Cardinals. But Ruth's surprising message to Colonel Ruppert, to the
fans of New York—to the sports followers
of America—struck me as a far more vital
story than anything or anybody having to
do with a World Series game. There will
be lots of World Series games, but never
another George Herman Ruth.

"If I am to remain in baseball in 1935,
it will be as a manager," the Babe continued. "Yes, that means I will not sign another player's contract with the Yankees. I
have reached the point at which it must be
manager or nothing. If I cannot get a job
as manager—and it must be in the major
leagues—Claire and I may spend next summer travelling in Europe."

It was a strange spot and a strange
time for the announcement. I had met Ruth
by accident. He had spied me from a car
window and had come down to join me in
my constitutional while we waited for our
special to start for Detroit. I had asked no
leading questions. He had volunteered the
information, and he delivered it with conviction, and determination and sincerity.
Apparently Ruth and Mrs. Ruth just had
made their decision.

"You're getting me into a transom"

July 28, 1943. There was the time when
the Babe quit the Yankees and we got an
exclusive on it. That never would have happened, the exclusive part, if the Babe didn't
have a juvenile's interest in engines. We were
waiting for the train to pull out of St. Louis
on its run to Detroit. It was hot in our
compartment.

"Let's go out and look at the engine,"
suggested the Babe.

It was one of those big, puffing mon-
sters. The engineer, of course, recognized
the Babe instantly.

"What's the Yankees going to do next
year, Babe," the engineer asked.

"I didn't give a damn what they do,"
the Babe snorted. "I'm through with them."

Thus the unidentified engineer was the
first to learn the great man had quit. Back
in the compartment the Babe told how he
had had a showdown with Jake Ruppert
. . . "It's Joe McCarthy or me" . . . and
how he had lost the decision and had
walked out for good.

The next afternoon in the Detroit
press box (it was World Series time) the
Babe was besieged by newsmen, whose ed-
itors were checking the story. Even the

Babe's own ghostwriter hadn't been informed. The Babe had had a bad night (so had we) and he sat there in the burning sun sweating prodigiously, and fanning his flushed pan with a scorecard. Finally he exploded.

"You guys get away from me. You're getting me into a transom!"

"I'll have to say Ty Cobb"

March 20, 1936. ST. PETERSBURG—Mr. George Herman Ruth wishes I hadn't written he is bitter at his old club—the New York Yankees.

"The only reason I haven't been over to the field to watch them practice is because I've been busy playing in golf tournaments," he explained. "I'd like to get somewhere as a golfer this year if I can. And besides, I'd rather see the Yankees play when they are a little farther along in their training. As a matter of fact, I've bought a box for Sunday's game."

This was the beginning of a catch-as-catch-can baseball talk with the great man as he sat in front of a wood fire, nibbling on a highball, in his home here. It was a cold, moist evening and he had ordered the hired man to brew some heat that could be applied both on the inside and outside of a man.

Mr. Ruth tried to explain why he left the Yankees to join the ill-fated Braves last year. The critics called this a stupid move, pointing out that all he had to do to ultimately become manager of the Yankees —his burning ambition—was to sit tight and pursue a policy of watchful waiting.

"I would have been content to stay with the Yankees as a coach, or a pinch hitter for a couple of years longer if anybody had given me the slightest encouragement that when the proper time came I would be given a chance to run the club," he says. "But this encouragement never came. On the contrary, it was made very plain that I was never to be considered. That's why I took the Boston proposition. It turned out bad, but it was the only step I could make."

Some of the traditional amiability of Mr. Ruth returned when he began to discuss baseball matters less personal. . . . "The greatest ballplayer I ever saw? Well, I'll have to say Ty Cobb. He could do more with a bat than any player in my time and I don't suppose there ever was a base runner like him. They'll tell you he wasn't much of a fielder, but he was good enough. I know he took a lot of base hits away from me out there."

Who was the greatest fielding outfielder? . . . "Harry Hooper, of the old Red Sox. No doubt about it. He could do anything any other outfielder could and on top of that he was a great position player. His instinct for knowing where the ball was going to be hit was uncanny. I'm sure, too, that he made more diving catches than any other outfielder in history. With most outfielders, the diving catch is half luck. With Hooper it was a mastered piece of business."

Mr. Ruth thinks Happy Felsch, of the notorious Black Sox, had the most powerful and most accurate throwing arm of his day. . . . "You writers used to say Bob Meusel had the best arm in baseball, but if you check back you'll find he didn't throw many base runners out. He had a powerful arm, but it didn't come close to Felsch's for direction."

Getting around to the pitchers, the great man said he'd have to split them into sections. . . . "Walter Johnson had more speed than any pitcher I ever looked at. Old Eddie Plank was tops when it came to control. He could knock a bead of perspiration off your brow with a pitch. There have been many fine curveball pitchers, but the best curveball I ever saw was thrown by Walter Beall of the '24 Yanks. Beall lacked control, and that's what kept him from being a sensational pitcher. The best catcher I ever saw was Ray Schalk, of the White Sox. He did everything a catcher is supposed to do and did it perfectly. You writers don't give that fellow the recognition that is his due."

The great man joined the graybeards in naming his all-time infield. He put Hal Chase at first, Nap Lajoie at second, Hans Wagner, short, and Jimmy Collins at third. The best double play combination?... "That's easy. Stanley Harris and Roger Peckinpaugh, the year Washington won its first championship. There never were two infielders who worked together better as a unit than those two."

By this time the fire had burned down and the highball glass was empty. Mr. Ruth bellowed for more fuel. . . . "The sunny South!" he snorted. "Say, I saw more sun in the subway last winter than I've seen down here for two months."

There Was a Case on Ice in the Bathroom

June 23, 1944. "I've been in so many hospitals they ought to make me a doctor," Babe Ruth boomed as he got ready to leave Orthopedic, to which he had come to have a cartilage yanked from his right knee.

"This must be the 20th, maybe the 30th time I've been in a hospital," the great man added. "When something happens to me it happens all over. Even when I get a hangnail they say, 'Get the big bum to a hospital.'"

This appears to be more or less true. Consider the contemporaneous cartilage. In size and form it looks like a frosted frankfurter. "Largest I ever saw," the nurse whispered. Which should not be surprising. The Babe was never one to do things on a minor scale.

When we called he was overflowing a regulation hospital bed, propped up in a cloud of pillows, smoking a bowl-shaped pipe. At his side on a table stood several perspiring bottles of beer.

"I haven't had a belt of whiskey or smoked a cigar since April," he volunteered, running a prodigious paw through his hair, now fast turning gray. Switching to a pipe and to beer (there was a case on ice in the bathroom) constitutes the Spartan life for the Babe.

The unanchored cartilage, an evil-looking thing, swam about malevolently in a Mason jar. The Babe fingered the jar tenderly.

"I should have had the damned thing taken out in 1918," he said. "That's when I got it."

Al Schacht, the baseball jester, was a visitor. He had brought the Babe two thick steaks for his dinner that night—his one meal a day, by the way.

"Well, nobody can say you rushed into this operation," commented Schacht. "How'd you get it, anyway?"

It developed the Babe was playing for an industrial team during the last war in Baltimore. He hit one inside the park, scored standing up, but his spikes caught in the rubber.

"I went head over appetite," he remembered, "and when I came down I heard and felt something crack. I intended to have it taken out before the next season started, but somehow I just didn't get around to it. It got worse and worse, and that's why I used to quit in the sixth or seventh inning in later years." The Babe paused and shrugged. "I guess being a damn fool about it cost me two or three more years in the game."

Cartoon by Willard Mullin

Schacht, who used to pitch for Washington—and was a better pitcher than he's given credit for—boasted the Babe never got a home run off him. . . . "And I'm the only pitcher who can say that."

The Babe launched a monumental yawn, and the white iron bed trembled.

"I don't remember hitting against you much," the Babe said, and there was no trace of discourtesy in his tone. "Cicotte —Eddie Cicotte, of the White Sox—he was the one I couldn't get a homer off. I must have hit .700 against him—a million singles and doubles, but not one homer. Just wouldn't stick one in there for me."

Schacht flashbacked to the Babe's last year in baseball, 1935, when he was lured into the National League on the proposition that he was to be vice president, assistant manager and right fielder of the Boston Braves. The party who thought that one up was Judge Emil Fuchs. All he had in mind, of course, was to exploit the Babe.

The illusion lasted for only 28 games, but before the Fuchs scheme trickled through the Ruthian skull the great man had himself one last glorious fling at the plate—he hit three homers in one game.

"That's the day you should have quit," commented Schacht.

The Babe nodded, then added, "I should never have fallen for that guy's baloney. That was the first mistake." There was bitterness in his voice.

The nurse returned with a slip of paper.

"One of the patients downstairs, a little boy named Haney, is leaving the hospital today. Been here six months. His mother wants your autograph for him."

The Babe put down his bottle of beer, readjusted his blubbery frame, took the slip and John Hancocked it with a flourish.

"Well, the kids haven't forgotten the old guy, anyway," he laughed. Kind of flat it was, too.

It turned out Schacht was the only old ballplayer who had visited him during the two weeks he was in the hospital—and until the Babe came along they were paying off ballplayers in cigar bands.

"Jeez! I hope he makes it"

August 14, 1948. Jack Dempsey is, like everybody else, deeply moved by Babe Ruth's magnificent struggle to live.

"Did you know the Babe and I once met in the ring?" he asked.

This, indeed, was news.

"Not in a real fight, or anything like that. A sparring match. Three or four rounds down in Florida, Palm Beach, one spring. We did it to help Sam Harris and George Jessel. They were running some sort of charity bazaar. The Babe wasn't too bad, at that. Told me later he'd always wanted to be a fighter."

"Did you let him have one?"

"Of course I did. You know me. Right off. First punch. Shook him up good, too."

That's the way Dempsey was. Whether he was fighting or merely working out, he took charge, or tried to, with the first punch. It wasn't meanness or viciousness. Rather psychology. Once you establish you're the boss, then you can operate the way you want to.

"There was more to it than that," Dempsey, sitting in his attractive Broadway restaurant, corrected. "I don't care how good you are, you never can be sure the other fellow isn't better. Not until you've found out for yourself, you can't."

At this point the venerable Jim Dougherty, who refereed several of Dempsey's notable fights, came in with the early morning newspapers. The headlines cried: "Ruth Gains in Fight for Life."

"Jeez, I hope he makes it," Dempsey murmured, cushioning his head in his hands.

[Williams was vacationing on Cape Cod when Ruth died, so there are no further stories. Ruth had sent word that he was to be a pallbearer, but Williams, evidently unnerved by this particular death, pretended he had not been reached in time.—P. W.]

17

A Note on Appetites

"A ballplayer who will eat an umpire must be hungry"

January 16, 1929. In recent years, Mr. Bob Fothergill has supplanted Mr. Ruth as baseball's widest girth. You hear and read more of Mr. Ruth's girth these days than Mr. Fothergill's only because the former has a more practical sense of publicity. When Mr. Ruth sheds a pound he sees to it that it is a news story, but Mr. Fothergill can drop a ton and you never hear of it. This is one of the differences between New York and Massilon, Ohio.

Mr. Fothergill is as fine a fly catcher and as competent a batter as you'll find in the league. His barrier to greatness is a Graf Zeppelin belt line. He is a living example of what confirmed Republicanism and full dinner pails will do for you. It has been said of him that he covers more ground standing up than two Tris Speakers in full flight. Warming the bench this year he will look like the Four Horsemen, the Volga Boatman and two other fellows all in one.

Upon the heaving contours of Mr. Fothergill's embonpoint two Detroit man-agerial careers have already crashed. Ty Cobb could do nothing with him, or it. George Moriarty managed to melt him down to 256 pounds and claimed a moral victory.

Under Moriarty for a time Mr. Fothergill was subject to fine and suspension without salary if his weight exceeded a stipulated poundage. This had the effect of compelling the diamond dinosaur to practice dieting in a grim way.

One afternoon in the slanting sun of a late July day the diet ended, suddenly and summarily. Mr. Fothergill, protesting against the injustice of a called third strike, took a bite out of the fleshy part of umpire Bill Guthrie's upper left arm.

The incident convinced Moriarty of the complete futility of his task.

"A ballplayer who will eat an umpire must be hungry, or something," philoso-phized Moriarty. And thereafter Mr. Fothergill was allowed to eat whatever and whenever he pleased.

18

The 1929–1931 A's

The Second Great Team

March 5, 1929. FORT MYERS, Fla.—The Jason of the American League, eternally seeking the golden fleece of another championship, is here equipping his crew for its annual cruise in the uncertain waters of baseball.

Mr. Cornelius McGillicuddy has riches, peace of mind, health, happiness and about everything that is needed to round out a full career, but he refuses to step down as manager of the Athletics.

Everybody knows the reason: He wants to be in one more World Series. It has been 15 years since he sat back in the dugout wigwagging to Oldring, Strunk and Murphy in the outfield to play back or in. It has been 15 years since he moved his infielders—McInnis, Collins, Barry and Baker—around like pawns, shifting them a foot this way against curveball hitters and a foot the other way against fastball hitters, pulling them in close to cut a run off at the plate or pushing them back deep to play for double plays. It has been 15 years since he sat with bony hands on angular knees and nodded instructions to Plank, Coombs, Bender, Pennock, Shawkey and Bush. The old man wants that thrill again—just once more—and then Eddie Collins, his present first lieutenant, can have the team and the many irksome responsibilities that go with the daily conduct of it.

For the last five years the sportswriters have been predicting the current year would be his last, that he had grown too old for the job, that he had lost his enthusiasm and interest. But always the old man came back—just as he is back this spring, as alert, eager, nervous, fidgety, hopeful and fearful as ever. To those who were born and nourished in a baseball cradle the business is not easy to desert. Paradoxically, it is hardest to desert when it seems easiest, when there is nothing to gain—nothing that needs to be gained, except, possibly, the realization of a dream. And maybe that is everything, at that.

Howard Ehmke's submarine delivery. — *NBL*

Why Mack Used Ehmke

December 16, 1929. When Mr. Cornelius McGillicuddy sent Howard Ehmke out to pitch the first game of the World Series last fall he astonished the baseball world. Ehmke was the last pitcher anybody figured would be chosen for such a strategically important game. Prior to the Series he had not pitched for weeks, and when the team left for its last swing through the West the tall right-hander was not even permitted to go along.

Why, then, did Mr. McGillicuddy decide to throw Ehmke against the Cubs in the first game? "One of these days I'll tell that story," Mr. McGillicuddy smiles when you ask him about it. To my knowledge I don't believe he has yet told the story to anyone. But here it is, and it comes from Mr. Edward Trowbridge Collins, the assistant manager of the Athletics.

"You may recall"—this is Mr. Collins speaking—"that Connie took Ehmke out of a game with the Yankees late in the season. This was the game in which the Yankees scored 13 runs and Ruth hit one out of the park with the bases full. After the game Connie said to Ehmke, 'That's the last game you will ever start for us until you come and tell me you are ready to pitch. You were not ready today. You knew it, and you should have told me so when I sent you out to warm up.'

"Right after that series we started West. Connie told Ehmke he needn't bother about packing. 'We don't need you,' he explained.

"When we got back Ehmke put on a uniform again and worked out, but to all outward appearances Connie didn't even know Ehmke was around, and most of the ballplayers figured he was through for the year. We had just about cinched the pennant when Ehmke came up to Connie again to ask if he was going to be allowed to pitch another game for us, and Connie answered him in the same words: 'When you tell me you are ready to pitch, I will use you.' Finally we cinched the championship and moved on to Chicago.

"The morning of the first game we had a general meeting with all the players in Connie's suite. This was at eleven o'clock. It lasted about 30 minutes. When it was over, all the players drifted out. That is, all but Ehmke. Connie and I were standing over by a window, with our backs turned, discussing some further details about the game, which was then only a couple of hours away. I didn't even realize that Ehmke was still in the room. But evidently Connie did. At any rate, he suddenly turned,

looked at Ehmke and asked, 'Is there anything you want to say to me, Howard?'

"Ehmke stood in the middle of the room, with his hat in his hand. 'I just wanted to ask if you plan to use me in the Series,' Ehmke said.

"'You know what I told you. When you are ready to pitch I will use you.'

"'Well, I'm ready to pitch, and I'm ready right now.'

"'All right, Howard; you pitch the game today.'"

Mr. Collins breaks the thread of the yarn at this point to report that he almost swooned on the spot, so great was his astonishment at the audacity of the aged leader of the Athletics.

"You see, Connie makes a study of his men," he said. "He knows most of them better than they know themselves, and he knows Ehmke better than any of us do. He knew that Ehmke would be ready if he said he was. He knew that under the circumstances Ehmke would pitch as he had never pitched before. This is why Connie is the greatest manager in baseball; with him, knowing the game is not nearly as important as knowing his men."

I don't suppose it is necessary to repeat that Ehmke justified Mr. McGillicuddy's daring move by stepping out and turning in one of the greatest games ever pitched in the history of World Series baseball; not only did he turn the National League champions back, he fanned 13 of them to set a new record.

The Ten-Run Inning

October 14, 1929. The boys are still jabbering about that 10-for-10 inning the A's put on to pull the fourth game out of the raging flames after trailing by eight runs. It is unlikely that anything can possibly happen in the innings that are yet to come that will match this mad batting onslaught of the American Leaguers, when 15 men

went to the plate and 10 of them scored in one inning.

None of the experts seemed quite decided just where to place the blame for the Cubs' collapse. Mr. Joe McCarthy is criticized by some of the second-guessers for leaving his starting pitcher, Root, in too long. Root pitched to seven hitters in this inning, and six of them hit him for solid wallops, among which was the hardest and longest home run of the Series. When Mr. McCarthy took him out four runs had crossed the plate and two runners were on the bases, nobody was out and the entire Cub team was in a state of panic.

Yet it is likely that if it had not been for a capricious sun Root might have got by the inning all right and gone on to win by a fairly decisive score. Wilson lost two fly balls in the sun, and one of them went on to the back wall for a 30-cent home run.

No fair-minded filbert could fail to recognize that it was strictly an American League sun. Local astrologers, peering at the gentleman through elongated binoculars, claim he was garbed in the livery of a Philadelphia player and that he even shifted his position on signal from the A's dugout, responding instantly to the mysterious wigwags of Mr. Cornelius McGillicuddy's scorecard. Old Sol, as he is affectionately known to his fellow Elks, was easily the hero of the A's sensational victory. Indeed, anyone with sufficient brass might be disposed to say that he rose to the occasion brilliantly.

Hack Wilson never was a Speaker in action, but he would have gone through that game with a perfect average if the sun hadn't blinded him at a devastating moment. I'm kind of sorry the fates kicked him around. Wilson belongs to that school of ballplayers Ring Lardner immortalized. A big, laughing, honest, egotistical and lovable human. I don't think I'll ever forget the picture of him leaving the grounds here Saturday. The whole world had crashed around him in that grisly inning when Haas' hit went through him for a home run.

He came through the gates with his big bearlike head slumped down on his chest, looking neither to right nor left. An unlighted cigaret dangled from his lips. He walked through two long lines of jubilant fans, but for the moment there was a brief commiserating silence. It was impossible to escape the misery of the man.

At his side toddled a three-year-old youngster, a boy known all around the league as "Little Hack." The youngster hung to his dad's hamlike paw. As he ran, almost, to keep step with the man he tilted his small head upward and said something, and the man reached down and picked him up in his enormous arms and kissed him

"Nuts to you, Mr. Mack"

June 24, 1942. "Remember that day we were playing Cleveland?" remarked Lieutenant Mickey Cochrane.

"And Bob Johnson overran a line drive in left field?" laughed Mr. Jimmy Dykes.

"That's the day," the lieutenant picked up. "One of the Clevelands hits a ball out there and Bob tries to make a shoestring catch. The ball goes through his legs for a triple. There's a man on and, of course, he scores, and now the tying run is on third. Did I remember to tell you there were two out at the time? Grove's boiling, but he

strikes the next guy out and we win.

"Now we are back in the dressing room and Mr. Grove is putting the blast on plenty. 'What kind of left fielder does this team have? What does he use for a head,' and . . . well, you know Grove. It goes on and on.

"Presently Connie Mack spoke up, and I don't have to tell you about Mr. Mack. About how quiet and placid and even-spoken he is, and how he hates profanity, even slang. 'Now Robert,' he said,

The Big Three of the 1929–1931 Philadelphia Athletics pitching staff:
Rube Walberg, Lefty Grove, George Earnshaw.—*NBL*

very soothingly, 'the boy couldn't have caught the ball in the first place and, after all, we did win. Besides that, may I say you storm and fuss too much. You get everybody excited. It would be much better if you controlled your temper and went along with the rest of us.'"

Lieutenant Cochrane nudged Mr. Dykes and laughed: "You remember, don't you?" Mr. Dykes, pulling at his inevitable cigar, nodded and smiled.

"Well, Grove looked at Connie and screamed, 'Go along with the boys! I'm the guy who wins 30 games a year for you and I'd like to say this: nuts to you, Mr. Mack!'"

The lieutenant nudged Mr. Dykes again. "Remember? Connie stretched his

long, lean neck out, looked Grove in the face and practically shouted, 'Nuts to you, too!' At least nine of our guys went into a swoon. They couldn't imagine Connie saying nuts."

Mr. Dykes flicked a bale of ashes from his cigar. "You don't mind if I tell Williams you cleaned that one up a little bit, do you?" he commented dryly.

P.S.—Just what did the priestly Mr. Mack say?

[A later column explains that what Mack actually said was, "To hell with you." Mack was not the only saint to prove human at bottom. Granny Rice's wife told my mother that Granny cursed like a sailor—but only in his sleep.—P. W.]

Lefty Grove

May 6, 1936. The young man looked at the withered patriarch who sat in the big chair shaking with palsy and said, "Dad, didn't you used to tell me about a baseball pitcher named Lefty Grove when I was a little shaver bouncing around the neighborhood?" The old pappy guy nodded his head.

And the young man continued, "Wasn't he a tall left-hander who pitched a long time for Baltimore in the International League and an even longer time for Connie Mack's Athletics, and wasn't he the fellow who used to strike out as many as 300 hitters some seasons?" The old rooster nodded again.

The young man went back to the script: "Well, Dad, this will give you a belt. There's another Lefty Grove around and he's pitching for the Boston Red Sox, and right now he's the hottest thing in baseball. The hitters can't get a loud foul off him. He's pitched five games and won 'em all. Listen to this . . ."

The young man sprayed the room with sizzling statistics. He told how the new sensation had pitched a two-hit shutout against the New York Yankees to open the season; how he followed with a three-hit victory against the Washington Senators and then another easy win over the Yankees. Two days later, as a relief pitcher, he held the Chicago White Sox runless in one and two-thirds innings. After which he blanked the Cleveland Indians 6-0 and yesterday he held the Detroit Tigers scoreless, 2-0.

"You see, Dad, this Lefty Grove of our time must be a wonder," went on the young man. "Not only have three of his five victories been shutouts but he has allowed only one earned run in 44⅔ innings, or in all the innings he has pitched. This run was a homer by Myril Hoag, of the Yankees. Anyway, the figures show he has pitched only one bad ball all season, and you'll have to admit that's real pitching."

The old graybeard listened with a tolerant smile. Finally he wheezed, 'You through, Sonny? This here Lefty Grove you are talking about is one and the same critter. The very same one I used to tell you about in the nursery. What I can't understand is how anybody and particularly this here Hoag ever got a home run off him in 45 innings. Hoag wouldn't have got a home run off the Left Grove of my time in 45 years. But otherwise it sounds very much like the same Lefty, and I have no doubt at all but what it is."

Foxx's 61 Homers in 1932

March 15, 1940. SARASOTA—We sat in the crude pine-board dugout of the Boston Red Sox training camp and gnawed the gristle with James Emory Foxx of Sudlersville, Md., today. It was one of those hot, steamy days. A resinous goo worked itself up through the pine boards and crystal balls of honest sweat trickled down Mr. Foxx's soccer-ball face.

"You look light," we remarked.

"Down to 182. Lightest I've been at this stage in 10 years. Been playing a lot of golf this winter."

Mr. Foxx was a big chubby country kid when he came up to Connie Mack's Philadelphia Athletics in 1925. What were

Jimmy Foxx has just hit a home run in the first game of the 1929 World Series.
The catcher is Zack Taylor of Chicago.—*NBL*

the important changes that had taken place in the game since then?

"The rookies have it easier, I think. The newcomers today are big-leaguers the moment they arrive in camp, or at least they think they are.

"Every one of the veterans steps aside and lets them have their own way. I think the old custom was better—better for the kids. The veterans pretended they didn't know the rookies were around. The softening-up process had already begun to set in when I came up, but even so the veterans made you realize your place. It was days before I got a chance to take my turn in batting practice and it would have been many more days if Connie Mack hadn't led me to the batting cage himself. And he carried the bat."

Mr. Foxx had a fine year at the bat last season and led the league in home runs, though this total was only 35. This would seem to suggest that it was getting tougher and tougher to make home runs and that Babe Ruth's existing record of 60 would never be topped.

"Oh, some strong young kid will come along and break it one of these days. I came close in 1932, you know. As a matter of fact, I actually did break it, but a barbed-wire arrangement set up outside the Shibe Park to keep kids from climbing the fence blocked me. I hit three balls that went outside the park; they hit the wire and bounced back on the field. They were just as legitimate as any of the other 58 home runs I hit but they didn't count."

The discussion was detoured to pitching. Mr. Foxx said it was easier to hit curveball pitching than fastball pitching, and, in the same breath, revealed he managed to do better than fair against the blinding slants of Cleveland's Bob Feller.

"Is Feller the fastest pitcher you ever hit against?"

"Hell, no! He's fast and his ball takes off, but I've swung against must faster pitching. See that old guy out there throwing to the hitters?". . . We looked and it was Mose Grove, now 40 and gray, who is still one of the Red Sox pitching dependables.

Billy Evans, the reformed umpire who now runs the Red Sox farm system, was sitting on the bench.

"Jimmy's right. There have been a number of pitchers who were faster than Feller. Grove was only one of them. There was Vean Gregg, Joe Wood, Ed Walsh and, of course, Walter Johnson, who was the king of speed."

Mr. Foxx toweled his dripping chin. . . . "As long as you're going to put it in the paper you might say for me that Feller's fast enough. I don't mind telling you it's not exactly a cinch to stand up there in front of him."

Mickey Cochrane

August 9, 1938. It would be interesting to know what Mickey Cochrane's thoughts are as he wends his way to that Wyoming ranch to spend the rest of the baseball season away from the familiar hurly-burly of the diamond.

Mickey has just been released by the Detroit Tigers in the most surprising move of the year. Everybody said the Tigers never would release Mickey. He had won them two championships and put them into the World Series for the first time since 1909. It was Mickey's managerial feats backed up by his brilliant catching that changed an indifferent baseball city into a mad, howling bedlam. During that period Mickey was the biggest thing in town —even bigger than Ford. Indeed, he came close to being the town itself.

When the Tigers came home from a road trip thousands jammed the railroad station to cheer them, but most of all to cheer Mickey. Representative civic, religious and social bodies vied with one another in their efforts to honor him. But all this, it is well to remember, was when Mickey had the Tigers up there, when he was winning. He didn't do so well last year and the hysteria cooled down. He was doing worse this year when the surprising blow fell. Noth-

ing is so fickle as hero worship. Mickey must have known this all along. And now, of course, he knows it better than ever.

As the wheels of the train heading for Wyoming sing a dirge of harsh realism, Mickey's thoughts must concern themselves with the caprices of fate. Mickey has always been one of the nice fellows of baseball, pleasant, generous, industrious; he took his job seriously, but never himself.

In the beginning Mickey seemed to be the golden-haired boy of fate. He was a college hero and a campus idol. He went into professional baseball and practically from the start he was a star. It wasn't long before he had taken Cy Perkins' job away from him as first-string catcher of the Philadelphia Athletics—and Perkins was still a first-string catcher himself. Mickey and Perkins got along well from the start. Instead of being irked by the sudden success of the youngster, Perkins went out of his way to show Mickey the ropes of big-league catching. And later, when Mickey moved to the Tigers as the head man, he brought Perkins along with him as his assistant. This was the first chance he had to show his appreciation in a practical way. It was typical of the man.

Mickey Cochrane in action as catcher. — *NBL*

Before Mickey had moved to the Tigers he had begun to build up a modest fortune, something he could fall back on when his baseball days were ended. He had saved more than $100,000 and had high hopes of adding to it. Very high hopes because all of it was invested in gilt-edged securities that couldn't miss. Then the panic hit him and he was wiped out.

In 1934 Mickey went to the Tigers. The late Frank Navin bought him for $100,000—had to go out and borrow the money to close the deal, too. Almost from the start the Tigers progressed under Mickey. They won two championships in a row and, in between, a World Series. The city went wild. All the glittering exploits of Ty Cobb were forgotten. The king was dead and the new king, of course, would live forever in the hearts of the people —and the club owners. Navin died and

his business associate, Walter Briggs, took over the franchise. One of the first things he did was to change the name of the park from Navin Field to Briggs Stadium, a modest, self-effacing gesture.

A year ago the Tigers fought their way back into the pennant fight and were moving at high speed when, one hot afternoon, Bump Hadley of the Yankees lost control of a high hard one. That night Mickey lay in an uptown hospital hovering between life and death. The Hadley pitch had caught him in the head and produced a multiple fracture of the skull. All night long Cy Perkins walked up and down in front of the hospital, smoking one cigaret after another.

Mickey recovered but his playing days were over. From now on he would have to be a bench manager. That was all right.

Other bench managers had done well, and besides, Mickey was sitting pretty in Detroit.

The moral is as old as the hills. When you are on top you are great. When things start breaking against you you are just another guy. Here's your hat, and go out through the tradesman's entrance. Baseball, being a business, has always been like that and always will be.

Yes, it would be interesting to read Mickey's mind on his way west. Here's a fellow who never did anybody a wrong, who saved his money, only to lose it through no fault of his own; who had a brilliant career cut short by a thrown ball that almost sent him to his grave, and who now is unceremoniously booted out of his job. To him life must appear a very strange game indeed.

19

Hack Wilson

A Plumber

August 16, 1931. There are a lot of people who would rather watch Babe Ruth hit a long fly than see Hack Wilson smack the ball over the garden wall. One is an artist, the other a plumber.

A Field Hand at Heart

September 15, 1931. Mr. Wilson is a squat-sized, bull-necked gent who is no brighter or dumber than the usual run of professional sports headliners. He is amiable enough, but for the most part his temperament is regulated by the number of base hits he gets. He likes to sit up with the boys and inhale tubs of ale and tell Mike and Pat stories, of which he has a limitless fund, totalling two. His stand on sleep is that it is a fine thing if taken in moderation. Generally speaking, Mr. Wilson is what you would call a good fellow. He isn't especially vainglorious, and I imagine he would be just as content hitting home runs in Saginaw as at the Stadium. I don't suppose he was ever quite able to adjust himself to his new sphere of influence. Fundamentally Mr. Wilson is a field hand at heart.

A Short, Stumpy Geezer,
Built Close to the Ground Like a Toadstool

August 9, 1934. They handed Hack Wilson his unconditional release over in Brooklyn yesterday. This wasn't surprising. He wasn't hitting the size of his collar. Still, even in his best years Wilson didn't do quite that well. His collar was prodigious. The boys called him Great Neck. Wilson was a short, stumpy geezer, built close to the ground like a toadstool. . . .

Babe Herman of Brooklyn and Hack Wilson of the Cubs in 1930.—*NBL*

Why Casey Admired Hack Wilson

December 4, 1948. WASHINGTON—Tumult and turmoil have been running the bases here all week. An unprecedented open draft was put into motion; big-league players, demanding a cut in club earnings, were angrily denounced; a group of minors threatened to strike over pensions; suddenly and surprisingly, the head of the American League up and quit.

But through it all Casey Stengel, the Yankees' 68-year-old manager, has been holding daily court in the hotel lobby, regaling his colleagues with hilarious tales, startling transient onlookers with generous gesticulations, moving all and sundry to awe at the inexhaustibility of his speech and memory.

At almost the same moment Tom Yawkey, Red Sox owner, was announcing that he would get out of baseball before he'd turn over 20 percent of his gross to the hired hands, the most important thing in Stengel's life was the arrival of Joe Judge . . . and this, of course, reminded him of the day Boom Boom Beck refused to leave the pitcher's box.

"Judge was there," rasped Stengel. "He was my first baseman. We [the Dodgers] were playing the Phillies in their dinky park and Beck wasn't getting 'em out, so I had to get him out.

"'Gimme the ball,' I said.

"'No. I want to pitch, to one more hitter.'

"'You give me that ball,' I repeated, rough like.

"'I'm not going to give you the ball. Not until I pitch to one more hitter anyway. And that's that.'"

This was a first-time predicament for Stengel. Never before had one of his pitchers defied him in this manner. . . . "I'm wondering if I've got to throw the young man down and take the ball away from him, because after all I've got my managerial prestige to think about, when, all of a sudden, he rears back and fires the ball to right field and it bounces off that short fence and . . . "

Here Stengel paused briefly for confirmation from Judge. . . . "You was there. And tell me this: Did you ever see Hack Wilson make a better throw?"

Sudden detours and the introduction of seemingly irrelevant characters are common to Stengel narrations. But in due time continuity emerges.

"Wilson is playing right field and is bored with it all, which I can't say I blame him, considering the kind of ball we was playing. So when the ball bangs into the wall and bounces back on to the field, Hack thinks it's a base hit, which is understandable, because if it ain't a base hit what's it doing bouncing off the wall out there?

"Well, Wilson fields the ball and does what any right-fielder in his right mind would do, he cuts loose with a throw to second to keep the runner on first from advancing, only there ain't no runner there, but it was the right play, just the same, and, I repeat, a great throw."

20

When the Dodgers Were Daffy

Wilbert Robinson

March 12, 1930. CLEARWATER—The most conspicuous person in the training camp of the Brooklyn Dodgers is Mr. Wilbert Robinson, manager of the club which finished a dawdling sixth a year ago. It is no difficult feat for Mr. Robinson to attain a degree of conspicuity because he is, taking him circumferentially, the largest manager in baseball. Indeed, I recall having read somewhere in the higher literature of the sport that he is the dinosaur of the dugouts.

On very hot Florida days Mr. Robinson is a distinct boon to the community, and mothers bring their young out-of-doors to allow them to play their childish games in the soothing shadows cast by the gentleman's superstructure. The spectacle of hordes of children scampering around in this vast shaded area is very moving to behold, and it is characteristic of the generosity of Mr. Robinson and his deep interest in the woes of humanity that each spring sees him becoming beefier and bulkier.

The visitor to the Dodgers' camp finds Mr. Robinson garbed in a turned-down Panama hat and knickers which seem to have been cut from the mainsail of a three-masted schooner. He is out on the field booming guttural exhortations to the demon athletes. "Show me some of that old pep!" he roars, and the tall palms that fringe the field rock and sway from the force of the blast.

At one stage of the proceedings yesterday Mr. Robinson waddled down to the warm-up box to watch the veteran Dazzy Vance throw a few, suggesting, as he moved over the sandy stretches, a plump dromedary laden with a cargo of choice beefs and suets. Mr. Robinson studied Vance with a critical eye for a few minutes and nodded his assorted chins approvingly. "Old Daz is right this year," he commented. "And when Old Daz is right he's right."

Mr. Robinson has a way of presenting these technical matters with a crystal-like clarity and an open-face lucidity that make every detail easily understood by the layman.

Ebbets Field

July 24, 1930. No more pop bottles at Ebbets Field! The thirsty customer quaffs his favorite beverage out of a paper cup, and realizes how futile an instrument of protest a paper cup can be. It seems that during the recent series with the Cubs a couple of bottles were cast in the general direction of an umpire.

The banishment of the pop bottles in Brooklyn already has had a deleterious effect on Harry Stevens' receipts. It develops that when pop is served out of paper cups the fans aren't so thirsty. It seems that hitherto many of the Brooklyn enthusiasts bought their pop not so much for the thirst quencher. Apparently they get a bigger kick out of the game if they have an agency for direct action right at hand. The bottle is more effective than the squawk. There is no getting away from the fact that the pop bottle is an essential part of a highly geared baseball enthusiasm. It is the symbol of vigorous, keen thought, civic fervor and ever-ready protest.

The bottle has a peculiar significance in Brooklyn. Were there a baseball crest for the Dodgers it would show a pop bottle rampant on a field strewn with umpires.

The Birth of the "Bums"?

March 22, 1932. ST. PETERSBURG— There is still some question as to what the Brooklyns should be called this season. They used to be known as the Robins but Wilbert Robinson is no longer with the team. They were called the Robins after Robbie.

A Brooklyn fan is a rabid soul, no matter where you find him. Geographical frontiers in no way affect his flaming emotions. Yesterday the Brooklyns lost their fifth game of the spring season. It was a particularly disheartening defeat.

They were shut out by the Boston Braves, who are in the process of demonstrating that they can be worse in March than they are in July. In case you didn't know, everybody is kicking them around down here.

Well, anyway, after the shutout a large, red-faced gent got up out of a box and came over to the press stand. "If you fellows are still trying to dope out a name for the Brooklyns I can help you," he raged. "Call 'em the Bums."

I am happy to report that this suggestion did not go over so well with the industrious young men in the press stand. Indeed, I do not believe they even heard it. At the moment it was offered half of the young men were debating the respective merits of the Culbertson-Lenz bridge systems and the other half were deploring the unkempt condition of Florida's putting greens. As for your correspondent, he was wondering who the snappy-looking blonde sitting back of first base was and where she came from. Possibly she was hitchhiking to Miami. Apparently there is a law against any young people visiting St. Petersburg.

[Willard himself said he heard a cabbie call the club "our Bums" in 1938, but it's hard to imagine he hadn't heard and absorbed this earlier story.—P. W.]

Spring training, Florida: Dazzy Vance and a stylishly attired Wilbert Robinson.—*United Press International*

Dazzy Vance

March 28, 1939. It isn't easy to talk about the new Brooklyn Dodgers when one of the old Brooklyn Dodgers is around. This happened to be the pleasant situation today. Arthur C. Vance, the erstwhile Dazzler, had the floor. Mr. Vance toiled for the Dodgers when they were the Dodgers —back in the days when Pegler christened them the Daffiness Boys.

"Robbie was as daffy as the rest of us," admitted Mr. Vance with a wide, reminiscent smile. He was referring to amiable Wilbert Robinson, who wet-nursed the Dodgers through 18 years of strife and hilarity. "The only person he was afraid of, or paid any attention to, was his wife. He

always called her Maw. She knew baseball pretty well, and when we'd drop a tough game she'd give Robbie the dickens. She'd say, 'Why didn't you do this,' and 'Why didn't you do that?'

"One day we were playing the Cubs, and Robbie started a second-string pitcher, and he got his ears pinned back before the first inning was half over. Robbie just sat there on the bench with his hands folded across his stomach as if he were enjoying the shambles in the pitcher's box.

"Finally he got up and walked over to a box where Maw was sitting. He put his hands on his hips, stuck out his neck and sneered, 'Now I hope you are satisfied,' When he got back to the bench he snorted, 'What makes these women think they can tell men how to play baseball—'"

It seems that in those days practically everybody tried to tell Robbie how to play baseball. There was a time when even the great Babe Herman tried his skull at masterminding.

"And darned if it didn't work, too," recalled Mr. Vance, as he touched a match to a fierce-looking tobacco which caused less hardy bystanders to retreat in terror. "We had lost six or seven in a row when the Babe, writhing in the throes of an inspiration, suggested to Robbie that he pick the starting lineup out of a hat.

"'Schoolboy stuff,' scoffed Robbie.

"'Well, we're playing schoolboy baseball, anyway,' commented the Babe.

"Anyway, Robbie succumbed, and we won a ball game. The next day we used the hat formula again, and we were brutally beaten. After that game Robbie turned to Herman and barked, 'From now on you play the outfield and I'll manage this ball club.'"

We seemed to recall that in the old days the Dodgers were made up of two clubs—one which endeavored to interpret the game, and another which stressed the warming qualities of good fellowship.

"Oh, you mean the Big Four," laughed Mr. Vance. "I don't know whether you ought to write about that or not. It wouldn't make good reading for the youth of the land."

By degrees the details of the only secret organization ever connected with a baseball team were revealed. To qualify as a member of the Big Four a player had to ignore all training rules, especially those which pertained to sleep and liquid refreshments.

"The membership was restricted solely to those who had the makings of a first-class bum," stated Mr. Vance with what seemed to be high pride.

The Big Four met secretly, usually in the back room of a friendly speakeasy.

There was a membership committee which carefully passed on qualifications of aspiring brothers. The initiation rituals were more expensive than impressive, since the newly inducted brother was always compelled to pick up the check.

"Jess Petty, the pitcher, was the only member we ever had to blackball," said Mr. Vance. There was an understandable note of apology in his voice. One does not like to talk of a fallen brother.

"Petty stayed out all night in Chicago, and Robbie caught him and fined him," continued the depressed Mr. Vance. "He tried to get back in for years, but we would have no part of him." Throughout the remainder of his career Petty remained an untouchable to members of the Big Four. He had committed the one unpardonable crime. He had been caught.

"And he would have been one of our most illustrious members," sighed Vance, sadly. "He was a real good man."

As a member of the old Dodgers Mr. Vance was not only the exalted ruler of the Big Four but the Man of Magic. Time after time he rescued moody Dodger hitters from a batting slump by uttering mysterious words of magic over their bats. We asked the gentleman how he accounted for his strange powers.

"I am the seventh son of a seventh son," began Mr. Vance dreamily—"Oh, hell, you know how ballplayers are. They'll do anything to get out of a slump. One day I told Lefty O'Doul I could help him. I took his bat and gave it the old abracadabra. He hadn't had a hit for five games. That day he got three. From then on I was Mahatma Vance."

Mr. Vance believes ballplayers are children at heart, and are helped by simple applications of psychology. He found that out himself when a torn shirtsleeve made him a pitching monster in the eyes of the opposition. One day in Cincinnati Mr. Vance was at bat. Adolf Luque was in the box. He threw a fastball in close, and as Mr. Vance tried to pull away from the plate the ball caught the end of his sleeve and tore it to the elbow.

"I kept on pitching with the torn shirt," relates Mr. Vance, and "pretty soon the fans started to yell. They said the hitters couldn't see the ball, that the fluttering strands of the sleeve obscured their vision. This gave the hitters an idea, and they started to complain, too.

"Well, all of a sudden I found I had an asset in the torn sleeve. Hank Deberry, our catcher, helped me; he would growl to the hitters that he couldn't see the ball, either. This was just a gag, of course, but it kept the hitters worried. Anyway, from then on I always managed to have a torn sleeve when I pitched."

We mentioned that such outright cunning was in open conflict with the established traditions of the Daffiness Boys. "But you must remember it was not planned," Mr. Vance hastily corrected. "It was the outgrowth of an accident."

Lefty O'Doul

March 15, 1933.   Mr. Francis J. O'Doul, the Brooklyns' star slugger who led both leagues in hitting last year with .368, was talking about quakes.

"I can remember the one we had back home in 1906," said Mr. O'Doul, "and although I was only nine years old I'll never forget it."

"That's one thing about Irish quakes," interjected Mr. Casey Stengel, "you never forget them."

"Say, you never forget any kind of quake," insisted Mr. O'Doul, who was eager to get along with his personal reminiscences as a veteran survivor.

"But the Irish quakes are very different," persisted Mr. Stengel. "They have singing and food and cigars, and it's all sort of pleasant like."

It became evident that the two gentlemen were not talking about the same thing. In fact, Mr. Joe Judge, the first baseman, made bold to suggest that this was the case, adding:

"While I have not been following the conversation with unflagging interest, I am prompted to believe from the fragments which have assailed my ears that Mr. Stengel confuses quakes with wakes."

"Oh, you mean quakes!" exclaimed Mr. Stengel.

Everyone seemed content to let the matter stand, and Mr. O'Doul got along with his story about how he lived through the 1906 holocaust to become ultimately the idol of merry old Flatbush.

There wasn't much to the story, except that Mr. O'Doul can still remember seeing bricks flying through the air as if they were feathers and that people who were sleeping were blown right out of their homes, beds and all, some of them without being disturbed in their sleeping, although, as Mr. Stengel commented at this stage, "It would be easier to believe that stuff about the beds if you saw it."

Mr. O'Doul spent the past winter in Japan teaching the collegians how to hit. They have a quake over there almost every afternoon, but for the most part they are mild tremors—"so small that over here we would throw 'em back in." Still, on occasions a real tremor hits the empire, "and if you happen to be on the ball field you can see the diamond bounce up and down."

"Say, that's nothing!" cut in Mr. Stengel. "Did you ever try to play on the diamond at Bradenton?"

Your agent thought it high time to swing the conversation back to the Brooklyns—that having been the original theme, anyhow—and what he learned was that everything is going to be pretty much all right at Ebbets Field this year, provided:

"We get the pitching. Yep, we gotta get the pitching."

One of these days your agent, just for the novelty of it, would like to talk to some manager or ballplayer and be told that there is enough batting and fielding and running strength to win regardless of the pitching. A manager with nine Ruths in their prime would hesitate to say he had enough batting power to offset a suspected weakness in the box, because that is one of the traditions of the business. The Brooklyns are stronger behind the plate, in the infield and in the outfield, but if they are to get anywhere this year, "they gotta get the pitching."

And a good way to get the pitching is to get it the way Mr. O'Doul got it last year—with a full swing from the hip. A few more Mr. O'Douls hitting .368 or thereabouts and the Brooklyns might have finished out in front in '32 instead of nine games back.

Babe Herman

December 22, 1931. They tell a story on Mr. Herman which I always thought typified the gay mental abandon of his club. Mr. Herman approached one of the newspapermen in a hotel lobby and complained to him about the personal character of his writings.

"I wish you would lay off'n me," said Mr. Herman. "I don't mind so much on my account, but the missus has funny ideas."

While he was talking, Herman reached into his coat pocket and took out the stub of a cigar. "Got a match?" he asked. But before the newspaperman could come up with a match Mr. Herman, who had proceeded meanwhile to puff, experimentally and with vigor, cried out: "Never mind. It's lit!"

A Daring Outfield Maneuver

January 27, 1932. Has anyone told you about the national baseball school, located in Los Angeles? It is a school where the young are taught how to smack the apple and carry the mail around the sacks.

They say it is the only one of its kind in the country. In one respect it certainly must be, because I note that Mr. Babe Herman, of Brooklyn, is a member of the faculty.

Now, Mr. Herman is all right in his own way—and one of the indictments against him is that he generally is in his own way, especially when he gets on base. But somehow it is not easy to envision Mr. Herman as a professor in a baseball school, not even with the ranking of D.B., which in academic circles is Doctor of Bone.

Mr. Herman is an individualist. Conventions have never meant anything to him. Until Mr. Herman came along baseball was a stencilled routine, a daily repetition of the civil war pattern. There had been no Marx, Tolstoy or Shaw to pioneer radical innovations.

It was Mr. Herman who introduced the three-base or triple out to baseball, easily the most outstanding contribution to base running the art has known in more than 80 years. There are some critics who make mockery of the stratagem, but that is only because the professor is ahead of the times.

The three-base or triple out consists of retiring the side on a base hit. Obviously it is effective only when the bases are full, nobody is out and the batter hits a triple. It can be executed only with a complete detachment of mind and an absolute cessation of thinking. Preferably the batter, in such circumstances, should imagine himself to be in a rowboat at sea playing a mandolin.

It is a tribute to Mr. Herman's inventive genius that up to now he is the only major-leaguer who has thoroughly mastered the play, although there have been many who have tried with great earnestness. As Mr. Wilbert Robinson used to say, "There is only one Babe Herman." Old-timers used to say that about Pop Anson and later about Ty Cobb.

Mr. Herman is also known as the author of the skull bounce, a daring outfield maneuver which many critics believe is too fantastic ever to become a permanent part of the game. I advise these critics not to be too dogmatic in their judgment. The skull bounce will last at least as long as Mr. Herman's skull, and, being one of his devoted followers, I trust that will be a great number of years.

The skull bounce is not as involved as the three-base or triple out, yet it is not altogether simple. It consists of standing directly under a high fly ball, waiting until it descends with a comforting bang upon the skull and then trying to catch it on the rebound. Fellows like Speaker and Simmons say this is not only foolish but that it is injurious to the baseball, but Mr. Herman, who is, to repeat, far ahead of his times, has evolved the theory that it is much easier to catch a ball that has bounced once than a ball that has not bounced at all.

Now what is going to be the result of Mr. Herman's missionary work among the youngsters who want to learn how to play big-league baseball? Once graduated, what kind of baseball will Mr. Herman's pupils play? The answer seems obvious; they will play Herman baseball. I think this is something to look forward to with keen interest.

One thing that recommends the Herman system, as taught and demonstrated by the professor himself, is that no thought is required. Or very little at the most. For almost a century only one system has prevailed in baseball—the Abner Doubleday. That this system is not entirely without flaws was proved by Connie Mack back in 1914, when he developed the perfect ball team—and the customers walked out on him. They'd never walk out on the Herman system. They might have to be carried out, but I don't imagine they'd mind that. Anyway, by all means let's give the Herman system a trial. A trial by jury in necessity, but a trial nevertheless.

[Herman was more than a clown. He had a lifetime average of .324 and one year he even hit .393, although—with typical Dodger luck—he didn't win the batting title. The problem was that it was 1930, and across the river a Giant named Terry was hitting .401.—P. W.]

The End of Prohibition

March 16, 1933. MIAMI, Fla.—Stirred by national ardor and civic pride, members of the Brooklyn baseball club will hold a formal keg party one night this week in a ceremony of patriotic beer drinking. Since guzzling has been made patriotic, Mr. Joseph Gilleaudeau, who is down here looking after the social phases of the club, feels the Brooklyns should set the pace.

This is the first time in the memory of the world's oldest reporter that the management of a baseball club has called its athletes together in the midst of a spring training season and compelled them to tear into the foamy stuff or suffer the consequences.

I am told that Mr. Gilleaudeau entertains no fears about the loyalty of the Brooklyns and that he is confident, when the call comes to advance with unsheathed steins upon the embattled Pilsener pots, every man jack will will respond with alacrity and parched throats, determined to save the country at any sacrifice.

From what I can gather this is to be in the form of a light workout—a sort of practice drinking session—the purpose of which is to better acquaint the athletes with their grave responsibilities to the new administration. None of the young men will be expected to save the country by his own individual efforts all in one night, and particular steps will be taken to see that no such martyrdom, however admirable, is attempted. In fact, the plan is to hold the young men in check as much as possible so that they will have something left when the big national drive begins after legalization.

The action of the Brooklyns indicates definitely that baseball may be counted upon 100 percent in the happy scheme to drink the country back to prosperity. The surprise is that Colonel Jacob Ruppert and his Yankees did not swing the first bung starter. His attitude has been rather mysterious, and I am forced to admit there has been widespread criticism. It is one thing to join up wholeheartedly with a patriotic campaign and quite another to enroll for crass commercial purposes. There are sinister insinuations abroad that the Colonel is a beer profiteer, and that all his posturings on patriotism are just so much sour yeast.

"If the Colonel was really one of us—a soldier in the field—he would have a keg of dark brew in the Yankees' dugout right now," said a loyal suds blower as he released his grip on the billiard table and slid gently to the floor amid resonant burps.

The prebigoted era, when the athletes dunked their cheese and rye bread in bowls of bock, was an era of healthy bitterness and rowdy drama. Whether beer will bring the spirited, swashbuckling player back to the diamond, who can say? At the moment I think Mr. Casey Stengel speaks for the whole fraternity when he declares:

"My only regret is that I have but one set of tonsils to give to my country."

21

Rabbit Maranville

"Guess who's the ape"

March 7, 1931. When Jim Thorpe was sold to the Boston Braves Mr. Rabbit Maranville, then a youngster, was short-stopping for the team. Thorpe and Mr. Maranville struck up an immediate friendship. Their outlook on life was strangely similar. They both liked to look upon the Pilsener when it was pale.

The Buck Herzogs invited Thorpe and Mr. Maranville to spend a certain Sunday with them. The lady prepared a large feed for the distinguished guests. When it came time to eat neither Thorpe nor Mr. Maranville was to be seen.

"You go out and find those fellows and bring them into the house," commanded Mrs. Herzog. "I am not going to allow my dinner to get cold."

The Herzogs lived on a big farm, so Buck set out to see what had happened to his two teammates. He found them up in a tree, leaping from limb to limb.

"What the heck are you guys doing up there?" yelled the astounded host.

"We're playing Tarzan and the Apes," answered Mr. Maranville. "Guess who's the ape."

Herzog reported that the eats were ready and ordered them to come down to earth. By way of reply the giant Indian and the midget infielder climbed still higher among the branches and began to sing.

Herzog threw stones at them, but this had no effect. "If you guys don't come down I'm going to get a shotgun and take a bang at you!" threatened Herzog. This was a cue for a loud and prolonged guffaw from the two mischievous gents who had gone to nest in the treetop.

Finally Herzog decided on strategy. He brought out a bottle of very rare rum and placed it under the tree. "If this doesn't fetch 'em down nothing will," grumbled Herzog.

It fetched 'em down, all right. Or almost down. Mr. Maranville scrambled down to the first tree limb and with a graceful sweeping motion seized the bottle with one hand, and then went scurrying back up the tree to join his less agile but thoroughly delighted mate.

And for the next hour they sat high in the sky, drinking to the health of their generous host.

A youthful Rabbit Maranville of the Boston Braves and Everett (Deacon) Scott of the Red Sox. — *NBL*

"As good as it ever was"

March 25, 1935. A shrunken little old man sat in my room today, swung his left leg back and forth from the knee vigorously and said, "See, it's as good as it ever was."

The little old man was Rabbit Maranville, dean of the big-leaguers, and he was referring to a multiple fracture suffered in an exhibition game a year ago. He slid into home plate, was blocked and the leg snapped. The shattered bones protruded from the flesh, and so ghastly was the spectacle that his fellow workers on the Boston Braves turned their heads. It was seconds before any of them made a move to go to him. Finally big, lumbering, emotional Shanty Hogan went to the plate, cushioned him in his arms and whispered, "You scored the run, anyway, Rab."

"Who was going to stop me?" snapped the gallant little veteran, biting his lips. "Gimme a cigaret."

Letters of sympathy poured in. One day there were 786. And so many rabbits were sent to him—live ones and stuffed ones— that the hospital had to assign a special attendant to handle them. This demonstration of affection surprised the veteran. That these people, most of them total strangers, were interested in him inspired new courage and determination. . . . "I'll be back at second by July," he announced.

But he wasn't. Something went wrong with the bone-setting job, and the leg had to be rebroken. This time the cast wasn't removed until late August. The season almost over, playing was out of the question. For weeks he hobbled around on crutches. Later a cane was all he needed, and finally he could walk a bit without support.

One night at home the radio was on. The melodies of a hot band filled the living room. The veteran sat in an easy chair beating time with his feet. A few moments later he found himself on the floor going timidly through the jerky patterns of a jazz dance. To his delight nothing happened. . . . "From then on I danced three or four hours a day," said the Rab. "I didn't have anybody to dance with, so I danced alone. People used to come into the house, look at me and go away shaking their heads. They thought I was nuts. But all the while I was getting my leg in shape."

After some days the Rab extended his home-training exercises to practicing sprints from a crouch position. . . . "I used to start from the kitchen and run through the house to the front porch. But I finally had to give that up when the missus showed signs of agreeing with the neighbors."

I had seen the Rab at fielding practice in the morning, and the sadness I felt as I watched him hobble stiffly around second base was intensified as he sat there in the chair detailing the gritty fight he had made to come back. I knew, too, how Bill McKechnie felt about this little old man. . . . "For the first time in my life I wish I wasn't in baseball," said McKechnie. "When the time comes I must tell Maranville he is through."

That time will come on opening day. Leslie Mallon will be at second base—a fair-to-middling ballplayer. There is nothing else McKechnie can do.

"How'd you think I looked out there this morning?" asked the Rab. I told him, "Fine." What else can you say. The Rab reminded me that he had replaced Wagner at shortstop in 1912. . . . "And you know the Dutchman was still a great hitter. Something went wrong with his legs."

That's the history of veterans. Something always goes wrong with their legs. In the Rab's case that something was more disastrous than is usually the case. But, like all veterans, the Rab refuses to admit he is through. As he got up to go he pawed out sharply with his rebuilt leg and said: "She feels swell. I can hardly wait for that opener."

[*Maranville, unfortunately, was* through. *The 1935 season was his last. He appeared in 23 games, and batted a dismal .149. —P. W.*]

22

The Gas House Gang

"I'm surprised at you, Frankie"

January 26, 1935. Mr. Frankie Frisch is not quite sure whether a baseball manager should try to think or not these days.

It is the custom of most managers to call their players together before a ball game and go over the hitters. "Well, we are doing this one day last summer," relates Mr. Frisch, "and I am giving the boys some very inside information on the team we are to play. I am particularly stressing the hitters and I am addressing my remarks directly to my pitchers. I start with the lead-off hitter and I go right down the line pointing out the weaknesses and strengths of the various men. I think I am doing an excellent job, when Dizzy gets up and cracks, 'Oh, hell, why waste all this time talking about pitching. There's only one way to pitch. Just go out there and blow 'em down.'" Mr. Frisch admits this was a most embarrassing moment for a mastermind.

What kind of fellow is this strange Mr. Dean? "Well, he ain't strange at all. And I wouldn't call him cocky, either. He simply believes in himself. He has the notion he can throw a baseball past any hitter that ever walked to the plate and he operates

on that theory. As you may have noted, he is not backward about saying so."

Despite the fact that Dean does not lend himself very readily to masterminding, it is obvious that Mr. Frisch has a deep admiration for him. . . . "Nothing ever bothers him. We had to beat Cincinnati in our last game in order to cinch the pennant. I was plenty worried and showed it. Dizzy came back to the bench after warming up. He knew what was on my mind. He broke out in a laugh, jerked my cap off, ran his fingers through my hair and said: 'I'm surprised at you, Frankie. Don't you know who's pitching for us today? Old Diz. These fellows will be lucky if they get three hits.' What are you going to do with a man like that?"

In the eighth or ninth inning the Reds loaded the bases with none out. Mr. Frisch, who like all managers makes a business of worrying, came in to the box. . . . "I started to talk to Dizzy. I said something about bearing down, getting the side out, the game over and all that sort of thing. . . . He stood there on the mound tossing the ball in the air, catching it one-handed, waited until I had finished and smiled: 'Frankie,

Paul Dean, Dizzy Dean and St. Louis Cardinals manager Frank Frisch. Note that Frisch's right foot seems to be in a cast of some sort.—*NBL*

you go back and play second base; let old Diz do the pitching.' Of course there was nothing at stake but the game that was to decide whether we got into the World Series or not. What are you going to do with a guy like that?"

"You can't have my run"

June 22, 1949. I thought I had heard all the Dizzy Dean stories that have ever been told but I came across one a while ago that was new to me. The big right-hander spent a couple of seasons here in Houston, a Cardinal farm unit. Houston was playing Fort Worth and Mr. Dean, who always fancied himself an excellent hitter, got a home run in one of the earlier innings. But along about the fifth or sixth he got into a jam and filled the bases and the manager, one

Joe Schultz, took him out. Instead of going to the showers Mr. Dean went directly to the scoreboard, climbed a ladder and removed the one-run marker he had contributed. Then he returned to the dugout.

"And just what was all that funny business about?" demanded the manager.

"Twarn't no funny business," groused Mr. Dean. "If I can't pitch you can't have my run."

"S-l-u-d"

April 22, 1950. The smart set has adopted Dizzy Dean. To the bistro snobs the old pitcher's Tobacco Road argot is just too, too killing for words. To the pseudo-intellectuals he is a droll realist uttering great truths in an unadorned mud language. But to most of us the senior member of the famous pitching team of "me and Paul" is simply a pleasant fellow with been-there experience who gives you an adequate picture of what's happening on the ball field.

The Dean tongue is pure literary inspiration. I happened to be sitting next to him in the St. Louis press box the day he invented the very inspired "slud." I was doing a series on his daring experiments in the field of phonetic symbols and my ears were alert to any new sounds. A Brooklyn runner beat a throw to one of the bags. . . . "He slud in and was safe."

"Never heard you use that one before," I beamed at the Great Man.

"What?" he answered, a bit coyly, it seemed.

"That word, slud."

He laughed. "Well, that's just what the boy did, he slud."

Realizing I had been present at the birth of an etymological miracle, an adventure given to few mortals, and wishing to be sure that all the details be accurately recorded, I asked:

"How would you spell it?"

"S-l-u-d. Just like you'd spell slud," he informed.

I note since this arrival here he has stated the correct spelling is s-l-o-o-d. New York affects some newcomers that way. Makes 'em pompous.

I regret to state that Dean is not yet altogether at home in television, a new medium for him, and the decision to force the commercials on him slows up his natural artistry and eloquence. At one stage following a sweaty hand-to-hand grapple with an awkwardly worded commercial, Old Diz grumbled:

"I don't see why I have to read all them commercials. Why don't they just let me tell 'em to drink the beer."

There must have been a million screen fans all over the metropolitan district who stood up at that moment and cheered.

Pepper Martin and the Musical Mudcats

March 24, 1938. BRADENTON, Fla.— Frank Frisch, the old Fordham Flash, sat on the lawn in front of his hotel pulling away at a cigar that was too big to be a baseball bat and too small to be a flagpole. Someone over in Tampa had made it up especially for him. Frisch was talking about his club, the St. Louis Cardinals, and how he expects to make a real good catcher of Don Padgett, outfielder by trade.

"And a funny thing about him," said Mr. Flash, "the simplest play back of the bat is the one he has most trouble—"

A gay, rollicking voice cut through the night air, rising high above the managerial utterances of Mr. Flash.

"And now, ladies and gentlemen, the Musical Mudcats will present that gripping classic of the hills, 'Willie, My Toes Are So Cold.'"

Six St. Louis Cardinals who made the 1935 National League All-Star team in 1935.
Left to right: Burgess Whitehead, manager Frank Frisch, Pepper Martin, Rip Collins, Joe Medwick and Dizzy Dean. — *Associated Press*

There followed a mad series of blasts, moans, sighs and loose, unclassified noises that somehow managed a rugged harmony and Mr. Flash explained, with a gesture of heavy weariness, that that was Martin and his mob. Which proved to be true. Mr. Pepper Martin and his orchestra, minus one artist at the moment, were brewing the regular nightly concert on the veranda of the old hotel down near the bay.

The Mudcats specialize in hoedown stuff. The touching lamentation about the cold toes of Willie's friend is an example. Under the magic baton of the old maestro, who is Mr. Martin himself, the boys bring out the beauty, feeling and warmth of these musical gems in a manner that leaves their listeners limp.

The Toscanini of the baselines is assisted by Mr. Frenchy Bordagaray at the washboard, Mr. Robert Weiland at the jug, Mr. Fibber McGee at the fiddle and Mr. Lon Warneke at the guitar, or git-tar, as the boys pronounce the name of the instrument. The old maestro is a git-tar man himself. Mr. Warneke wasn't able to be present at last night's concert. His wife had just presented him with what the poets call a bundle from heaven, out in Arkansas, and he has had to absent himself for what is hoped will be only a little period. "Warneke had a tougher time getting Martin's permission to leave the band to see his new baby than to leave the club," said Mr. Flash. "If it isn't one thing with him it is another."

This seems to be approximately true. The Pepper Pot must have action. He tears through life in much the same way he tears around the bases. Or used to when he was faster. He is an earthy, robust person with

Carrying the Torch. —*cartoon by Willard Mullin*

a teeming zest for living. About the only thing he can't do is yawn. He never has the time.

He drove to camp this year in one of those tan, lacquered things called a station wagon. Oklahoma City was his starting point. He had a mattress in the wagon. When he felt sleepy he pulled over under the trees along the road and staked himself to a generous portion of shut-eye. A few years ago he rode the rails to camp in the best approved hobo fashion. He didn't do this to save the money the club had advanced for railroad expenses. There's nothing cheap about John Leonard Martin. It just wasn't any fun riding to camp in a Pullman. Anybody could do that.

With a shudder, Frank Frisch recalled a bus ride the Cardinals had taken down here a year ago. They were headed across state for the east coast.

"I guess we were bowling along at about 70 miles an hour," said the manager, "when I heard a loud, sharp report. I was sitting up near the driver. We were pretty sure it was the backfire of a motor.

"Pretty soon there was another explosive blast. This time there wasn't a car within miles of us. I heard somebody say, 'There goes another,' and with that the roaring blast sounded again. It was Martin banging away at birds. He had been trying to hit 'em on the fly from a lurching bus."

The old maestro always carries his rifles with him. Four or five at a time. When he arrived here this trip it was long past midnight. The trip in the station wagon had been a long, hard one. Nobody would have mistaken him for the dapper Anthony Eden.

In fact, John Leonard looked exceedingly tough. The time of his arrival was calculated to arouse a certain suspicion to begin with, and when he slammed down his arsenal the porter turned loose a scream of terror. And when the ineffable Pepper Pot registered as "Baby Face Martin," even the drowsy room clerk must have expected the worst.

Well, that's John Leonard for you. This year he's the life of the party with his Mudcats. You are likely to see him on any of the streets strumming his git-tar, with Frenchy Bordagaray or Fibber McGee passing the hat. Anything for a laugh. The other day the Mudcats were rehearsing in the locker room at the ballpark when Sam Breadon walked in. Breadon is the owner of the club. He'd just as soon the boys keep their mind on baseball at the park. The Pepper Pot happened to turn, saw the owner, and by way of beating him to the punch, if any, he laid down his instrument, walked up to him and in a very firm manner said:

"Mr. Breadon, I want to talk to you. I want it understood that none of the Mudcats is to be sold or traded this season. You can't expect us to build up a fine musical organization and have you ruin it. It isn't fair to us and isn't fair to art."

"Yes, sir, that Martin, he certainly is a card," said Frank Frisch, while off in the distance sounded the clamorous strains of "Possum Up a Gum Stump." . . . The Mudcats were still going to town.

23

The Bronx Bombers

Joe McCarthy

October 20, 1936. The gracious Mrs. Joe McCarthy was not very pleased at the way her cocktail party was working out. She was entertaining a number of well-known guests, including the celebrated Dr. Dafoe, in her nicely appointed living room, and her husband was in the kitchen with a group of his friends.

"Joe," she demanded, "will you please get those men and come in here? We have company."

"Just a minute, mamma—

"Now there was a play in that game Pearson pitched you fellows up in the press box overlooked altogether, and to my mind it was the most important play of the World Series."

Mr. Joseph Vincent McCarthy was speaking, of course, of the recent baseball struggle between his Yankees and the Giants. The kitchen visitors, who seemed to be fascinated by the purr of the icebox motor, were rehashing the games and singling out some of the more dramatic turns.

Mr. Lou Gehrig, the big first baseman, who had peeled down his shirt sleeves and was doubling as a waiter—a calling for which he seemed to have a singular genius—had insisted that the catch Burgess

Whitehead made of Joe DiMaggio's liner in the first game was the best individual feat in the Series. . . . "If it hadn't been for that catch we might have won the ball game and the Series in straight games," the Iron Horse said.

"That was a fine play," Mr. McCarthy admitted, "but the play I'm talking about was different. If it had failed we might have lost the ball game—and the Series."

Mrs. McCarthy appeared in the doorway. "Joe McCarthy, are you coming out of this kitchen?"

"Just a minute, mamma—

"The score at the time was 4 to 1, Yankees," continued the laird of the manor. "Leslie opened the eighth with a pinch single to left, and Moore followed with another single to the same spot. Two on and none out. Bartell punched a grounder between second and first, Lazzeri came up with it and Pearson ran to cover first. If Pearson hadn't handled the throw perfectly—a Hal Chase couldn't have handled it any better—the bases would have been filled with none out, the tying runs would have been on, and there's no telling what

Joe McCarthy of the Yankees and Connie Mack of the A's, Opening Day of the 1940 season. —*NBL*

would have happened from then on. Yes, sir, to me that was the payoff play of the Series, and you can have—"

"I'll have a little more ice in this, if you don't mind," said Mr. Quentin Reynolds, the short story writer. "And how about that Hubbell? How did he look to you guys down on the field?"

"If you're speaking of the first game, we don't know how he looked," said Mr. Gehrig. "We didn't even see him. At that, you know, we practically beat ourselves in the first game. We were hitting at headlines."

"What do you mean, hitting at headlines?" asked Mr. Ray Schalk, the only major-league catcher who ever made a put-out at first, second and third base with a chest protector on.

"Here's what I mean," said Mr. Gehrig. "We had read so much about Hubbell's

screwball that we were all but mentally whipped before we took up our bats. We had got in a frame of mind where we were pretty sure Hubbell threw something that no living batter could hope to hit. That's why we were swinging at so many bad balls."

"Joe McCarthy!" . . . It was the missus again. . . . "This is positively the last time I am going to ask you and these men to get out of my kitchen. Now will you please—"

"Just a minute, mamma—

"You guys weren't hitting at headlines," interposed Mr. McCarthy. "You were hitting at one hell of a pitcher, so don't try to alibi yourselves."

"Well, we hit him the next time, didn't we?" insisted Mr. Gehrig.

"Maybe so," nodded Mr. McCarthy,

"but I notice you guys didn't exactly murder him in that second game, either."

"He's one of the best pitchers in baseball for setting up a hitter," said Mr. Gehrig. "Before you know it he has you in a hole. Then he will come through with a pitch that is probably a bad ball, and because you are desperate you will take a cut at it and make yourself look pretty foolish indeed."

"That reminds me, how about some fresh setups around this place?" urged Mr. Reynolds, who was plainly on the hunt for an inspiration.

A number of ladies and gentlemen, headed by Mrs. McCarthy and Dr. Dafoe, started streaming into the kitchen.

"If we are going to have our party we may as well have it here," sighed the lady of the house. "These bums will be here all night."

Psychic Nudges

August 25, 1938. As an individual McCarthy is a pleasant, sociable fellow with no pretenses or conceits. He is as hard a loser as John McGraw ever was but he never shows it in the open clubhouse. He waits until the next day, when he has cooled out, to take an individual or the club to task. For a baseball employee he is immensely wealthy. Can probably write a check for $300,000, but lives unassumingly. It wasn't until last year that he hired a chauffeur. Feared his friends would think he was putting on airs.

McCarthy will tell you without blinking an eye he is psychic, that spiritual messages come to him in the early hours of the morning and that he obeys them faithfully. It was one of these psychic nudges that moved him to start the injured Pearson against the Giants in the '36 World Series, and Pearson won a 5-2 game.

"How do you get these psychic messages?" a puzzled reporter asked.

"Prepaid," laughed McCarthy. "That's the best part."

First Flush of Fame

December 4, 1930. I understand Mr. Gehrig no longer takes himself seriously. When the first flush of fame fell across Mr. Gehrig he was almost impossible.

I recall a newspaper photographer pleading with him for an hour to pose for a picture in the Southern training camp. When he finally posed it was with great annoyance and reluctance. By this time the photographer had become provoked himself. He snapped the great man's picture, handed him the plate and told him to mix it with his beef stew for lunch. On that particular day I had more respect for the photographer, whom I had never seen before, than for the man who had given Mr. Ruth his closest run up to that time for the home run championship.

But I am becoming captious. As a drummer boy I was like that myself the day I shook hands with General Lee at Appomattox.

Lou Gehrig taking batting practice at St. Petersburg, Florida, 1929. The catcher is Matty Matthews. —*NBL*

The Iron Man of Baseball

January 9, 1932. It might be argued that when Lou Gehrig finds out how good he was last season he will build a strong barricade against the lures of Colonel Jacob Ruppert and Ed Barrow. This is contract time, and Gehrig soon will receive his 1933 papers. However, Lou is not the sort that holds out. And he believes that Colonel Jake has a fatherly interest in him. Lou is impressed with the fact that Ruppert has done pretty well by him thus far.

The past year saw a change in Gehrig as a man. He mellowed and he smiled more. He threw off a feeling that perhaps was shyness, perhaps aloofness, maybe a tendency toward overintrospection.

When you realize that Gehrig is the iron man of baseball— that he has the longest streak of unbroken play—his value increases. And then there is the fact that he is big, that he is powerful and the best physical specimen in the majors—and no doubt the best conditioned. In short, this bird from Eighth Avenue and West 112th Street is quite a ballplayer.

"Suppose there hadn't been any baseball"

February 18, 1938. Lou Gehrig, the Iron Horse of baseball, was sitting on the dais waiting, with others, to pay oral tribute to Johnny Neun, new manager of the Newark Bears. And he fell to talking about baseball and his career.

"When I tell people I'm just a big lucky guy they don't seem to believe it. They put it down to modesty and persist in asking how I got where I am in baseball. But I'm not trying to be modest or anything like that; I've been lucky. You must be lucky to last a long time in the majors."

I remember Ty Cobb had told me the same thing shortly after he had retired. "I was lucky," he said, "in the sense that I never was seriously hurt."

That's what Gehrig means when he says he has been lucky.

Gehrig is the type who would pay to get into a ball game. To him everything about the game is simply grand. He can't wait for a new season to begin and hates to see an old season end.

"Of course, I've got ample reason to like baseball," Gehrig admitted. "Look at what it's done for me. It has enabled me to give Mom and Pop ease and security in their old age. One year Mom had to have three goiter operations. We wouldn't have been able to give her the best of everything during those dangerous days if it hadn't been for baseball.

"Pop's in his 70s now, and he doesn't have to work. Every fellow looks forward to the day when he can help repay his folks for the privations they went through to bring him up. I know my limitations as a man of the world, and I know I couldn't have even hoped to do these things for Mom and Pop if it hadn't been for baseball. And, another thing, I met Eleanor through baseball. Gosh, when I think of all the things baseball has done for me I get frightened. Suppose there hadn't been any baseball."

This is a more or less verbatim report of Gehrig's remarks. His enthusiasm for the game and his appreciation for the benefits that have come to him from it are almost juvenile in their warmth. You'll go a long way before you'll meet a more genuine, whole-souled, human fellow.

Sooner or Later

March 16, 1939. ST. PETERSBURG—The older newspapermen sit in the chicken-coop press boxes around the grapefruit circuit and watch Lou Gehrig go through the laborious movements of playing first base, and wonder if they are seeing one of the institutions of the American League crumble before their eyes.

They watch him at the bat and note he isn't hitting the ball well; they watch him around the bag and it's plain he isn't getting the balls he used to get; they watch him run and they fancy they can hear his bones creak and his lungs wheeze as he labors around the bases. Every mental note they make contributes to the broad conviction of physical disintegration. On eyewitness testimony alone the verdict must be that of a battle-scarred veteran falling apart.

We sought out Joe McCarthy, the

Murderers' Row, style of 1936–1937: The Yankees' Bill Dickey, Lou Gehrig, Joe DiMaggio
and Tony Lazzeri.—*Associated Press*

manager, for a little comfort on the subject yesterday. Gehrig has long been McCarthy's ballplayer. He thinks he is the greatest ballplayer of all time. He puts him ahead of Ruth and Cobb and Wagner and all the rest. This is a tender subject with McCarthy. He has seen the same thing the newspapermen have seen. He realizes, too,

Gehrig is getting along in years, and inevitably the time will come when he will be forced to turn to him in the dugout and say, "You had better sit this one out today, Lou."

That will be the death sentence. Sooner or later it comes to every great player in the game.

"Something organically wrong"

June 22, 1939. There are some things you can't do much, if anything, about. Illness is often like that. Obviously we have Lou Gehrig in mind. Not even his incredible du-

rability, which enabled him to shatter every endurance record known to the game, was strong enough to fight off the insidious ravages of a strange malady; in the end this tremendously strong young man just had to acknowledge defeat to an unseen foe.

Just the other day we were talking to Ed Barrow, president of the Yankees, and he said, "There must be something organically wrong with Gehrig. I've been in baseball 50 years and I never saw a great hitter go to pieces all at once before. The last thing the great hitters lose is their ability to hit the ball." He pointed out that Babe Ruth hit three home runs in one game only a few weeks before he retired for all time.

Well, there's no longer any mystery about Gehrig. He's not a well man. Nothing happened to him that couldn't have happened to a bookkeeper, an accountant or a headwaiter. Sickness just overtook him. Bad as it is, we should think Gehrig would feel relieved. At least he knows now where to start from. The lingering oppressive uncertainty, which kept him in a continuous mental stew, has been lifted. He knows now he has a fight on his hands, and since he never was the kind to take a fight lying down, he isn't likely to let this one whip him.

"The luckiest man alive"

July 6, 1939. Always it was said Gehrig had no color. Perhaps he didn't. Certainly he lacked the rumbling thunder and majestic presence of the Babe and the glint and glitter of Cobb; he seemed content to do the job well and let it go at that. It never occurred to him that an eccentricity, a mannerism or a theatrical touch would make him stand out, and if it had he would have scorned the thought.

But the other day at the Stadium Gehrig rose to dramatic heights, naturally, spontaneously, from the soul and the heart.

The thing called color became a cheap, tawdry affectation in the clear, honest emotion with which the ailing athlete acknowledged his gratitude.

No Barrymore could have touched the hearts of his listeners more deeply than Gehrig did when, with broken voice and tear-stained eyes, he said, "I'm the luckiest man on the face of the earth." It was a dramatic emotional triumph that could have been achieved only by a tremendously sincere and grateful man.

"My three pals"

September 26, 1945. It did look a bit strange seeing Eleanor Gehrig sitting back of a desk poring over football data and in other ways functioning as the secretary-treasurer of the new football league which has come along to challenge the long monopoly of the professionals. Of course, the only reason it seemed strange was that she has always been identified with baseball. When you thought of her you thought of

her late husband, the famous Lou Gehrig, and when you thought of him you naturally thought of baseball.

There is only one picture on Eleanor Gehrig's desk. It isn't a football picture. It's a smiling head picture of the incredible Iron Man of baseball, who succumbed to an insidious germ at the peak of his career on June 2, 1941.

Lefty Gomez. — *United Press International*

Mrs. Gehrig has now reached a point where she can discuss the tragedy with restrained emotion.

"You know, he always believed he was coming back to the Yankees. Only one thing worried him. He'd look up from his reading or whatever he was doing and ask, almost with a note of alarm, 'Now tell me honestly do you really think Joe McCarthy will make a place for me?' You see that was his home, the Yankees. I doubt that he ever would have played anyplace else had he lived and had to make such a decision."

Gehrig never realized the nature or the inevitability of the disease which struck him. "It may have been that we were hop-ing for some sort of miracle, or that we thought it would be better for him if he didn't know. In any case, we never told him. It was hard, but there was some small comfort in knowing he was able to develop and hold on to a philosophy of cheer and hope. I'm sure it would have been so much worse if he had nothing at all to cling to."

Moisture spread over Eleanor Gehrig's eyes as she recalled the approach of death.

"It was about ten o'clock in the morning. We were standing around his bed. The doctor, my mother and myself. Lou looked up and smiled. 'My three pals,' he said. That was all. He never spoke again. A minute or so later he slipped into a coma. At ten o'clock that night he was dead. I'm sure I know the instant he died. He worked his features into that old familiar smile of his —like the one you see here in the picture on my desk—and that was the end."

Lefty Gomez

June 16, 1936. The story is that Mr. Goofy Gomez, the baseball bowler, is very irate because the Yankees have had two flat-feet tailing him. "They must stop this or trade me," Mr. Gomez is quoted as ultimatuming.

It develops the person responsible for this reprehensible procedure is Mr. Ed Barrow, business manager of the Yankees. When the pitcher developed a pitching weakness which defied the science of medical men, the unsympathetic Mr. Barrow decided to approach the case from another angle.

Ignoring the constitutional rights of a free citizenry, Mr. Barrow called in a couple of sleuths and, in effect, said: "I'm paying this guy $20,000 a year to win ball games for us, and he isn't winning 'em. I want you to camp on his coattails every minute he's away from the Stadium. Maybe you can crack this mystery for us."

In due course Mr. Gomez was called into the office of the heartless executive.

"Your arm any better?"

"It seems OK, but I just can't get going."

"Well, I'll tell you what's wrong with you and your arm. . . . "

And with that the Fiend in Human Form reached into his desk and pulled out a report which traced in detail Mr. Gomez's activities for the last 10 days—or rather nights. The report showed the pitcher had been hanging around the Broadway hot spots and getting home with the milkman, to use a figure of speech.

"That's what's wrong with your arm," growled Mr. Barrow. "That's why you are blowing up in the sixth and seventh innings. There's nothing wrong with your arm. It's your head. Better guys than you have lost their fast one in those joints. Get wise to yourself."

"Watching a great pitcher go over the hill"

March 20, 1943. ASBURY PARK—There has been very little sunshine in the lives of the Yankees this spring, a circumstance which makes the absence of Señor Lefty Gomez all the more distinctly felt.

The señor, as is well known, was a gay, cheerful, witty soul, one of the most popular of all the Yankees, and to his post with the Boston Braves he carries the best wishes of all his old teammates. Not only has a Yankee fixture been torn down and carted

away but in the process an extraordinary pitching team has been shattered: the team of Gomez and Murphy is no more, and probably never will be again. It is saddening to see these fine old relationships dissolve. We think we can now imagine how Weber and Fields felt.

The other half of the act, Johnny Murphy, was sitting around the lobby today trying to peer through the greasy fog which swirled in from the ocean. . . . "It's too bad the Goof isn't here; he'd brighten the joint up a bit," mused Mr. Murphy.

This started the Society of Sitters and Lobby Loungers on a tour of the life and habits of Mr. Gomez.

Art Fletcher remembered a time the Yankees were playing the Red Sox in Boston. The umpires were Quinn and McGowan. The latter is a full-fledged dean of his own umpire school. It is one of those mail-order approaches to wisdom.

"It was late in the season and Joe McCarthy decided to see the game from the grandstand," continued Mr. Fletcher. "This was always an open invitation for the Goof to do his stuff; McCarthy never encouraged his clowning.

"Well, when the game started the Goof appeared in the dugout with a cane, a tin cup and pair of dark glasses. He ignored McGowan and fixed his attention on Quinn.

"'Quinnie, oh, Quinnie. Look, I got my diploma. I'm a graduate from an umpire school.'"

The president of the Sitters Society and Lounge Loungers is Paul Krichell, who now has the floor.

"I had to work like the dickens to get that Johnny Broaca of Yale to sign a contract with us. Finally it comes the day when he pitches his first game for us in the Stadium. We are playing a double-header. Gomez pitches the first game and shuts 'em out. Broaca starts the second.

"I'm sitting in one of those upper boxes between home plate and third base; I'm sitting with Ed Barrow, the boss, the fellow who had to okay the bonus check I give this Broaca, the bum. Keep in mind I'm talking of Broaca, not my boss. You know how it is. I want this bum to look good. If he looks good, I look good.

"So what happens? He passes the first three guys and has three straight balls on the next guy, and just then an usher touches me on the shoulder and says, 'Mr. Gomez wants to see you right away. Says it's very important.' Well, I'm not looking any too good to my boss at this moment, so I get up and quickly follow the usher.

"It seems like I follow him all the way to Albany. For some reason I'll never know the Goof has taken himself a seat in the lower stands at the far end of the right field foul line. By this time my bum is getting his ears pinned back for fair.

"What in the hell do you want?" I bellowed.

"I just wanted to know, Mr. Krichell, how you'd feel right now if you'd discovered me instead of Broaca."

For hours the members of the S.S. and L.L. sat around spinning yarns about the Goof. Mr. Murphy had little to add. "You ought to know a million funny stories about the Goof," someone remarked. Mr. Murphy wrinkled his brows and scratched his forehead.

"There's nothing funny about watching a great pitcher go over the hill," he said. And got up and walked away.

George Weiss

January 25, 1952. NEW HAVEN—They say if the home town goes for you you are all right. George Weiss must be all right. This is the home town of the Yankees' general manager and the natives gave him a banquet and a gold medal last night.

"The food he'll keep," observed a dour baseball writer who had come down from New York for the affair, "and the medal he'll probably try to trade for a first baseman."

Weiss is generally accepted as the mastermind behind the Yankees' long run of success. Out of the rich soil tilled by Weiss and his scouts came a seemingly unending flow of blue-ribbon products. Since 1932 the Yankees have won 12 pennants. From '36 through '39 they won four in a row. Another period, '41, '42, '43, they made it three straight. Last fall they made it three hand-running again, and as the records show, there's no law which says they must stop there.

Ruth went. The Yanks still won. Gehrig died. The Yankees still rolled. Now DiMaggio is through.

"What will happen to us now?" a charming, anxious, ardent Yankee fan was asking in Leone's the other night. An eavesdropping sports columnist made bold to answer.

"Nothing, lady, as long as they still have George Weiss."

———

24

Bill Terry's Giants

A Pretty Fair Sort

May 26, 1931. Even the fact that he once warbled a determined baritone in a church choir and has never abused an umpire sufficiently to be booted out of a ball game does not keep Mr. William Harold Terry, of Memphis, Tenn. and the Polo Grounds, from being a pretty fair sort of ballplayer.

A year ago Mr. Terry was the only regular in the big leagues to bat over .400, and in recognition of this accomplishment, together with the comforting fact that he no longer sings in choirs or in Pullmans, he will be presented with a large ornamental hunk of silver tacked on a mahogany block by the local baseball writers' guild up in the Harlem sometime this afternoon.

This will formally confirm the critical judgment of the press box that last season Mr. Terry was the most valuable player in the National League and that as such he should have something to remember it by, although, being a practical young gent, Mr. Terry is more likely to remember that this said performance yielded him a new contract of $25,000.

I do not wish to convey the impression that Mr. Terry is utterly soulless or devoid of sentimental appreciation, but it so happens that he is, among other things, a businessman, actively identified with Mr. Rockefeller's oil interests, and his training has taught him that you cannot buy T-bone steaks with loving mugs or draw interest on such conceits in the bank.

Still and all, Mr. Terry is something of an artist on the ball field, both at the bat and around first base, where he habitually performs, and the boys who ought to know tell you that he ranks with the great first basemen of all time—right along with the Chases, the Sislers and the Chances.

There are two things that Mr. Terry does on the diamond that are unmatched by any other first baseman: (1) He can screw his spikes into the bag and stretch out further for a badly thrown infield ball than anybody else, and (2) he can make a double play, second to first, a very difficult and thrilling maneuver, with greater certainty and deftness than all the others.

He is a six-footer and supple, and this helps in the stretching play, but the perfected technique is something else. It is a shameless thing to record and practically indecent, but Mr. Terry, although a Southerner, ascribes his success to sheer labor. "I wouldn't want it to get around, but it's

New York Giants manager Bill Terry is about to be ejected from a game, for the first time in his career, by umpire Bill Klem, *1937.—Associated Press*

a fact," he meekly confesses.

Happily, there are extenuating circumstances. Roger Bresnahan, the old Giant catcher, virtually forced him into it. Mr. Terry started out doing a serious job of first basing at Toledo. Bresnahan had the club at the time. In the forenoon he used to take Mr. Terry to the ballpark and work him by the hour.

"Bresnahan threw so many balls in the dirt trying to make me stretch that it got so I thought it was against the rules for an infielder to make a good throw," said Mr. Terry.

One of the most difficult plays a first baseman has to make is the double play,

which starts with the first baseman fielding a ground-hit ball and throwing to second to head off a runner. This done, he must scramble back to first to take the return throw from the shortstop.

Mr. Terry—dark-haired, pleasant-faced, soft-spoken and discriminating as to dress—doesn't like to talk about what the other players can't or can do.

"They say I make the play pretty well now, and I guess I do. But I remember one game in Toledo, when I hit the same runner three different times. Wilbur Good was the runner. I hit him twice in a row trying to make the play between first and second, and the next time up I hit him again, although he didn't even get to first. He slammed a line drive into my hands, and with a flourish of pep or something I shot the ball back to the plate—and damned if I didn't hit him before he got out of the batter's box."

Nine Rahs and a Locomotive

July 18, 1934. This seems to be as good a time as any to tear off nine rahs and a locomotive for Mr. Bill Terry, the young Southerner who replaced the great McGraw —replaced him at McGraw's own wise suggestion, if you recall. A lot of people don't like Mr. Terry; they say he is colorless, self-centered and grasping. Well, maybe he is, but right now he comes close to being the best manager in the game.

I sat down in the lower stands with the customers and watched the games yesterday. Lon Warneke was turning back the Giants in blocks of three. Critz had flied out to open the fourth. Mr. Terry was next up. A gentleman sitting back of me said, "Here comes the old sourpuss. Get a load of him. At that he's just as liable to bust one into the stands as not." The words had scarcely rattled through his molars before the Giants' manager had driven a home run into the left-field pavilion. There may not have been much affection in those remarks, but there was considerable respect.

Mr. Terry's smash tied up the ball game. I watched him as he trotted around the bags. There was not the slightest show of emotion. The crowd stood and bellowed. Mr. Terry nudged the bill of his monkey hat briefly in response as he crossed the plate and then continued solemnly to the dugout, his lips tight, his brows knitted.

This was merely a part of the day's work with Mr. Terry. I think he would have been happier if the crowd had received the home runs in chaste silence. After all, he was supposed to hit when he went to bat, wasn't he—so why all the giddy whoop-de-doo?

Mr. Terry happens to be like that, constitutionally. He's neither volatile nor vivacious. He wouldn't know how to be what is called a showman if he tried. Compared to Ruth in this respect he's a bush-leaguer. I suspect mass popularity either bores or frightens him.

Possibly like Gene Tunney—and he reminds me a lot of Tunney—he would like to be a crowd idol, but lacks the formula and it doesn't interest him enough to try to find it. He's an intelligent young man with a sound sense of values—and to him baseball is a business and not a field day for Rotarian exuberance.

If Mr. Terry does not go over big with the crowd, I can assure you he stands aces back-to-back with his players. That's one of the main reasons for his success as a manager. Whether this fraternity spirit may be attributed to business soundness or personal charm that only his intimates know, I can't say. But it is a fact that every man on the squad is for him from who laid the rail, as they say down in his home town of Memphis.

Carl Hubbell

April 29, 1933. The pitching sensation of the majors at the moment is Mr. Carl Hubbell of the Giants. The boys have managed to score just one run against him in 32 innings. For 25 consecutive innings he

Carl Hubbell pitches to Gib Brack of the Phillies, 1939. Harry Danning is the catcher,
Beans Reardon the umpire.—*Associated Press*

has pitched shutout baseball.

Mr. Hubbell is a tall, angular person with not a great deal of heft. He does not impress you as the type of pitcher capable of heavy burdens. Yet he is the truck horse of the Giants. Not only does he start ball games, but he goes in and finishes ball games.

Mr. Hubbell's chief stock in trade is what the boys call the screwball—a ball that fades away from the hitter and takes a sharp drop. Generally it cannot be thrown

with great speed, but the Giants' star manages to get quite a bit of smoke behind the delivery.

Because he throws the screwball so often the critics are saying that Mr. Hubbell will not last, that the strain will cut his pitching days short by two or four years. The only one who does not seem to be disturbed about this is the pitcher himself. "I can throw it all day," he says, adding, "and besides, it's my arm."

Sixteen Straight

September 24, 1936. In winning his 16th consecutive game in Philadelphia yesterday, Carl Owen Hubbell, the screwball wizard

of the Giants, achieved pitching heights which are denied even to the great Christy Mathewson, who quite generally is rated as the greatest hurler of all time and whose right to that designation is disputed only by Walter Johnson.

Hubbell lost to Bill Lee of the Cubs on July 13 even though the Bruins got only two hits. Then he began to win. With the sheer artistry of his pitching he lifted a whole ball club out of the doldrums. On July 13, the Giants were in fifth place, threatened by the sixth place Braves, 10½ games behind the pace. The day before Horace Stoneham had admitted that his Giants looked terrible, that even a first-division finish was very problematical. But among the Giants there was at least one ballplayer who believed in himself: Carl Hubbell.

At the All-Star game in Boston, Hubbell was fooling around in the outfield before the competition. A certain American League star exchanged greetings with Carl and asked, "What's wrong with your ball club, Carl?" Hubbell fairly snarled. "There is nothing wrong except that the boys don't

think they can win. They already have picked out the best roads for driving home." Carl hurled an extra-hard ball to his warm-up companion and spat derisively on the Braves Field greensward.

It was that ball club, which had picked its road home, which Hubbell picked up by the determined force of his pitching. The Giants rose, peg by peg. They won 15 in a row, and always Hubbell was in the van. They were pulled and tugged until Hubbell had them in the No. 1 spot. And there they have stayed—and from there they will pass into the World Series with the Yankees next Wednesday.

To me, Hubbell is the greatest pitcher of the year by so big a margin as to destroy all thought of competition for the distinction. To me, he is one of the greatest pitchers of all time. It is no soft job for a pitcher without a fireball to hang up 16 in a row.

To me, the pennant victory of the Giants is the greatest one-man job in the history of modern baseball.

Ott

May 10, 1939. Someone once said versatility is the badge of mediocrity. This isn't true in baseball. Every once in a while you come across a do-anything ballplayer who is a standout star.

Hans Wagner was one—and in John McGraw's book Wagner was the greatest ballplayer of all time. Wagner could play any position, including catcher, and once, for a gag, he pitched.

Everybody knows Babe Ruth was a superlative pitcher before Ed Barrow, now president of the Yankees, made him over into an outfielder because he wanted the use of his thunder stick in every ball game.

The business of changing Ruth from a pitcher to an outfielder did not exactly tax Mr. Barrow's genius to the limit. He merely told Ruth to pick up his glove and

go out to the meadows. Mr. Barrow could have sent Ruth to first base and the chances are he would have become known as one of the leading first basers of all time. He had the footwork, the fielding skill and the arm. In short, he was a natural ballplayer.

Mel Ott fits into this category. He's a do-anything ballplayer. And it's a good thing he is. If he wasn't the Giants would be in a much unhappier state than they are. True, he hasn't completely plugged the hole at third base, but he has been a great help.

The enemy clubs know he isn't a third baseman by trade and they direct their attack at him—as the Cubs did yesterday—but Ott gives every play an honest wrestle, and he succeeds more often than he fails. Next to Stanley Hack he is still the best

Mel Ott demonstrating his unusual batting style.—*NBL*

third baseman in the league, which, of course, is a pretty sad commentary on the third basemen as a group. And when you consider Ott is the best right fielder in the game, very likely the best the Giants ever had, you marvel that he is able to come in from the outfield at a moment's notice and play the bag at all.

In recent years most of the success of the Giants has depended on two men—Ott and Carl Hubbell. If they were to win Ott had to hit and Hubbell had to pitch. It may be that Hubbell is on the way out, though there was a glint of the old master's magic in his brief appearance as a relief pitcher the other day.

Ott remains the one dependable, the anchor, the life-saver. The Giants had lost seven out of ten when the manager, boasting "the greatest team ever put together," brought him in from the outfield on May 1 to stop the panicky retreat. It stopped. The Giants won five out of their next seven —eight, including yesterday's.

In the first game he played at third base this year he hit a home run in the ninth inning with two on and one out. This was against the Cincinnati Reds. The Reds were leading by 7 to 5 at the time. His home run won the game, ended the panic and gave the team a vital breathing spell.

Ott has been one of the great players of the game for a number of years, but for some reason he hasn't danced spectacularly in the headlines. This is probably because he isn't a headline guy at heart. He just goes about his business doing his job and doing it well and leaving the circusy flourishes for the others.

It is something more than a coincidence that he and Hubbell have roomed together for years. They are both cut from the same fabric. Quiet, affable, likable fellows, with simple tastes and simple pleasures. The glitter of New York life never touched either of them. They have taken success and the loose adulation of unknown thousands in stride.

So softly do the ballyhoo drums play in the life of Ott that if it wasn't your business to keep track of such things you would be surprised to know, for example, that only three players in the history of baseball have hit more home runs than the little guy, who seemingly threatens to kick himself in the chin with his right foot every time he sets to swing at a pitch. Yet this is true. Only Ruth, Gehrig and Foxx top him. It seems to us Chuck Klein, of the Phillies, has drawn more headlines in his time as a slugger than Ott, but the records show that Ott has hit all of 60 more homers than Klein. They also show he has hit a hundred or so more than Joe Medwick, but here the comparison isn't altogether fair. Medwick is still a comparative Reginald Recently Arrived.

For the last three years Ott has been the leading home run hitter in the National League. Pie Traynor, of the Pirates, says he is the most dangerous man in a pinch in the league, first because he is the hardest to fool and second because he is liable to drive the ball out of the park any minute.

Year in and year out there is such a wide difference in the home run totals in the two leagues that supremacy in the National doesn't receive much press attention. In these days, when 60 is par for the course, it is hard to get excited about leaders who

hit 40. But the top man in any circuit is always entitled to credit, and Ott has not only been the National's Mr. Big with the lethal stick for three straight years but has been threatening for many years. Twice he tied for home run honors—in 1932 with the aforementioned Klein, and in 1934 with Ripper Collins.

Another time . . . on the last day of the season in 1929 Ott and Klein were tied, each with 42 homers. The schedule brought their two teams, the Giants and the Phillies, together in a double-header. Some 10,000 spectators assembled to see the duel between the two hitters. The game meant nothing. Klein hit one over the right field wall in the fifth inning to take the lead. It was now up to Ott; he had to hit one to draw up even again and two to go to the front. He did neither. The truth is he didn't get another ball to swing at all day. The Philadelphia pitchers conspired to protect Klein's lead. They did this by walking Ott six times in a row.

This absurdity reached a ridiculous climax in the ninth inning of the second game. The Giants were leading, 11 to 2. The bases were filled. Ott was up. It was his last chance. Phil Collins was the pitcher. And what do you think he did? He deliberately passed the little guy and forced in another run.

That's one way to stop him from hitting, but fortunately for the Giants, there's no convenient way to keep him out of the lineup, and so long as he's in there "the greatest team ever put together" by the manager must be conceded a chance.

[Ott took over as manager of the Giants when Bill Terry was kicked upstairs in 1942, and stayed in the job a year after he retired as a player. His best finish was third, in his first year; he averaged about sixth. After he left in mid-1948 Leo Durocher came over from Brooklyn to take over, and the old Giant era was over.—P. W.]

25
Hank Greenberg

A Human Darning Needle

March 13, 1930. The best story in the camp of the Detroit Tigers is that of Henry Greenberg, a human darning needle, who plays first base, is only 19 years old and has never had any sort of league experience. Young Henry came to the Tigers from the campus of New York University, where he is, in a manner of speaking, still a student.

He was a freshman when Jean Dubuc, the old pitcher, lured him from the Bronx in broad daylight and under the regal beaks of the Yankee management. It develops that Greenberg was propositioned by the Yankees but ultimately chose the Tigers, and thereby hangs a tale.

Mr. Paul Krichell was the Yankee scout assigned to the task of bringing Mr. Greenberg into the fold. Mr. Krichell is a German who is very fond of native cooking. Those who are close to the gentleman know how difficult it is to persuade him to eat anything else. But when there is an important duty to perform Mr. Krichell will make any sacrifice.

In the case of Greenberg, he decided upon a campaign of sociability. Together with the Missus he visited the Greenberg home, met the boy's mother and father, and

sat down to a menu prepared especially for the Greenbergs. It was a fine menu, but it was lamentably deficient in kraut and sausage and lager.

Still, Mr. Krichell sat through it, and demanded more. There being something of the martyr in him he returned at frequent intervals and repeated the ordeal. He seemed to be getting along splendidly with the elder Greenbergs—so splendidly, in fact, that a weekend party at Atlantic Highlands was arranged and Mr. Krichell was invited to go along.

There is a rumor that before he went he gorged himself on German victuals, but whether or not this is so your correspondent has been unable to verify. But it is a fact that he went along and a good time was had by all, and Mr. Krichell came back to the city feeling more than a little pleased with his rare diplomacy. In another day or so he would have a contract drawn up and submit it to the Greenbergs assigning the services of young Henry over to the Yankees. Yes, everything was all set, as the boys say, and Mr. Krichell went over to the corner delicatessen and ordered a Westphalia ham and three rolls of his favorite cheese.

Seven future Hall of Famers were on the American League All-Star team at Griffith Stadium, Washington, D.C., in 1937. *Left to right*: Lou Gehrig, Joe Cronin, Bill Dickey, Joe DiMaggio, Charlie Gehringer, Jimmy Foxx and Hank Greenberg. — *United Press International*

It was at this point that the sinister Mr. Jean Dubuc entered the drama. Mr. Dubuc went direct to the young player himself and said: "I want to sign you for Detroit. I will give you $6,000 for your promise to join and $3,000 more the day you report." So far as anybody knows, Mr. Dubuc did not trouble himself to spend a single evening around the dining table of the Greenbergs. Perhaps he wasn't hungry. At any rate, young Henry, eager to try his hand at baseball anyway, said he would go to Detroit if his parents gave him permission.

This was not so easy to get. The elder Greenberg thought baseball was all right as a pastime but that it was no business. He insisted that young Henry remain in college and prepare himself for a career before the bar. It was then that young Henry told him about the $9,000 offer Mr. Dubuc had made him.

"You mean he wants to give you that kind of money just to go out and play with the baseball?" demanded the incredulous father.

"And that's just a starter," added the youth.

"Go and take it," begged the father. "I thought baseball was a game, but it's a business, and a very good business."

And so it happens that young Greenberg is here in Tampa trying out with the Tigers, and Mr. Krichell is over in St. Petersburg bewailing all that time he lost away from downtown rathskellers.

"I have nothing against young Greenberg," confesses the charitable Mr. Krichell, "but if he winds up as the bat boy for

How'd That Kid Do Today? — *cartoon by Willard Mullin*

Cedar Rapids he can expect no sympathy from me."

Young Greenberg is not likely to wind up as a bat boy anywhere. Every critic has pronounced him an excellent prospect. He has all the mannerisms of a big-leaguer. He fields well, takes a fine cut at the ball, is fast, and his one ambition is to be a baseball star. It's hard to see how he can miss.

The Temper of the Man

September 14, 1938. When the customers call up their favorite newspaper these days they want to know how Hank is doing. Henry, of the Bronx Greenbergs, is stepping high, wide and handsome along the home-run trail, and they want to see him keep it up.

With four in his last five games, giving him a total of fifty, Greenberg definitely is breathing warm on the record held by Babe Ruth. The fans know it, and they talk about it. Naturally, Hank does also, but it would interest most of the anxious phone inquirers to discover that the Tiger first-sacker thinks less of it than anyone else.

"You know," Greenberg explained recently, "I'd trade my chances for a home-run record to get the runs-driven-in record. Last year I only missed Lou Gehrig's American League mark by a run. I'd like to beat Hack Wilson's 190."

That's the temper of the man. He's a ballplayer's ballplayer, a fellow who would rather help the club's attack than pile up an outstanding individual record. Such a point of view may be the very thing which will carry him beyond Ruth's mark. Thinking in those terms, Greenberg will not press for those extra eleven homers (one every two games from now on) which he needs to establish a record. And not pressing is half the job.

It would be interesting right now to note the day-by-day reactions of one George Herman Ruth, the coach, to Greenberg's current effort. Mr. Ruth, who has a tendency to go sulphuric at very short notice, might not be quotable. At the same time, the Babe's facial expressions in answering questions would be worth describing. The big fellow is a child at heart, and he undoubtedly would reveal the pathos of a small boy about to lose a prized possession, because if there is any segment of his career as a player of which he is proud it's his home-run record. Still, you can bet the Babe would be among the first to congratulate Hank.

[Greenberg lost four years to the war, so his totals are less revealing than these percentages: career home run percentage, 6.4, ninth on the all-time list; career slugging average, .605, fifth on the all-time list. —P. W.]

———————

26

A Pair of Indians

Earl Averill

June 7, 1929. Mr. Averill appears to be quite a ballplayer. He broke into the league by hitting a home run off Earl Whitehill, the Detroit southpaw. It was in the first inning and on his first trip to the plate. When he came back to the dugout he asked Roger Peckinpaugh, the Cleveland manager, who that pitcher was. When he was told it was Whitehill he grunted, "Yeah, I've heard of him."

The next day he belted a home run off George Uhle, the Detroit right-handed ace, by way of showing that he played no favorites.

Mr. Averill came up from San Francisco. He cost the Cleveland millionaires $50,000. It was one of those rare baseball deals in which money was used for money.

The announcement of the sale was made around noontime on a late August day, and Mr. Averill, riding to the local ball orchard, read the details on his favorite sports page.

Inviting tragic consequences, the ballplayer began to think, and finally reached the conclusion that he was entitled to some of the purchase money.

He waited until the field was about to start and then walked over to the manager

of the club and inquired, "Do I get any of that dough?" The club manager told him that he did not get any of that dough. Whereat Mr. Averill tossed his old black glove—these boys always use old black gloves—blithely over his shoulder and left the park.

"When you decide to give me some of that dough I'll come back," he sang out on his way through the dugout exit.

It so happened that the club was up in its ears in a rousing pennant fight and that Mr. Averill's services were sorely needed. In due time a truce was effected. Mr. Averill's sordid demands were satisfied and he returned to the lineup. It is a matter of record that he got some of that dough before he signed a Cleveland contract.

This episode attracted the attention of Judge Kenesaw Mountain Landis, who was trying to play a brassie shot out of a Louisiana sand trap at the time, and he promised to propose legislation at the next league meeting by which players will cut in on the swag.

The Judge may be wrong about this but somehow or other the players to a man don't think so.

Earl Averill.—*NBL*

"The way I look at it," comments Mr. Averill, who must be ranked with the great economic masters of history, "is that a player ought to get all he can."

Mr. Averill has none of the sartorial volcanics that mark some of the other players, nor does he carry his own spotlight and scene-shifting crew around with him. He doesn't even rate himself as a great ballplayer, or baseball as a particularly important and exalted calling. By profession he is a florist, and Mr. Stuart Bell, the Cleveland sports commentator, tells me you can get him more excited talking about the home life of jonquils than Lefty Grove's fastball.

You can, however, lure him to your zoo at the most meagre provocation—provided there are monkeys to be observed. Mr. Averill likes to observe monkeys. He thinks they are funny and very silly. They remind him of some baseball writers he reads. He spent yesterday forenoon at the Bronx Zoo, and the local citizenry probably will be pained to learn he was not overly impressed with the exhibits.

The monkeys in the St. Louis zoo, he thinks, are vastly superior animals. There is one out there, for instance, that reminds him of Umpire So and So. Only, of course, the monkey looks more human. There is another monkey out there that spurns the advances of all ballplayers except Mr. George Herman Ruth, a circumstance that is most repugnant to Mr. Averill, who is from the wide open spaces where everybody is just one big family and where such things as class barriers do not exist.

"To me a monkey is a monkey," explains the philosophical Mr. Averill with great profundity, "and I think a monkey ought to look on all ballplayers the same way."

Mr. Averill himself is smallish as to build, but his shoulder development is enormous—a heritage of rigorous outdoor existence in his native state of Washington. The dugout dope on him is that he lacks the necessary fire, imagination and ambition ever to be a great ballplayer. He is said to be a perfect fielder, a speedy base runner and a better than fair hitter, with added gifts.

The razzle-dazzle of the big show has left him yawning. Each new town around the circuit is Des Moines as far as he is concerned. He didn't care about seeing the Woolworth Building; he had already seen it on a postcard. Half the time he doesn't appear to know who is pitching. He will line out a long hit off an enemy pitcher in one of the late innings and then inquire, "Who's that guy?"

The suspicion exists that this may be a pose. If it is it is the only one he has. Otherwise he seems to be thoroughly normal. Still a number of pitchers who have tried to slip a fastball past him this season claim he isn't.

[Averill is a Hall of Famer who, despite his consistency and lifetime .318, is no longer much of a household word.—P. W.]

Bob Feller

April 4, 1940. Control has been bothering Feller since he arrived in the majors. Last year and the year before he gave more bases on balls than any other pitcher in the league. Still, it is significant that he improved sharply in this department last year, passing 66 fewer hitters than the preceding year.

This year may see him having that one tremendous season the critics have been predicting for him. He is a youngster who works hard for perfection. He gathers more pitching savvy as he goes along, and in due time he will get his control where he wants it. When this happens he will be doubly tough, and goodness knows he's tough enough now.

Feller is not the first Clevelander to work a no-hitter. As a matter of fact, Cleveland pitching, dating from way back, has had a glorious background. Old Earl Moore gave Cleveland its first no-hit, nine-inning performance and, incredible as it may sound, was beaten. Held hitless for nine innings in a tie game, the White Sox got to Moore in the tenth and beat him. This was in 1901.

Addie Joss, who probably was the best pitcher any Cleveland team had until Feller came along, worked in two no-hitters, the first, in 1908, being what the boys call a perfect game: that is, no man reached first base. This was also against the White Sox. His other no-hitter came in 1910, and once again the White Sox graciously cooperated in the exploit.

Dusty Rhodes, Ray Caldwell and Wesley Ferrell were three other Clevelanders who beat Feller up to the mythical Hall of Fame. Caldwell's game was especially noteworthy since he was considered a shopworn has-been at the time, having been released by the Yankees. His retaliation took an epic

A youthful Bob Feller. — *NBL*

turn when he proceeded to set his former teammates back without a hit a few weeks later.

We talked with Caldwell after the game, and he professed to be surprised. . . . "You know I didn't have a thing on the ball out there today," he said. In point of blinding stuff and darting breaks he was correct, but he did have control and that can be very important to a veteran pitcher.

Old Mose Grove of the Red Sox continues to be one of the marvels of the game. It took Feller's no-hitter to grab the spotlight away from him and his two-hit mastery of the Washingtons. It was his 574th game as a big-leaguer and one of his best.

Grove is now 40 years old. Feller has just turned 21. There's a wide gap between the two in years, but both are masters, one with his savvy, the other with his remarkable arm power. If Feller can escape injury and sticks to his knitting he ought to be good for another 18 years.

Grove was a Feller type when he broke in. He threw the ball past the hitters. Jimmy Foxx, who has hit against both Grove and Feller, tells you Grove, at his peak, was much faster. It wasn't until Grove's arm started to backfire on him that he resorted to soft stuff and cunning.

What makes him effective now is that he can still show the hitter a fairly fast ball once in a while. This enables him to keep the hitter slightly off stride. He can never be sure just what the old man is going to pitch. And for a left-hander he has amazing control. This makes him a fine spot pitcher. Last year he passed only 58 hitters. The year before it was 52.

Wouldn't it be funny if this G.A.R. veteran and Master Feller fought it out for the pitching wreath this year? Could happen, too.

[*In 1940 Feller was 27-11, led the league in wins and strikeouts and had a 2.61 ERA; Grove, in his next-to-last year, was 7 and 6 with a 3.99 ERA. Overall, Feller ended up with six 20-game seasons, in each of which he led the league. Like Greenberg, he lost four years to the war. Had he not, he certainly would have won more than 300 games, and might very possibly have led the league in wins for an incredible nine straight seasons.—P. W.]*

27

Two Executives

Larry MacPhail

May 20, 1936. The reddest of the Cincinnati Reds is Leland Stanford MacPhail, general manager of the team. Mr. MacPhail is not only red as to hair but in the eyes of his National League colleagues is red in the Marxian manner as to his baseball philosophy.

He is the gentleman, as you have been told before, who pioneered night baseball in the major leagues. To most of the magnates night baseball is not looked upon with any great favor, but MacPhail insists the time will come when it will be the universal vogue. . . . "Baseball by day will never pass as a regular thing, but within five years every club in the majors will be playing a set number of games at night. There is logic behind night baseball," continues Mr. MacPhail. "You attract people who are unable to attend games in the afternoon, people who are either unable or have been uninterested. You cater to a new element, and in due time a certain percentage of this new element becomes interested in the afternoon offerings, too."

The first night game held here—and it was the first ever played in a big-league park—lured more than 30,000 people. The crowd overflowed onto the playing field, restricting the movement of the outfielders. One young lady, in the flush of the general excitement, seized a bat and stepped to the plate demanding a chance to hit. A good time was had by all.

"But do you call that baseball?" Mr. MacPhail was asked.

"I've seen World Series games where they had overflow crowds which handicapped the players, but nothing was said about it. When the crowds rushed the field for our night openers the critics called it a circus. Now if you are talking about the young lady who wanted to bat, I think I can explain that. She had watched fellows like Freitas, Kowalik and Jorgens [all three were pitchers] swing, and very properly she had an idea she couldn't do any worse. As a matter of fact, I'm sorry we didn't sign her ourselves. We could use her right now."

He'll Never Get Over the Shock.—*cartoon by Willard Mullin*

Larry and the Kaiser

January 20, 1938. The man who tried to kidnap the Kaiser is the new boss of the Brooklyn Dodgers. Somehow this seems entirely fitting. It is at least consistent with the extraordinary traditions of this strange baseball outfit.

On the night of January 8, 1919, Captain Leland Stanford MacPhail, of the 30th Division, was a member of a party that invaded Holland with the idea of bringing the fugitive warlord of the crushed German army back alive. It wasn't Mr.

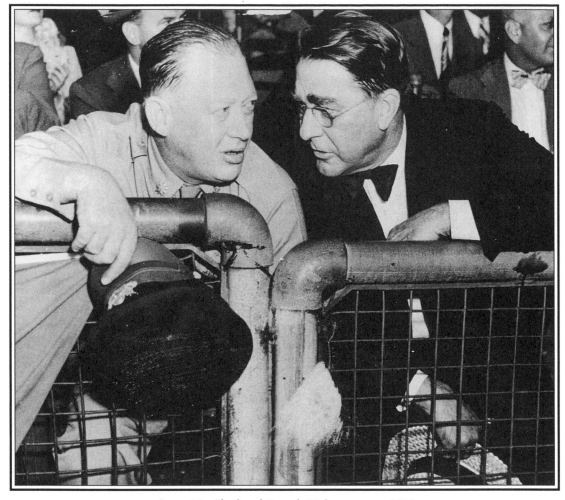

Larry MacPhail and Branch Rickey, 1943.—*NBL*

MacPhail's idea to kidnap the Kaiser that night. It was Colonel Luke Lea's. Mr. MacPhail just happened to be the Colonel's adjutant and he went along. The officers managed to get themselves armed with credentials and crossed the border into Holland, where the Emperor was hiding out. They pretended to be newspapermen seeking an interview.

But Lea and his accomplices wanted the old buzzard in person. All the allies except America had gone on record they intended to get him and try him as an instigator of the war. Lea and his pals decided on direct action. It developed the Kai-

ser was too well protected in his retreat, and the most spectacular enterprise of the world war came to naught.

Well, not exactly to naught. Somebody made off with a heavy bronze ashtray that belonged to the Kaiser, and that somebody is the new boss of the Daffiness Boys of dear old Flatbush.

"It's still around here someplace," smiled Mr. MacPhail. "I knew nobody would believe me when I got back to America and told 'em I was in the Kaiser's house, so I decided to bring along something to make my story stand up."

Branch Rickey at a Louis Bout

August 10, 1935. No other sport event comes close to an important heavyweight fight in public appeal. And this despite the fact it is the rowdy, dirty-faced urchin of all sports, where larceny is not unknown and vigorous policing at all times is deemed necessary. It may even be that much of its fascination lies in these sinister circumstances.

No other sports gathering brings together such a miscellaneous assortment of men. At the ringside in Chicago I saw men of the cloth, football coaches, medicos, statesmen, entertainers and baseball notables. And I have no doubt that the aristocracy of the underworld was liberally represented, too.

I don't know why but I was somewhat surprised to see Branch Rickey there. Mr. Rickey is a practicing YMCAer whose profession is baseball. He is the father of the chain-store system in the majors. As a player he would never put on a uniform on the Sabbath. As a later-day [*sic*] executive he never goes near the park on the day of rest. In short, he is not exactly the type you would expect to see sitting at the ringside urging another human to "go in there and bust his brains out."

I mention Mr. Rickey's presence merely to stress the universal allure of the loaded fist. The man won't go near a ballpark on a Sunday, but you can't keep him away from a heavyweight prize fight. If you happen to be an expert on riddles you may want to play with this one for a while.

Full Circle

August 14, 1945. The baseball career of Branch Rickey has become a full circle. Today finds the college-trained executive one of the principal owners of one of the sport's most valuable franchises, the Brooklyn Dodgers.

This is a good thing for baseball and, of course, for Brother Rickey. Like him personally or not, it cannot be questioned that he is one of the outstanding men in baseball, dynamic, whip-smart and far-seeing. Under the administration of Rickey, Brooklyn's baseball future is guaranteed for years. There are a few men closer to the game, none more capable in the field of operation.

The only rap I ever heard against the Brother is that he is charmed by the rhapsody of his own voice. I imagine this can be annoying at times, yet it scarcely constitutes a criminal offense. Moreover, the Brother has a compensating habit of packing his sonorous oratory with solid sense. Even when he is in one of his evasive moods, he is not without interest.

A Con Man

January 24, 1950. Rickey is a con man, brilliant, fascinating, erudite—but still a con man. I've been listening to him for 25 years. I've always been impressed, seldom enlightened. The trick of the con man is to

Jackie Robinson signs his 1948 Brooklyn Dodger contract with Branch Rickey.—*Associated Press*

weave a spell. In his field Rickey stands alone. Not since the days of William Jennings Bryan and Billy Sunday has any man fallen so deeply in love with the melodic quality of his own voice.

End of a Saga

January 19, 1954. The remarkable saga of Branch Rickey seems to be coming to a close. His youth program at Pittsburgh has collapsed. Nothing he tries works out for him. The wealthy owners have suddenly put him on a tight budget. So with a last-place team hopelessly mired, where does he go from here?

For the first time since he invented the farm system, he finds he must sell without regard to consequences. In other days he gave up only what he didn't need and at his own figure. His position was such he could let good men go, knowing he had adequate or superior replacements. This gave him a rating as a dealer which may have made him look shrewder than he was. When you are in a position to call the tune, the fiddler has no alternative.

The farm system made Rickey. A brilliant, far-seeing man, he was the first to realize the advantages of going to the source for material. His idea was born of necessity. He had no money to work with in St. Louis, so he substituted a resourcefulness and unflagging energy. There was no way to copyright the farm system, and in due time every club had one. Eventually Rickey was out of St. Louis. Sam Breadon, the Cardinals' owner, found he could get along without him.

"He costs me too much money," Breadon told me.

Rickey's next stop was Brooklyn and here he introduced another first, the Negro ballplayer. Because of its impact on society and contribution to humanity this was vastly more important than the farm system. It also put Rickey back in business.

Without Robinson, Campanella and Newcombe, Rickey could not have had a winner in Flatbush. Certainly not in the relatively brief time he managed it. Rickey is a man of honor, integrity and compassion. It would be grossly unjust to impugn his motives here, just as it would be naive to disassociate him entirely from any consideration of selfish interest.

In any appraisal of Rickey as a baseball man it is necessary to call attention to the two factors that made him a success as a builder, which is the intent here. When Rickey had lost the farm-system edge, Breadon no longer regarded him as indispensable. Now that the Negro player is commonplace in baseball, Rickey has lost another edge, and what other new channels are left for him to explore?

28

Johnny Mize

You Never Can Tell

February 1, 1950. See where Old John Mize just inked his Yankee slave papers. You know, Old John's something of a rarity. Loves to play baseball. Really does. I believe he'd actually pay to play if he had to.

Well, maybe he wouldn't, but even so it can be truthfully stated that Old John's one ballplayer who is nuts about the game. You'd be surprised how many of the headliners aren't. They get their hits, pitch their games, collect their dough and that's that. Once the game's over they can't be bothered about baseball. Don't even want to discuss it. Too boring. Their golf? Oh, yes, they'll give you a stroke by stroke account.

I never saw Old John that he was too busy to talk baseball. Indeed, I never saw him when he didn't practically insist upon talking baseball. It could be knowing fans, elderly tourists, eager youngsters, Old John was always happy to oblige. And most of the time he seemed to be having as much fun as his admirers.

I think Cincinnati was the place. Two youngsters had engaged Old John in an almost endless baseball catechism. It could scarcely have escaped their notice that he was an inveterate cigar smoker. Next morning there was a small box in his hotel box. It contained two cigars. From his young friends. And you may be pleased to learn Old John's the type who thought the gesture was pretty swell.

Old John hasn't got many more seasons to go. He's 37. If the Yankees hadn't been up to their ears in a scorching flag race late last summer and needed all the help they could get, they probably wouldn't have given him a tumble when the Giants put his contract up for sale. True, they didn't get much use out of him as a first baseman, but his pinch hit in the third game of the World Series was the turning point.

The Yankees can be counted upon to get some use out of Old John. Just how much or in what capacity remains to be seen. It is hard to picture him as a regular

Johnny Mize at bat.—*Chicago Today*

first baseman on a team that has championship aspirations. Still, you never can tell. If nothing else Old John ought to be able to earn his cakes just sitting around talking baseball. Nobody in the trade does it better or makes it sound more like a big wide-eyed kid telling it.

29

Joe D

In the All-Star Game as a Rookie

August 8, 1936. Before the start of yesterday's contest Joe DiMaggio was the principal topic of discussion wherever you stumbled across a group of National League players or supporters. They wanted to know all about the Yankees' sensational freshman who was burning up the American League with his hitting, fielding and throwing.

Well, they haven't seen the real DiMaggio yet. His performance in the "dream game" was the effort of a badly frightened youngster who was fortunate enough to be singled out as the "goat" because he made two glaring misplays that contributed to the National League scoring and failed to hit safely in five tries, twice when

a base blow would have put the American Leaguers back in the ball game.

Young Mr. DiMaggio was nervous as a deb at her coming out party. He was scared stiff and admitted as much after the clubs had quit the field. Gehrig, Gomez, Bill Dickey and the other members of the Yankees present couldn't understand the sudden change in the lad who had taken all games in stride this season.

I suppose it just wasn't the lad's good day. The sad part about it was that it had to happen to him at a time when he wanted to show at his best before a critical audience to justify his being there. Still, I don't think there's any danger of his being waived out of the American League.

In the World Series as a Rookie

October 8, 1936. Young Joe DiMaggio didn't exactly emerge from the Series as the bright particular star, but he performed in such a manner as to win the applause of everybody, including the Giants. He hit .346, and he might have done even better

if he hadn't been overswinging, trying too hard for extra base hits. Besides which his fielding was sensational. It will be a long time before a World Series gathering sees a more thrilling catch than he made of Leiber's titanic drive out near the center-

Joe DiMaggio hitting in his 43rd consecutive game, 1941.—*NBL*

field bleachers at the Polo Grounds. Already baseball men accept the loose-limbed Italian as the best center fielder in baseball, and he has been in the league only one year. "I think he's as good as Speaker ever was right now," said Clark Griffith, of the Washington club.

The Gionfriddo Catch

October 6, 1947. A lot of things happened in that game yesterday, a tense, tough, thrilling game, a game made to order for the customers. DiMaggio (J.) was robbed of a home run by the most remarkable catch I ever saw, World Series or no. Some anonymous character on the Brooklyn team leaped clear out of the park to take a home run from the only real big-league ballplayer in the series. You never saw anything like it. It was indescribable, so why be stupid and try to describe it? Later another Brooklyn outfielder took a home run away from Tommy Henrich. Dixie Walker they call him, but he just happened to be where he should be to catch a long ball from a left-handed hitter so I couldn't get too excited about that.

A few words about DiMaggio. These other fellows who pose as Yankees ought to bow deep as they pass this man today.

DiMaggio and Mickey Mantle, Mantle Day, Yankee Stadium, June 8, 1969. — *NBL*

He is so much the best. So much the best in all baseball. The supreme artist. You'll never hear of him making a great catch for the simple reason that he doesn't know how to make a catch look great. Or even difficult. The ball is in close. DiMaggio is there to take it. It's hit nine miles away. Somehow DiMaggio is there to get it. So easy. So effortless. This is an okay Series from the fans' point of view. Excitement, drama, fight, hustle, all that sort of thing and, mostly, it's been on the part of the Brooklyns. But the big guy, the top guy, the pro guy . . . that's DiMag. I think even the Brooklyn addicts hated to see him robbed of that home run.

"Didn't you think so?" I said to one of my younger heirs, aged 10 going on 11, a confirmed Brooklyn rooter, seeing his first Series game, by the way.

Answer: "Mr. DiMaggio has robbed plenty of people, too, hasn't he?"

I said the young man was a confirmed Brooklyn rooter.

"You'll have to make a change"

September 1, 1950. There must come a time when Joe DiMaggio will have taken his last cut at the ball. Inevitability crowds him more and more. Yesterday found the classic baseball star grudgingly giving ground against the insidious enemy again.

I was sitting in the dugout engaged in

a scholarly discussion of the Paleozoic age with Casey Stengel when DiMaggio, who had been taking exploratory swings in the batting cage, paused on his way to the locker room and said:

"Case, you'll have to make a change."

The Yankee manager looked up. "The knee again?"

DiMaggio frowned. "Both."

I followed DiMaggio into the locker room where he paced up and down in front of his clothes rack.

"The left's worse than the right. I've been favoring both. That's why I'm not hitting. I can't get the upper part of my body into the swing. The pressure on the left knee is too great. You say it looks as if I'm swinging late? I am. A thing like this af-fects your timing. I don't know what to think, except this is one hell of a time to be out of the lineup."

As I say, the day must come when DiMaggio is through. It has to come to all great stars. I myself have witnessed the gradual decay of such immortal hitters as Lajoie, Cobb, Speaker, Heilmann, Sisler, Ruth and Gehrig. At first the fissure is imperceptible. Then it widens. Finally there is a crash and a long, brilliant career lies in ruins.

I doubt that DiMaggio will buck the unbeatable odds all the way. He is too prideful a man to permit himself to be seen in oafish attitudes and grotesque postures on the field. This may be his wrap-up year. Next must surely be.

30

Ted Williams

As a Rookie

March 31, 1939.   Williams is an outfielder and is the fair-haired boy of the camp. He is free and easy at the plate and swings in a true, sharp manner. He took complete charge of the American Association last year. He led the hitters in practically everything, including speed records for the dining room. Donie Bush says he can't miss. He managed him last season.

The young man is regarded as something of a problem. The name he carries may have something to do with this distressing condition. We, for one, have a sympathetic understanding. The Red Sox had him down here last spring but could not stand him. He got on everybody's nerves. Finally, Joe Cronin, the manager, called Bush by long distance and asked him if he could use Williams.

"I'd drive all the way from Minneapolis to get him," cried Bush. He knew all about the young man's eccentricities and pop-off tendencies, but that was all right; he also knew he was a ballplayer.

Bush was told to try to tame the young man down. It was an interesting but difficult assignment. One day in a tight game Williams reached second in the ninth inning. If he scored it meant the ball game. Bush was coaching at third base. Williams took a long lead.

"Watch yourself down there, shouted Bush. "If you get caught off base we're sunk."

Williams shouted back: "I got down here on my own and I'll get home on my own."

This is typical of the young man's disposition, self-reliance and feeling of importance. Or, rather, it was. Bush must have done a good job of taming him down. He's much more reticent and conservative this spring.

Ted Williams giving a demonstration to several Philadelphia Phillies, Sarasota, Florida, 1958.
—*Associated Press*

As a Soph

March 16, 1940. SARASOTA—One of the finest young hitters to come to the big leagues in a number of years is Ted Williams of the Boston Red Sox. We met him down here a year ago when he was fresh out of the bushes. A mutual friend in San Diego had sent us a letter asking that we talk with the youngster and "try to make him feel at home." We don't know yet whether Mr. James Wood Coffroth was rib-

bing us. Williams is the kind of tangerine who will feel at home any place, any time, including daylight saving.

He was standing near the batting cage swinging three bats when we introduced ourselves and told him about the letter. He paused briefly to shake hands, patted us cheerfully on the shoulder and said: "Well, the Williamses must stick together." Then he floated two bats in the direction of the dugout, stepped to the plate and hit the center-field wall on a line.

You couldn't call him a fresh young man, perhaps not cocky, either, but he wasn't short-changed at the self-reliance counter. He has the abandon, spontaneity and unpredictability of youth. Around the camp here they call him the kid. And that's what he is. But he's no kid when he swings a bat and there's no kidding about his hitting.

He's as natural at the plate as next day's dawn. A free, loose swinger with powerful wrists and forearms, he hits for tremendous distances. It's not entirely silly to toy with the dream that he may be a new Ruth in embryo.

There's nothing Williams would rather do than hit—except, possibly, discourse on the extraordinary virtues of San Diego, his home. Yesterday someone suggested going over to the Ringling Brothers lot, where the famous circus hibernates for the winter, to see Gargantua, the blue-ribbon gorilla.

"Say, if you want to see some really big gorillas go out to San Diego," boasted Williams. "We got the two biggest in the world in our zoo."

Williams rooms with Charley Wagner, one of the young pitchers. The other morning Wagner came to Phil Troy, the club secretary, and said he wanted another roommate.

"What's the matter?" asked Troy. "I thought you and Williams got along okay."

"We do. But he wakes me up at seven o'clock every morning. He stands in front of a mirror with a hairbrush, holding it like a bat, and he scowls in the mirror, like he's facing a pitcher, and he growls, 'Come on, you big so and so. Put it over the plate and I'll drive it down your throat.'"

That's a good picture of Williams' intensity, his absorption in hitting.

Jimmy Foxx is his idol, or at least one of his very pronounced favorites. Down here he stands behind the batting cage when old Double X is up and studies every move. Foxx likes him, too.

"He gave me a laugh last summer," recalls Foxx. "I hit 10 homers in seven days. When I hit the 10th he came to me, solemn as a sleepy old owl, and shook hands. 'You know,' he said, 'I always suspected you could hit, but now you've convinced me.'"

Williams is starting out with a heap of character and we hope the hurly burly of baseball leaves him untouched. Because of his great season last year the testimonial people rushed him. One wanted him to endorse a beer product and another wanted him to sing praises to a cigaret. The money he could have picked up was certainly not inconsequential.

"I don't drink beer and I don't smoke cigarets and I'm not going to say I do anything I don't." Needless to add, he didn't sign.

But his main, vital interest is hitting. His curiosity and studiousness are endless. He wants to know how Lajoie hit, how Hornsby stood, how Ruth gripped the bat.

"What kind of a hitter was Pop Anson?" he asked us suddenly yesterday.

We departed quickly, in a gathering gray melancholy. Pop Anson! How old did this kid think we were? Next thing, he'd be asking us about Abner Doubleday.

"A wonderful pair of eyes"

August 12, 1941. It looks as if James Emory Foxx is getting closer and closer to the end of a glorious career. He's hitting under .300. He may come back and have another good year, maybe two, but he's definitely in the veteran class. Still, he isn't worrying much. There's something of the philosopher about the big fellow from the hills of Maryland and he knows ballplayers don't last forever.

Right now he likes to talk about Ted Williams, the long drink of water who promises to be the first .400 hitter the majors have had in years. "I don't know when I've ever seen a better hitter than this kid," enthused Mr. Foxx, who may be accepted as an authority on the subject. "One of the remarkable things about him is that he never goes after a bad ball. He must have a wonderful pair of eyes. What's his weakness? I don't think he has anything approaching a weakness. He'll hit high balls out of the park and he'll undress infielders with line shots on low pitches. He's got every manager in our league daffy trying to figure him out. Some clubs play three infielders to the right of second base against him. Most of the clubs used to do that against Ruth, too. And I'll tell you something else, if the kid had Ruth's power—his muscular power, I mean—he'd out-Ruth the Babe. He'd hit .500, too."

Just before the game started we caught up with Mr. Williams himself. We wanted to know why he was hitting so much better this year.

"Don't let this get around," he whispered with boyish mischievousness, "but I'm smarter. Hell, I've been up here three years now and if a fellow can't learn to hit in three years he ought to throw his bat away. And another thing's helping me, I'm all full of confidence. I keep on saying to myself, 'Williams, even if nobody else thinks you can hit, you know you can, so go out there and do your stuff.'"

The young man's current batting average of .400-plus shows how convincingly he is able to talk to himself and how faithfully he follows the orders which he issues.

[Williams lost more time to Uncle Sam than any other great player, since in addition to his three years in World War II he served nearly two in Korea. He still hit 521 home runs. While he might not have passed Aaron or even Ruth had his career not been interrupted, his total probably would have been about 700, and the hitter with the best eye in history certainly would have broken the all-time record for walks. —P. W.]

31

Casey Stengel Across the Years

Casey the Raconteur

March 20, 1933. Humor is a precious thing in any profession—in baseball doubly so because of its rarity. And the Brooklyn club is privileged to have among its employees the standout humorist in baseball—Mr. George Casey Stengel.

John McGraw, regarded by most fans as the last word in items baseballic, was telling me at a dinner here the other night of Arlie Latham, the first of baseball comedians. "He gave me many a laugh," said McGraw, "and in return I'd be willing to give Arlie my last dime." Such is the price that so astute a judge as McGraw places on laughs in baseball. At the same affair Stengel sidled up to McGraw on the dais, whispered a word or two to his old boss, and slipped away, leaving Mac convulsed with chuckles. Jack Hendricks, former manager of the Reds, turned to me. "There's a guy," said Jack, indicating Stengel, "who gave McGraw more sleepless nights and more laughs than any other man in baseball. And the old man loves him."

It is doubtful if our hero, Mr. Stengel, will ever have that much dough to show for his humor, but it's not because he isn't worth it. Don't get me wrong, Stengel is not a clown, no more than Will Rogers is. Casey is gifted with homely humor, with a sense of the ridiculous and a spontaneity that makes his stuff surefire. Casey holds daily gab sessions in the lobby of the Miami-Biltmore, awed not a bit by its splendor. His leathery face, mobile and expressive, works overtime as he relates his experiences, actual and fancied.

Casey was the hero of the World Series in 1923, even though the Giants were beaten by the Yankees. He won two of the games with home runs, one of them by a 1-to-0 score. And he swears that the first home run, which he hit inside the park at Yankee Stadium in the opening game, almost prevented his getting married.

"How?" inquired the old Colonel, who by now had his second wind and was able to sneak in a question.

"How?" snorted Stengel, who really doesn't need questions to help him. "Here's how. All them big shot sportswriters, the syndicate guys, are covering the Series. And they sit down and bang out big lead-alls like this: 'Aged Stengel circles bases while his venerable dogs bark like bloodhounds'; 'Casey comes to bat from wheelchair';

Casey Stengel in 1922.—*NBL*

'Long white beard no handicap to veteran outfielder.'

"And lots of tripe like that—pardon me, Mr. Williams, was you one of 'em? And the family of the girl I'm engaged to has never seen me. And they read all this in the California papers. And when I go out there to get married they are raising hell with the girl, saying she was a fool to throw herself away on a man older than her father. And when they saw me they still weren't sure but what the sports writing guys had me tabbed properly."

This is just a sample of how Mr. Stengel spends his hours off the ball field. It doesn't do his act justice, for no typewriter has yet been invented that can record the facial gyrations of Casey as he illustrates his yarns. He's no Clark Gable to start with and when he gets through one of his workouts children are scared for miles around.

The No. 1 Baseball Guy

January 8, 1935. This being practically the dead of winter, to mention baseball is incongruous. Therefore, my friends, I will tell you of Casey Stengel. Casey is noth-

ing if not incongruous, but Casey is also baseball, probably baseball's most living, breathing, vital character at the moment. I realize that there is a guy named Babe Ruth, not to mention a couple of fellows named Dean, but, after all, Casey is the No. 1 guy around our town.

Casey is at once the Svengali and the Punchinello of his business. He clowns plenty, but how he can hustle when the chips are down! Casey is responsible for about 80 percent of the baseball writers' gags, but he doesn't limit himself to wisecracks. He can take a wornout discard, give him a heart-to-heart talk and improve on any monkey-gland transformation in the books.

Stengel's home at Glendale, Calif., is right out of a movie set. Swimming pool, tennis courts and all the other falderals without which no California home is considered complete. On the alabaster white ceiling of his living room is a heel print, which is as out of place as a Broadway columnist in a church. And what do you suppose is the reason for this defacement? Casey, who acts out every story he tells —and he tells 'em as long as his listeners can stand—told one about the kicking ability of Morley Drury, who played fullback for Southern California in the days when Southern California was a football team and not a geographical description. Stengel, to show his guests how Drury could kick, punted himself and lost a shoe in the effort. Mrs. Stengel, a charming lady, in the vain hope that the telltale mark might reform Casey, allowed it to remain imprinted on the ceiling. The mark remains unchanged, and so does Casey.

In addition to his insistence upon gesticulating his way through stories Stengel has the habit of dropping into strange phrases. If you aren't in touch with his subject you are lost. It is like listening to one of Catiline's orations in the original Latin. Casey calls mediocre players "clerks," rookies "sugar plums" and batters who can't hit with men on "lobs." He also calls them lots of other things which we won't go into here. He talks in bunches, so to speak, but he always knows what he's talking about. In which he has the edge on most orators and no small percentage of his listeners.

Lest you think Stengel talks in vain, let me go back and cite an example of his baseball wisdom. He was in my room the day before the World Series opened in Detroit. Proudly I told him how I'd picked Detroit to win the American League pennant and also the Series.

Said Stengel: "Nobody's going to beat these Cardinals. Joe, these are very rough boys that sneaked into this Series. They'll get right down on the ground and wrestle with you. To the Cards there's practically a year's salary at stake. They'll win this thing in seven games, with each of the Deans winning two."

I don't have to say how correct Casey was. He knew the Cardinals, just as he knows his baseball. That's why I nominate him for the No. 1 baseball guy of our town. He stays around here half the winter, makes no enemies and never ducks an issue. If you've got a better candidate let's hear from you.

Casey in Florida

March 24, 1933. BRADENTON—We sat on the bench with Casey Stengel the other day and watched his Boston Bees play the St. Louis Cardinals. It was a happy adventure. One moment Mr. Stengel is all business, the next all buffoonery. It surprised him to see John Leonard Martin join the umpires in the pre-game rituals at the plate. He hadn't heard the irrepressible Pepper had been elevated to the Captaincy of the Cardinals.

There was no representative of the Bees at the plate conference. Coach George Kelly had presented the umpires with the team's lineup and departed briskly as if to avoid embarrassing questions. Mr. Stengel explained that the Bees had no captain. . . . "We're just like the Mexican army," he said. "Everybody on the team is a major general."

Bob Sherrill, the Cardinals' pitcher, turned the Bees back without any runs for three innings. Twice the Bees hit into double plays to stop budding rallies.

"Hell, we don't need any practice, fellows," said Mr. Stengel, addressing the men on the bench. "We're in mid-season form already."

Al Simmons, the repossessed American Leaguer, weather-beaten of face and gray at the temples, hit Sherrill for a sharp two-base hit down the left-field line.

"Now a fellow like that may be a little help to us," nodded Mr. Stengel. "We don't get to see many two-base hits on this club. When one of our fellows gets a two-base hit we call him the king of swat."

Johnny Mize, the Cardinals' slugging first baseman, stepped to the plate and Mr. Stengel megaphoned through his cupped hands to Lopez, the catcher:

"Now you treat Johnny nice up there, Al. You give him what he wants. Put it right in there for him. All these people are out here to see Johnny hit, and we don't want to spoil their fun."

Lopez grinned, crouched behind the hitter, wiggled his finger to the pitcher and Shoffner tossed up a slow, wobbly pitch that looked as big as a melon. Mize swung furiously, topped the ball and it rolled lazily to Miller at short for an easy infield out. Mr. Stengel jumped to his feet. "I'm surprised at you, Al," he snarled in mock rage. "You deliberately tricked Johnny into making a mug of himself. That will cost you three million dollars."

Back in his seat, Mr. Stengel turned to us and in that sinister, confidential manner of his said: "We burn 'em up, don't we? Ha, ha, ha."

Then, apropos of nothing, he craned his neck in the direction of the Cardinals' bench and let out a fierce jungle shriek. . . . "Wooooooooooooooooo!"

Captain Martin roused himself from judicial concentration, glared at Stengel and thumbed his nose scornfully.

"Imagine old Pepper having to be serious," sympathized Mr. Stengel.

Managing in the Minors

March 22, 1948. LOS ANGELES — Your old friend Casey Stengel is managing the Oakland club in the Pacific Coast League. Mr. Stengel tells a baseball story which is quite popular out here. One of his scouts is supposed to have come in with a thrilling report about a young pitcher who had just worked a no-hitter. . . . "Why," beamed the scout, "they only got one foul off'n him." . . . "Get the guy that got that foul," Casey is supposed to roar. "It's hitters we need, not pitchers."

Casey Lands His Biggest Job

October 14, 1948. There was a time when managing the Yankees was considered steady employment, like explaining Mr. Truman's speeches. From 1918 to 1946 there had been only three and one of the three, Bob Shawkey, lasted but one term. Miller Huggins served twelve. Death stopped him. Joe McCarthy served fifteen and part of another. The mental tantrums of Colonel L. S. MacGenius stopped him. The Yankees are now breaking in their fifth manager since 1946. Including McCarthy, who resigned, they had three in 1946. Bill Dickey and John Neun were the two others. Then came Bucky Harris who survived two campaigns. He was requested to step down a few days ago in favor of Casey Stengel. . . . Charles Dillon Stengel, to be formal about it.

The appointment of Stengel did not come as a major surprise. It is said he was the choice of Del Webb who, with Dan Topping, owns the Yankees. This may or may not be so. I do not know to what extent Webb influences baseball decisions in the Yankee organization. In this case it would be unimportant, anyway, because George Weiss, the general manager, has always been a Stengel man. So, if Webb made the motion, you can be sure Weiss seconded it with enthusiasm.

Stengel will make the Yankees a splendid manager. How far he will progress depends, as always, on two basic things: the cooperation he receives from the front office and the quality of the material that is turned over to him.

Stengel has managed in the majors before, in Boston and in Brooklyn. The records do not describe him as outstanding. But he had bad clubs and nobody makes a reputation managing bad clubs. I saw the clubs in question and it was my judgment he got the most out of the material. There were even times when he seemed to get much more than was there.

Stengel has always had a friendly press. In those days it was interesting to speculate on what he'd be able to do with a good club. We all agreed he'd do very well, indeed. Now he gets his chance. Maybe those Yankees do not add up to a good club but they are certainly better than any Stengel's worked with in the past.

Stengel is fine lodge company, a delightful raconteur, a late sitter-upper. In telling a yarn he gesticulates furiously. Once, in describing a close play on the bases, he took off and went into an actual hook slide. What made this unique is that it was done on the ballroom floor of a hotel.

But make no mistake about Stengel the baseball man. There is nothing eccentric about him. And you will meet up with few men in baseball who are more intelligent. There isn't anything about baseball he doesn't know because he's serious about baseball and has made baseball his life's work. If the ruling brass let him alone and give him the players he'll do better than all right.

Managing Yogi

January 23, 1951. "I'm going to see that he's the highest-paid catcher in baseball," Stengel told me. The locale was Detroit in midsummer, the occasion a $100-a-plate dinner for the Ruth Memorial Fund under the auspices of young Spike Briggs of the Tigers. Stengel, Yogi and I were seated together awaiting the come and get it. There is never anything formal or conventional about a Stengel interview. His esteem for the mental agility of sportswriters, based on years of observation, cannot be too exalted. This would explain the labored gestures which he employs in stressing a point. He leaves nothing to moronic imagination. "Get up and show Williams how you throw to second," Stengel demanded.

There had been imperfections in the catcher's technique. Under the tutorship of Bill Dickey, Yankee coach, these had disappeared. Oblivious of gaping guests, Yogi,

Casey with Edna, 1964.—*NBL*

much in the manner of a trained animal acting on cue, stood, adjusted his stance, took a forward stride and threw out an imaginary runner. "Best catcher in baseball right now and I'm gonna see he's the best paid," grunted Stengel. Yogi was still standing. "Sit down," ordered the manager. Yogi sat down. I half expected Stengel to reach over and pat him tenderly on the head.

Edna Rebels

February 22, 1952. LAKE WALES—There comes a time when a wife wearies of endless baseball chatter, even the wife of a husband who has won three straight championships with the World Series flags to match. "If he does not quit baseball this year I'm going to leave him," insisted Mrs. Casey Stengel yesterday, "and I want you to put that in the paper, too."

"For 27 years all I've heard is baseball talk. This boy can't go to his right. That boy can't hit a curveball. You can run on this fellow. You can pitch to that fellow. One man is a Kraut Head, another is a Road Apple, and another is a Fancy Dan and last year I learned all about switch hitters because Mickey Mantle was on the team. If just once in a while we had some other topic of conversation around the house. Even a good messy ax murder."

After the baseball writers' dinner this year Mrs. Stengel persuaded Casey to fly to Puerto Rico for a short vacation. "I figured that change would do him good, that down there he wouldn't know anybody and we could get away from baseball. But the first night we are there he can't get to sleep. Not too far off there is a familiar muffled roar.

"'Sounds like a baseball game,' Casey said, peeping over the covers.

"I urged him to go to sleep. . . . 'It's probably some sort of festival. These people are great for festivals. They have them every night. Now turn over and get some rest.'

"Well, three hours later he's back in the room and telling me about a pitcher and shortstop he saw, and he's cursing George Weiss. . . . 'We have both of these guys signed up as prospects and Weiss don't tell me nothing about 'em and he knows I'm coming down here.'

"That was the end of our baseball sabbatical. Every day he's out at the ballpark, every night he's on the radio and in-between times he's giving interviews to the baseball writers, and it's just like being back home. This fellow can't go the the right. That fellow can't hit a curveball. And on and on and on.

"Flying back to the States two engines on our plane began to sputter and finally went dead. Casey was no little worried.

"'Think we're going to make it, Edna?' he asked.

"At that moment I was so angry I hoped we wouldn't."

Stengel the Banker

March 12, 1958. Sometime back Charles Dillon Stengel was named chairman of the board of the Glendale (Calif.) bank which is located in the home city of the Yankees' colorful manager. Of late there have been reports of a marked change in manner, attitude, even speech. A touring journalist has emerged from a press conference incredulous. . . . "This is tragic. Now everything the guy says you can understand."

Heretofore a Stengel press conference was distinguished by non sequiturs rampant on a field of incomprehensible jargon —a challenge to ear and nerves. Even so, it had its points. For one, the man could never claim he was misquoted.

As we sat in the dugout with the Glendale financier before yesterday's game with the Reds here, we noted still another sign of an altered personality. The plebeian "either" had been benched in favor of the more fastidious "eyether."

"Now as for my shortstop, all I can say at this stage is that eyether it will be McDougald or Kubek."

This was becoming embarrassing. Charles Dillon Stengel, the banker, was a bore. We had come to talk with Casey Stengel. Abruptly we blurted: "Who are you trying to kid about a 'close exciting race'? If Ford's arm is okay you will win in a romp." That did it.

Ole Case winked expansively and croaked: "You know how far we win by last year if he don't get hurt? From here to China. And let me tell you this, Ford's arm is sound as ever. They say I got trouble at first and third and out there in left field. That's a laugh. I got four good men that can play any one of them spots. Trouble? I'm like a feller that ain't got nothing but caviar to eat."

Don Larsen, the perfect-game pitcher, is the manager's current rave. . . . "Last year he wins five straight before we go into the Series. And I say to him: 'You can win 55 straight if you get your arm in shape quicker. Next spring I want you to report ready to pitch.' So, what does the feller do? Gets himself married to one of them little airlines hostesses, and when he reports I never saw him look so wonderful. I may even pitch him in the opening game. Yes, sir, Eddie Rickenbacker did a great thing when he invented aviation."

Yogi Berra popped into the dugout, poured himself a drink of water. . . . "You've met Mr. Berra, of course," said Old Case with an elaborate Emily Post gesture. "Mr. Berra is a capitalist now. Owns a bowling alley. If I'm nice to him maybe I can get his banking business."

Moving from second to short last year, Gil McDougald had been a complete success. Yet there was a question now that he would remain there. Why Tony Kubek instead? . . . "I didn't say Kubek is my shortstop. I said it would eyether be . . ."

Charles Dillon Stengel, the financier, was back. We bade him a swift adieu.

Casey Himself

July 29, 1960. Back in 1910, when Ole Case broke into professional baseball, Freud was still a rookie, Jung a little-leaguer, and there were no Jimmy Piersalls as such. There were only guys like Rube Waddell and Bugs Raymond . . . and Charles Dillon Stengel, aged 19, Kankakee (Ill.) outfielder, who looked as if he might develop into a pretty good hitter, but . . . "there was a lot of things I couldn't do, or done wrong. One of them was running bases. Instead of sliding into the bag I'd come in standing up and the manager showed me how to do it right and told me to practice every chance I got."

So young Case did his practicing in the outfield, during the game, between pitches. He'd place his glove on the grass, using it as a base, back away some 20 feet,

run and slide, going straight in, or hooking.

Ole Case, getting ready to celebrate his 70th birthday in the Stadium tomorrow, rubbed his chin reflectively. Perhaps he was thinking of the psychiatric inferences drawn from a recent Piersall antic when the Indians' controversial player engaged in a solo version of basketball in the outfield.

"I was improving my sliding out there, but one day the manager told me something that made me stop. What he told me was this: 'See that brick house on the hill beyond the fence? Well, that's a nut house, and if the fellow that runs it ever sees you, he'll come in here and throw a net over you, and I'm not sure it wouldn't be a good idea at that.'"

Casey Inadvertently Shows Why Maris Will Hit 61

February 8, 1961. Ole Case, via long distance from California, had finished a dissertation on free pinch hitters for pitchers (likes the idea) and now he was back on a

subject in which he still retains something more than an academic interest, Mickey Mantle. "Now I'm going to say something

Casey at the Bat.—*cartoon by Willard Mullin*

I never said before on account of which I had too much doubt, but with them two new clubs, which has to be bad ones, and the eight extra games . . . well, now I can say it and mean it."

What Charles Dillon Stengel proceeded to say was that this is the year Mantle will break Babe Ruth's 33-year-old record of 60 home runs.

"Now I'll tell you why," he continued. "(1) His attitude. Them people must have gave him a real nice contract. (2) He'll be hitting against tiring pitchers late in the sea-

son on account of the longer schedule. (3) Why shouldn't he break it? He's got more power than Staleen."

Ole Case had an afterthought. . . . "And this park out here where one of them new teams [Los Angeles Angels] plays will give him chances he never had before. If a fella like him just nudges the ball, it's a home run." There may be substance in much of what the Glendale Banker says.

Ole Case had still another observation. . . . "Maris will help beat the inten-

Roger Maris hits home run No. 61, Yankee Stadium, 1961.   *NBL*

tional pass. They ain't going to pass him to get to Mantle. If he can go all the way this year, and stay hot, that'll keep Mantle on his toes, make him more choosy and he won't strike out so much."

Too Old to Manage but Not Too Old to Think

March 28, 1962. ST. PETERSBURG—The local sheets had billed it as a historic occasion, one that was only slightly less momentous than the return of Napoleon from exile, and a reunion with the Grand Armies, of which he was once the commander-in-chief. At that, to Ole Case this first head-on clash with the pin-stripe troops he had led to 10 victories in 12 battles was a bit more than just another spring exhibition game. . . . "I hafta admit I liked winning this one," he croaked musically.

The Mets had just turned back the Yankees in the ninth inning, with Stengel, too old to manage but plainly not too old to think, outfinessing his younger successor Ralph Houk.

The Old Perfesser. — *NBL*

With the score tied 3-3, one of Ole Case's faceless characters, name of Joe Christopher, first up, tripled over Hector Lopez' head in left. Don Zimmer was out on a foul pop, and then Richie Ashburn was called on to pinch hit. The Yankee infield moved in to protect against a bunt. The day before Ole Case, who describes his present personnel situation as such that he's "gotta steal runs," had used the squeeze to beat the Tigers, 1-0.

But this time the bunt wasn't on. Instead, Ashburn lined the first pitch into short right center, and the game was over. Ole Case—oh, let's go all the way—the 72-year-old Napoleon, both fists jammed deep in his hip pockets, a grin on his weathered kisser, strode in jaunty defiance across the field.

32

Bobo Newsom

A Pitcher of Parts

June 8, 1946. What was good enough for FDR is certainly good enough for Louie Norman Newsom, who is inaugurating his own fourth term in Washington. You may recognize Louie Norman more rapidly as Bobo. He is a pitcher of parts and if there are times when all the parts do not seem to be properly arranged. . . .

We have had some odd characters in baseball who were dreadfully boring, but old Bobo is right off the boat, authentic stuff. Bobo is a man of massive size and vast good humor, but because of his flamboyant personality and disposition to regard himself as an uppercase genius—a combination of Einstein and Edison with a high hard one—he is not without his hecklers. Any time he takes the mound it is a signal for the bench jockeys to don their silks and pick up their whips. They really ride him good, too.

I suppose now that he's back in Washington the boys will be recalling a game he pitched against the Cleveland Indians. Modestly, Bobo refers to it as his Purple Heart game. And as an exhibition of grit it was not too insignificant at that.

Early in the game Earl Averill, Indian outfielder, hit a line drive which crashed into Bobo's kneecap. Bobo was able to get the ball and throw the hitter out. Then he toppled over theatrically and stretched out as if dead.

"Get up, you bum! You ain't hurt," yelled the jockeys in the Cleveland dugout.

Bobo heard them. He sat up and yelled back: "I'm hurt like all hell, but I can still beat you punks on one leg."

Well, he didn't beat 'em. But he stayed in and pitched. Among other things he fanned Hal Trosky, the Indians' power hitter, three times, got two hits himself and covered first base on a bunt. It wasn't until after the game it was discovered Averill's line drive had broken Bobo's kneecap. He was taken to a hospital and was out for seven weeks.

Some seasons later Bobo found himself with the Detroit Tigers, and on a pennant-winning team that was to play the Cincinnati Reds in the World Series. This was raw, red meat for Bobo—the World Series, the big crowds, the emotional whoop-de-do. Naturally he pitched the first game for the Tigers, and just as naturally he won it, and after the game he submitted to an interview, and with all the reluctance of a Connie Bennett demurely pro-

Bobo Newsom.—*NBL*

testing against too many closeups in a picture, admitted the Series was as good as over. "I'll win two more," he said, subduing a yawn.

Bobo's strutting was tragically slowed down before the next sun peeped over the Cincinnati hills. During the night his old man, who had come in from the South for the Series, died. There was speculation as to how the death would affect Bobo, for the fellow is actually sensitive and sympathetic.

He delayed his next appearance until the fifth game. "I'll win this one for the old man," he told newsmen before he left the locker room, and this was one time he wasn't showboating. Bobo won it for the old man; he shut the Reds out with three

hits. And then, with only one day's rest, he came back to pitch the final and deciding game. It took a Paul Derringer at his best to turn him back, 2 to 1.

"That was one I sure wanted to win," moaned Bobo.

"For the old man?" he was asked.

"Hell, no, for old Bobo."

A reasonable view. There is such a thing as overdoing it.

[In a 20-year career, Bobo Newsom pitched, in the following order, for these teams: Dodgers, Cubs, Browns, Senators, Red Sox, Browns, Tigers, Senators, Dodgers, Browns, Senators, Athletics, Senators, Yankees, Giants, Senators, Athletics. No kidding. You could look it up.—P. W.]

33

Stan Musial

"Me hit .400?"

May 8, 1957. Stanley Frank Musial, interrupted in the act of obliterating a steak in a midtown caravansary, smiled cheerfully and said . . . "Me hit .400? Certainly. All I gotta do is keep going like I am."

There being no swagger in the St. Louis star, this was properly dismissed as what is known in meteorological circles as airy persiflage. Still, he was off to his best start in years, and going into last night's game at the Polo Grounds, he was hitting .406.

Records show the baseball climate in St. Louis is singularly conducive to .400 batting averages. Rogers Hornsby with three and George Sisler with two, gave the Missouri metropolis a distinction unmatched in any other big-league community. Musial tends to the belief that

Hornsby's .424, recorded in '22, overshadowed all the others.

"First off, he was a right-hand hitter and that means the run to first base was a couple of strides longer for him. Next, most parks are built to favor the left-hand hitter in that the stands are easier to reach. Also, when the first baseman has to play close to the bag to hold a base runner, the hole between first and second widens proportionately, and that's another break the left-hand hitter gets the right-hander doesn't."

These remarks are typical of one of baseball's nicest and most generous men . . . who is, as anybody knows, a left-hand hitter himself. Hornsby, however, had at least one break that did much to offset the handicaps under which he played. No night ball. But no mention of this from Musial.

"I just came from mass"

May 15, 1958. Musial's quiet, orderly, conscientious application of exceptional talent has brought him rewards in friendship and admiration that far transcend

glory and raucous idolatry. Too often the nice-guy has little else to recommend him, lacking the spirit to challenge, the imagi-

The Man.—*cartoon by Willard Mullin*

nation to explore, even the grace to charm. Not this man; he has depth, warmth, style, character.

Still remembered is a story Dickie Kerr, Musial's first manager, told us. The locale a Florida camp, the day Sunday, the time 7:00 A.M. For some reason Kerr was up at this revolting hour and spotted Musial entering the hotel.

"So you been batting around all night?" the manager barked.

"No sir. I just came from mass."

[Musial's best year, 1948, is very revealing. He hit for average .376, and led the league in hits, doubles and triples, but he also hit a career-high 39 home runs. Like many great hitters, he could do it both ways, and in fact his lifetime collection of 725 doubles (second on the all-time list) is balanced by his lifetime slugging average of .559 (ninth on that list).—P. W.]

34

Some Yankees

The Two Mickey Mantles

March 20, 1959. MIAMI—In his opening presentation here Perfesser Stengel, eminent linguist, orator, raconteur, economist, platooner, lobbyist, world traveller and pennant monopolist had made no reference whatever to Mickey Mantle. Why?

"I do not go around talking about the money I got in my bank in Glendale, do I? I know it's in there. I know Mantle's in center field, too."

No reasoning could possibly have been more clearly and cogently stated, but, unfortunately, the minds of sportswriters are not notably quick, and besides, in times past, some not too distant, the Perfesser had been openly and stingingly critical.

"That don't mean I don't get along with Mantle. It's on account I admire him and appreciate what tremendous ability he's got that I keep after him. I want to see him be the greatest player in baseball. DiMaggio was the best ballplayer I ever managed. Mantle can be right up there next to him, and it's his own fault if he don't get there."

His own fault?

"The trouble with Mantle is Mantle. I said it before, and I say it again, there ain't nothing this boy can't do, and do

better'n anybody else. Every year he ought to lead this league in five different things. Nobody can hit a ball farther than him, left-handed, or right-handed either. Nobody can run from first to third faster, nobody can throw better, and nobody can catch better.

"But only one year since he's been with us does he put all these things together, and then he is the great star which he should ought to always be, if he don't get mad at Mantle and fight Mantle when somethin' goes wrong."

It is the Perfesser's considered judgment that the man has yet to be born with power enough to hit a ball over Mantle's head. Yet the realities of life in the Stadium prove him wrong.

"They don't hit it over Mantle's head. They hit it over the other guy's head . . . the Mantle which Mantle's mad at. He stands out there in center field, his arms folded, like this, giving this other Mantle hell, and then boom. . . . Somebody suddenly hits one, and on account of the fight he's having out there, Mantle loses a step starting, and then the ball is gone, and now he's madder than ever."

Wait Till They Stop Rolling.—*cartoon by Willard Mullin*

Since a manager must be many things to all players, the Perfesser was asked what remedial measures he's tried and to what effect.

"Well, last season in Boston when he bangs his fist against the dugout concrete after a third strike, I hand him a bat, and tell him to bang himself on top of the head with it, on account if he wants to end his career, he might as well do it quick and get it over with."

[Although Mantle's lifetime average is below .300, he is sixth on the all-time home run list with 536, and seventh in home run percentage with 6.6.—P. W.]

An Apple-Cheeked Rookie

September 23, 1950. Only time dreams are any good is when you are young. And, of course, they are much better when they come true. Like Whitey Ford's, for example. Up from the sandlots around here, Whitey, 21, an apple-cheeked rookie, is trying to pitch the Yankees into another World Series.

Whitey Ford, with baseball, has just beaten the Washington Senators for his 16th victory of the 1965 season. Mickey Mantle and Billy Martin look on.—*NBL*

Doing all right, too. Nobody's beaten him since he arrived from the Kansas City farm in June and he's won eight straight. On the last western trip, which was crucial all over, the youngster—he looks more like 17 than 21 and you find it hard to believe he's got a bride-to-be—was a combination of Hopalong Cassidy, Captain Marvel and Mandrake the Magician. Characters, no doubt, from his favorite comic books.

Where the big guys faltered and doom threatened, Whitey remained staunch and invincible until the enemy broke and fled and new hope dawned, just as it always does in youthful dreams, and the Yankees came back to the Stadium still the team to beat.

Whitey's dream has been so exciting —and the fulfillment so perfect—there are times when he can't make up his mind which he prefers the more: the land of fantasy or realism. Like the other day when he was scheduled to pitch the wind-up game in Chicago. He overslept so long he just did get to the park in time to take his preliminary pitches. The baseball writers were startled when they saw the sleepy youngster enter the dining room fully an hour after his teammates had gone to the park.

Larsen's Perfect World Series Game against the Dodgers, 1956.—*cartoon by Willard Mullin*

"Don't worry," Whitey yawned. "All I need to beat them guys is a cup of coffee."

Must have been strong. Let 'em down with only three hits.

[Ford, of course, went on to a great career that encompassed a phenomenal 11 World Series. Of necessity he got many "longevity" records for the Series, like most innings pitched and most strikeouts, but being in the right place had little to do with the 32 consecutive scoreless innings, which broke one of the marks of which Ruth was proudest.—P. W.]

Larsen's Perfect Game, Seen from the Press Box

October 9, 1956. And now the Mt. Everest of World Series pitching has finally been conquered.

You don't give much thought to the possibility of a no-hitter, much less such an epochal thing as the perfect game, until the seventh inning or thereabouts. Mechanically, you recheck your scoring to be sure. Then you find yourself inwardly hoping the guy makes it and you begin to feel the tension that is all around you.

I have my binoculars in the press box and I watch Larsen turn back the Brooks in the eighth and then walk to the dugout. If the immensity of the drama has caught up with him his features fail to reflect it. He is a good-looking man, with slightly prominent ears, and he chews gum, or whatever it is, with animation. He has an ungainly stride that is more yokel than athletic or military, and this seems to accent his easy-going "what's-your-hurry" manner. In the dugout his teammates studiously avoid him.

The Gay Swede has had some luck.

The Duke and Sandy Amoros narrowly missed homers. Mickey Mantle robbed Gil Hodges of an extra baser in center, and Andy Carey later frisked him of a single. Now it is the top of the ninth and Larsen is back on the hill moving inexorably yet dispassionately toward a date with destiny. And as he is stacking up the last three Brooks to make it 27 in a row, and official, the packed stands strain in a choked silence, suffering the sweet agony of crisis, praying it will be met and gallantly resolved.

Just like Stengel's been saying. He ain't got no pitching.

Billy Martin

October 6, 1953.   There is nothing about Billy Martin that is remindful of Yankee heroes of the past. Gehrig could have put him in his hip pocket. Ruth would have mistaken him for the bat boy. DiMaggio, in a whimsical mood, might have let him carry his glove. Be that as it may, no Yankee goliath of the storied yesterdays ever contributed more to a World Series triumph than the 25-year-old dead-end kid out of the slums of Oakland, Calif.

A year ago it was the Portuguese-Italian's frantic catch of a twisting, treacherous, wind-blown infield fly, the bases loaded and all runners running, in the seventh game that saved the Series for the Bombers, and yesterday it was his blazing single to center in the ninth inning that broke a 3-3 tie and gave Casey Stengel and the perennial American League champions a history-making fifth victory in the fall frenzy.

And no one was more delighted to see Billy the Brat, whose square moniker is Alfred N. Pesano, climax a .500-hitting spree made up of seven singles, a double, two

triples and two home runs, a record harvest for six games, than the Yankees' grizzled old manager, for Stengel can truthfully and pridefully say, in a baseball sense,

"Yes, Sir, that's my boy."

They came up together to the Yankees from Oakland. Stengel was managing out there when the skinny, cocky, assertive kid collared him in the local park and sold himself as a coming big-leaguer who couldn't possibly miss.

They call him "Stengel's pet," and there can be no doubt that the childless old gaffer has an admiration for the little toughie that borders on parental affection. Possibly Stengel sees in Martin's mad enthusiasm for the game, jaunty truculence and keen team spirit a reflection of himself when he was young. Stengel lived for baseball and the team, and nobody ever pushed him around.

The difference in the Series between the Yankees and the Brooklyns, who, alas, have yet to win one of these all-out tests in seven attempts, was Martin. His bat, a modest .257 force during the season, figured mightily and opportunely in each of the Bombers' four wins.

His three-run triple set up the Yankee victory in the opening game; his two-run homer proved to be the insurance the Yankees needed in the free-scoring fifth game and it was his clutch ninth-inning single, after a two-run Carl Furillo blast into the stands had tied the score, that pulled the deciding game out of the fire.

"That's the worst thing that coulda happened to Martin," Stengel grumbled good-humoredly after it was over. "I ain't gonna be able to live with the little so and so next year."

35

Assorted Dodgers

Hugh Casey

October 3, 1947. By now it is clear that this is a Series that is not going to inspire epic prose to the mastery of the men on the mound. It has reached a point where even one or two well-pitched innings establishes the fellow as a phenomenon and he is instantly compared with the all-time greats. A perfect example is Hugh Casey who pitched two and two-thirds innings, stopped a Yankee rally, was voted the winning pitcher in that dreadful 9-8 charade yesterday and, quite properly, by current standards, was the toast of Flatbush last night.

This, I hasten to add, is not to take anything away from Mr. Casey who pours a mean drink and serves an enticing mess of corn beef and cabbage in his own bar and grill on Flatbush Ave. As pitchers go, Mr. Casey is an ancient character. Six years ago this month he was trying to win a Series game from the Yankees. No dice. Two failures. But yesterday when the scorers came to the line "winning pitcher" they filled it out with Casey's name. He had at least pitched one perfect inning.

Dixie Walker

April 11, 1942. Mr. Dixie Walker occupies an important position in the eyes of the Brooklyn fan. He is the big hero—and for reasons only the B.F. can convincingly explain. At one time it looked as if he might develop into a real star but it never happened. Now in his 30s, it is reasonable to assume a large part of his future is behind him. Nevertheless he is the idol of Flatbush.

You can have the brilliant Reiser, who led the league in hitting, and the masterful Wyatt, whose pitching genius sewed up the pennant; Flatbush will take Mr. Walker.

What seems strange to outsiders is perfectly clear and defensible to the Brooklyn fan. It's probably something only a Freudian would get, since it ties up in one sense

Before the 1947 World Series. *Left to right*: Pete Reiser, Hugh Casey, Cookie Lavagetto, Peewee Reese, Dixie Walker.—*NBL*

with hatred—hatred for the Giants. What did Mr. Walker do to capture the affection of Brooklyn? He made three hits against the despised Giants the first time he faced them. That makes him an immortal.

In another sense it ties up with a sort of social neurosis, an elegant, smug New York vs. a plain, provincial Brooklyn. The social neurosis side is replete with case histories. There was the unpredictable Babe Herman for one and Van Mungo, the pitcher, for another. Babe was loved be-

cause he did so many things wrong. This made him human. Mungo was loved because he was always in trouble; that seems to be the fate of the common man and Brooklyn is understanding and sympathetic. All of which suggests that Mickey Owen, the catcher, who dropped the third strike which led to the Bums' defeat in the World Series, will never be forgotten. Indeed, we are surprised monuments haven't already been erected to his enduring glory in Prospect Park.

Carl Erskine

October 3, 1953. To those of us in the plank-board Ebbets Field press box who had seen Howard Ehmke, a surprise starter

for the AAA's, strike out 13 Chicago Cubs to set a World Series record on the afternoon of Oct. 8, 1929, this was like sitting in on a modernized version of an old pitching classic. Only the characters and the locale were different. At the end of the sixth inning yesterday Carl Erskine had fanned 11 Yankees and it was clear a new record was well within the grasp of the 165-pound Brooklyn right-hander.

From the opening scene it was evident that Erskine had overcome whatever it was that afflicted his sense of direction in the first game in the Stadium. He fanned the first two hitters, Gil McDougald and Joe Collins. In the second he got two more, Mickey Mantle and Phil Rizzuto. Two more fell in the third, Vic Raschi and Collins again. This was six to three, close to par.

The young man from Anderson, Ind., who was only three years old when Ehmke set his record, was sharp and forceful and his breaking stuff was responding as submissively as a politician to a labor boss. In the fourth Mantle went down again and before the game was over he was to go down twice more. Collins bowed for the third time in the fifth and was soon to join Mantle as a four-time loser.

And so it went until the Yankee top of the ninth which saw Erskine needing one more to tie and two to break Ehmke's record of 24 years standing. Rizzuto was due to lead off but Manager Casey Stengel, who lights candles at the altar of percentages, sent in left-handed hitter Don Bollweg, who promptly became an interesting statistic as the hitter Erskine victimized to tie the record.

Obviously Mr. Stengel wasn't going to let Raschi hit at this stage and just as obviously old Jawn Mize would be the pinch hitter. Getting rid of Bollweg was one thing,

but old Jawn, who still has the smoothest swing in baseball, 20-20 eyes and a jungle cat lust for young pitching blood, was quite another dish. And Erskine had reason to remember him with terror, for old Jawn had slashed him for a three-run homer just a year ago.

This was the largest World Series crowd in Brooklyn history, 35,270, and everybody in the park somehow seemed to know that if Erskine could humble the Yankees' ageless slugger he'd have his record. There was a tremendous roar when he got the first one past Mize. The stands seemed to vibrate as he took another prodigious cut and never did so much energy produce such a tiny result. Jawn had foul-tipped the pitch, barely ticking it.

Now the young pitcher, who could only last one inning in his first start, needed but one more strike and he was in the Hall of Fame. Old Jawn stood there at the plate, 230 pounds of power, slightly crouched, his massive bat poised menacingly back of his left ear, imperturbable as always, unmoved by the drama of the situation, indifferent, quite likely, even blissfully unaware, perhaps.

You couldn't tell from the press box whether the little fellow out there in the middle of the diamond (he's only 5 feet 10) felt the strain. If he did he didn't show it. To all appearances Old Jawn was just another hitter. Composed and calm, Erskine took his position on the rubber, went smoothly into his windup, delivered a breaking curve that danced capriciously out of the range of Old Jawn's ferocious swing . . . and Howard Ehmke's long-lived record was no more.

The Bum and Willard

November 13, 1953. Rebecca A. Brady, 714 E. Fifth St., Bklyn., writes:

For years you have been using the de-

rogatory term, "The Bums" in poisonous contrast to the inspiring, "The Bombers" for the Yankees. It is shuddering just to think of the pitiful contrast in connotations.

In this age when we all know something about psychology, we should realize people respond to the name they are called. If you have children you would not call them "Bums" if you expected them to amount to anything.

Every once in a while a protest of this nature arrives in the mail, but this is the first time it has been used to explain the Brooklyns' endless futility against the Yankees in the World Series. Wondering how Walter O'Malley, the president of the club, felt about the matter, I solicited his views. O'Malley answered by return mail:

Although your correspondent professes not to be interested in the origin of the term, for historical purposes it should be noted "The Bums" is a brain child of your Willard Mullin.

The Dodgers, you know, are not just a baseball team. They mean something to people who have never seen a game. The Dodgers are the symbol of the underdog, and well— so is The Bum. The exhortation, "Come on, you Bums," is not an opprobrium. Rather, it is an endearment.

Something of this quality is mirrored in the face of Mullin's character. There are signs of pain and turmoil in his features, on occasions, unhappily, bruises and contusions,

and, of course, he is in tatters: but always in his eyes is a look of bold defiance and prideful resolution. At the same time he is not without guile and often these noble aspects are masked by a sly, mischievous twinkle not unlike that which is to be seen in a disdainful urchin's eye as he cocks his rebellious arm to fling a brickbat at a silk hat.

No, I cannot lend myself to any squeamish campaign which has as its objective the demise of The Bum. So far as we in Brooklyn are concerned the fellow is here to stay.

You will note O'Malley indicates The Bum has a contract for life. This implies a position of preeminence without contemporary parallel, for no other individual in the Brooklyn organization, from top executive to bullpen catcher, has a contract that calls for more than one year.

To be sure, The Bum does enjoy certain advantages which set him apart. One look at his unkempt beard and disreputable clothes is enough to suggest that he is not exactly the highest-paid man on O'Malley's salary list. And apparently the only time he ever eats is when Mullin feeds him.

It may be, too, that The Bum owes his unique security to the fact that he has no wife. Anyway, there's no record she ever wrote O'Malley a letter telling him off, as Mrs. Dressen did.

Roy Campanella

January 29, 1958. Whether Roy Campanella ever catches again must be of less anxious concern to his fans than whether the roly-poly can come out of his near-tragic crash unmaimed.

In addressing a high-school dinner the Dodgers' stalwart once said: "Of course,

you got to be a man to play big-league baseball, but you got to have a lot of little boy in you, too."

If Campanella had been requested to sit down and do a thesis on himself he couldn't have composed a more faithful

Roy Campanella, Duke Snider and Gil Hodges. — *NBL*

description. To him baseball was a living, but first it was fun. So marked was Campanella's ardor for play and urgency to help that it was almost impossible to keep him out of a game. Often he'd play in spite of crippling injury.

Our use of the past tense is dictated by convenience and not by conviction, for we like to believe that somehow he's going to make it. At the same time, we must respect the plain truth that time had already begun to run out on him, that at best perhaps he had no more than one fruitful sea-son left. Even so, Walter Alston was counting on him. No more than a week ago he had said: "As of now, Campy is our No. 4 hitter."

But, however fate eventually deals the cards, Campy's position as a big-leaguer . . . a big-leaguer in every respect . . . can never be challenged. For years he was the best catcher in the National League. A great arm, a dangerous long-ball hitter, superb with the glove, an elixir to reeling pitchers, a most happy fella and a darn nice guy.

Don Drysdale

March 22, 1960. Don Drysdale, 24 on July 23, throws more strikes than Hoffa. The 6-6, 210-pound right-hander fanned 242 to lead both majors last season.

Drysdale now occupies the same terrifying position, as a hitter's nemesis, as Herb Score held before the Indians' flamethrower was disabled in '56, following consecutive strikeout totals of 245 and 263. Apparently only one thing stands between Drysdale and superlative achievement—control. Not of the ball, but of his temper.

In enemy dugouts they tell you he can "dish it out but can't take it." The first pitch to a hitter who digs in, or crowds the plate, is almost certain to send him sprawling, ashen-faced, in the dirt. That would be dishing it out.

But when the bench jockeys curve him with taunting epithets, the umpire lifts a magisterial finger in reproof or a teammate louses up an easy play, the Drysdale temper flares, he reaches for the 16-pound glower and his combative knuckles whiten. And that would be the can't-take-it reaction.

First time Roy Campanella saw Drys-dale pitch, he called him "sweet and mean," a colloquial description of his distinctive ability and his misanthropic disposition. A personal hatred for hitters, however, has always been common among pitchers. Drysdale learned the more subtle arts of the craft at the feet of a master, sinister Sal Maglie. What realists call the bean ball and euphemists the brush-back pitch was an integral part of the Barber's equipment.

Laughingly Drysdale recalls a day in Brooklyn when Maglie (they were teammates then) lashed him verbally for throwing a curve to a hitter leaning over the plate, a triple resulting. . . . "That's when you give him the hard, fast one," admonished his remorseless tutor. "Make the bum dance. If you don't, pretty soon you'll be selling apples."

Did the young man ever take dead aim at a hitter?

"Never, never in my life, I swear. . . . Unless, of course, the bum was digging in. When he does that, he's asking for it."

Donald Scott Drysdale, Maglie graduate magna cum laude, baseball's Abominable Snowman.

Robby

October 7, 1949. It is my belief that Jackie Robinson is the most dangerous player in the Series, because he can beat you so many ways. The only time he's been on base in the Series up to now was in the second inning yesterday—and he ultimately came home with the winning run. The addicts got a fleeting glimpse of his speed when he scurried from second to third on a short foul fly back of first.

The Yanks' chances of victory will diminish or expand in ratio to the number of times the young Negro gets on base, for their catching is none too expert and Robinson has an unsettling effect on pitchers.

The Key Man

April 7, 1951. Duke Snider and Gil Hodges have the power to turn a game upside down without notice, but even so Jackie Robinson looms as the key man in any strategy designed to bring pitching and hitting closer together. He's the one player on the team—in the league in fact—who is just as dangerous on base as at bat. Last year he wasn't in shape. He didn't run. He stole only 12 bases against 37 in the year before. And it's not too severe a criticism to say he cost the Bums the pennant.

This spring Robinson is streamlined and in the Florida games I saw he was fencing with the pitchers, drawing leads and bringing into play the tactics which made him such an upsetting influence and such a vital factor in Brooklyn's '47 and '49 flag wins. If Robinson elects to play all-out baseball—which, by his own confessions, he didn't last year—he will help the Bums' pitching simply by driving the enemy pitchers crazy with his frenzied fakes and exasperating calisthenics on the lines.

Peewee Reese

March 20, 1940. Mr. MacPhail said that his manager, Leo Durocher, still one of the best ballplayers in the league, probably would have to spend most of his time on the bench this year.... "How's he going to keep young Reese out of the lineup?" he demanded.

Reese is the kid shortstop the Brooklyns bought from the Boston Red Sox after the latter outfit had bought a whole ball club just to get his contract. The story has already been told in this space how Joe Cronin, the Red Sox manager, was unimpressed the first time he saw Reese and ad-

vised his disposal. That's how Brooklyn happened to get him.

"Reese will definitely be in our starting lineup at short," continued Mr. MacPhail, "and I predict he will be the most sensational newcomer of the year in both leagues." Still, if Reese can send the brilliant Durocher to the bench he must be better than fair.

[Leo did get into 53 games at short that year, to Reese's 83, but in 1941 Peewee took over the job for good.—P. W.]

Leo Durocher

March 2, 1943. The rejection of lippy Mr. Durocher by the army on account of a defunct ear is a man-bites-dog item. It helps to explain, incidentally, how the gentleman was able to endure his own endless chatter down through the years. Presumably he couldn't hear himself talk.

But if Mr. Durocher's hearing equipment suffered collapse, it is horrifying to contemplate the effect his flow of oratory had on umpires and others who came within his wavelength. Truly, these hapless victims must live in a world of torture.

Back from Siberia

April 21, 1948. The return of Leo Durocher from the salt mines of baseball's Siberia found the Giants in a sympathetic, compassionate mood in their opener at the Polo Grounds yesterday. They looked at the humble, contrite Durocher, with butter melting in his mouth, and they gazed upon his missus, the lovely Laraine Day of the cinema, sitting in a box dandling a small flaxen-haired child on her knee, and they went soft all over. Naturally they didn't have the heart to take the ball game. They gave it to Mr. Durocher and his Brooklyns to take across the bridge with their compliments.

Mr. Durocher's reacceptance into baseball society was devoid of ceremony. There was no anointing with oils, churchly services or offering of incense for the repentant sinner. Since his formal return was being made on the grounds of the usually belligerent Giants it would not have been surprising if the pew holders had demanded elaborate proof of his right to mingle with the blessed. A mixed outburst greeted his first appearance on the field. There were cheers and there were boos. Durocher spent the afternoon walking nervously from one end of the third-base coach's box to the other. Napoleon was like that too. He couldn't think unless he was on his feet. Only once did Leo break out with familiar gestures and gab, when a boxholder picked up a ball on an overthrow at first base. The umpires listened to him tolerantly for a spell and then told him to go roll his hoop.

Chuck Dressen

February 16, 1960. The last of baseball's gifted whistlers is calling it quits. In his new capacity as big chief of the Braves, Charles Walter Dressen will manage from the dugout, instead of the coaching lines, as has long been his custom.

"To be able to whistle real good," explained Dressen, "you got to be standing up. Sitting down, you don't get the proper effect. Besides, it don't look dignified."

Countless eardrums in both leagues have been shattered by shrill Dressen blasts, as the little fellow went into his act back of third base, exhorting friendly hitters, distracting enemy pitchers, harassing innocent bystanders. For years the whistle has been his trademark.

Old-timers contend Hughey Jennings, who managed Ty Cobb in his early Detroit days, reached a higher pitch. Others maintain Al Schacht, as coach of the Red Sox, had greater range.

"I didn't hear Jennings," lamented Dressen. "Schacht I did, and he never impressed me. No artistry. Like listening to a hawk. Myself, I tried to emulate the clear, sharp timbre of the American eagle, which is at once commanding and inspiring. Patriotic, too."

The 61-year-old mastermind, who left the Dodgers to assume jurisdiction over what is said to be the most uninhibited club in the majors, shrugged. "I always did my best, even when I had a sore throat. I am content to be judged by posterity."

Opening Day Brooklyn lineup, 1954. *Left to right*: Junior Gilliam, Peewee Reese, Duke Snider, Jackie Robinson, manager Walter Alston, Roy Campanella, Gil Hodges, Carl Furillo, Billy Cox and Carl Erskine.—*NBL*

Walter Alston

November 25, 1953. Although baseball operations in Brooklyn have never been distinguished for their rational or even orderly aspects, the naming of an utter unknown, Walter Alston, as the new manager could not have but evoked surprise and shock among the faithful. "Alston? Who's he?"

Well, he is a young man who manifestly impressed the front office brass by his direction of Montreal, the top farm club, and the manner in which he handled those embryonic Bums. To get the appointment he stood up under the scouting of the entire executive family, from the president Walter O'Malley to head scout Red Corriden.

Assuming Alston has the basic requisites, as he must have, or else he wouldn't have survived such a searching examination, his appointment is probably as wise as any other could have been.

I happen to know, too, the front office is just as pleased Peewee Reese gave the job the back of his neck. Like the player himself, the front office believes he has at least two big seasons left, and it was feared the added burdens of managing would shrink his effectiveness in the field and at bat.

What about Peewee's managerial future now? Curiously, it is almost entirely in the hands of the unknown newcomer. If Alston should fail, the popular pressure on Reese, a year older, to accept would be all the greater. But if Alston gets a "Busher Joe" string going the Peewee may never get to be a manager.

[Years as big-league manager: Alston 23, Reese 0. —P. W.]

———

36

The Shot Heard Round the World

"Dodger caps, 25 cents"

October 2, 1951. There was a note of sullen contempt in the voice of the young vendor as he stood in the gloomy rotunda of the old Brooklyn ballpark and made his final pitch to the resigned fans who were shuffling toward the street.

"Here ya are! Dodger caps, 25 cents. Used to be a buck. Get 'em while they last."

The indication was they would last until next spring, anyway. There was no frantic rush to buy. But somehow the incident seemed aptly to symbolize the mournful destiny of the Dodgers, in early August the soundest investment on the pennant board, now a sadly deflated stock scarcely worth listing.

The Dodgers had lost the first game of the current National League playoff. They had lost on their home grounds, and the next two, if two were needed, would be played against the Giants in the Polo Grounds.

The Dodgers, their pitching shattered in their magnificent desperation stand against the Phillies the day before, had started Ralph Branca, who had been undependable in recent weeks. It was a game that called for a Roe or a Newcombe, but neither could lift an arm, so heavy and

crowded had been their down-the-stretch chores.

A young right-hander who scorns superstition, Branca took the mound, as usual, with a large "13" on the back of his shirt. This time it was not so much an ominous symbol as an agonizing reminder that on August 11 the Dodgers were leading by 13 games, their advantage so commanding that the race was virtually over.

Branca pitched well enough to win in normal circumstances. Two home-run balls beat him, one to Bobby Thomson in the fourth with a runner on, the second a solo to Monte Irvin, purely decorative, in the eighth. The Dodger hitting was more to be faulted than Branca's pitching.

The Dodgers came into the game emotionally and physically spent. They had played life or death baseball for 14 innings on Sunday to hold the surging Giants even and force a playoff. They were hoping for the breaks and possibly an easy game. They got neither.

Very likely Jackie Robinson never received such a whole-hearted ovation, even in Brooklyn, as when he came to the plate for the first time in the second inning. This in recognition of the indisputable fact

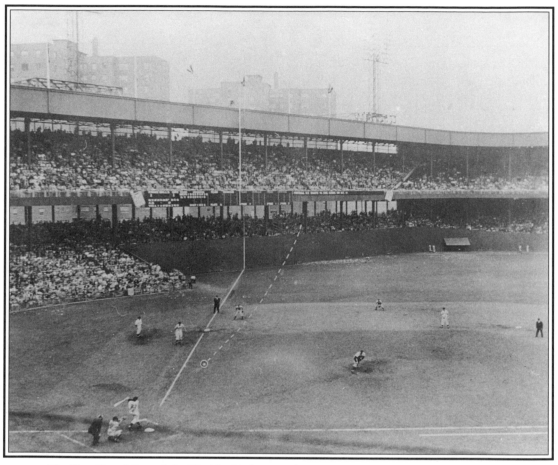

The Shot Heard Round the World: third game of National League playoff, Polo Grounds,
October 3, 1951.—*NBL*

that he, singlehanded, had kept the shell-shocked Dodgers in contention. But the exhausting labors in the Philadelphia melodrama and the emotional letdown had hit him, too. There were no more miracles left in this fiery competitor's frame. A scratch single past first was his maximum contribution, and even this was wasted.

"Where's Dressen been hiding this fellow?"

October 3, 1951. Consider the position Charley Dressen found himself in yesterday. His pitching was impoverished. He couldn't use Newcombe or Roe against the Giants and Branca had gone down the day before. It really didn't make much difference. One pitcher would be as good or bad as another. It had to be a guess. Clem Labine might do it. The 25-year-old right-hander from Woonsocket, R.I., won four straight when he came up mid-season from St. Paul. But then there was that frightful start he made against the Phillies last month.

The Phillies blasted him for a grand-slam homer in the first inning. Dressen hadn't liked the way the young man looked in that situation, so he took him out of rotation and sent him to the bullpen. The inference was clear enough: the young man was in the kennel. He didn't start another game, not until yesterday.

And that happened to be the biggest game the Dodgers had been in since 1946 when they found themselves in precisely the same situation against the St. Louis Cards, a playoff game they had to win. They failed then but not yesterday. Young Labine saw to that.

One run would have been enough to win for him, and indeed, so hopeless was the Giant attack that Jackie Robinson's two-run homer in the first inning actually settled the issue, a sharp, curving liner that barely cleared the lower left-field barrier.

Only once was this remarkably composed young man in serious trouble. That was in the third when the Giants filled the bases and Bobby Thomson, whose explosive bat had figured so vitally in the Giants' win in the first playoff game, was up with two down. Labine audaciously broke a 3-2 curve over the plate and the Staten Island Scot swung with massive futility.

It was no wonder that at this point the press box, crowded with out-of-town historians here for the Series, wondered out loud:

"Where's Dressen been hiding this fellow?"

It was a question even Dressen couldn't have answered or would have had an embarrassing time trying.

Ralph Branca Began Striding Toward the Mound . . .

October 4, 1951. For some minutes under the haze-draped skies in the old Polo Grounds it looked as if the capricious gods, who had picked up the Giants in their darkest hour last August, had decided they had carried the implausible fantasy too far and that the time had come for a semblance of sanity. And so when the Brooklyns scored three in the eighth in the third playoff game yesterday to end the unmitigated nonsense, crushed romance shook the hand of firm realism and in the moment of mixed emotions there was on both sides not only understanding but appreciation for a wonderfully inventive script.

The mockery had extended through the seventh, the game a deadlock at 1-1. There were runners at first and third with Jackie Robinson up and one away, a made-to-order situation for a squeeze and the prospects so inviting. In trying to keep the ball away from Robinson, Maglie, on the second pitch, threw so wide to the right of the plate the ball was unstoppable and Peewee Reese scored without a play being made on him. The Brooklyns got two more runs, and with Don Newcombe, the 200-pounder, rearing back and firing with disciplined and forceful efficiency, and his defense turning in one brilliant play after another—well, who would Charley Dressen pitch against the Yankees in the opening game today?

There is no reasonable way to explain what followed. It may be that the gods, viewing the shattered remains of baseball's gaudiest dream and catching some of the emotion which gripped the nation, had a change of heart and decided to write a happy ending to an incredible story that will be told and retold as long as the game is played.

A wakelike silence hung over the grounds as Alvin Dark, the Giants' captain, stepped to the plate to open the ninth. Even the Brooklyn loyalists, not particularly distinguished for restraint under any circumstances, seemed moved by the vast misery of their neighbors and assumed a

Out of the Book.—*cartoon by Willard Mullin*

deferential air which remained unaltered even when Gil Hodges' headlong dive failed to head off a single to right.

Don Mueller followed with another single to the same sector and the Giant fans began to breathe again, if ever so faintly. Monte Irvin, whose double had scored the Giants' only run up to then, added nothing to their vitality with a pop out, but a moment later when Whitey Lockman hooked a double to left a roar ensued. Maybe it hadn't all been a dream. Maybe it wasn't all illusion. Maybe—

This was as far as Dressen could go with Newcombe, who had come into the game with only two days' rest after heroic achievement in the Saturday-Sunday Philadelphia ordeals which, carried over, were to total 20 innings of scoreless pitching before the skein was broken. From the bullpen in far-off left field, Ralph Branca began striding toward the mound.

By now Mueller, who had sprained his ankle sliding into third, had been carried from the field on a stretcher and Clint Hartung was running for him. Lockman was still on second and the hitter was Bobby Thomson. It had been a wretched afternoon for the Staten Island Scot. He had been vulnerable in defense and witless on the bases. But he had been resolute in the batter's box.

Branca's first pitch was a strike. His second never reached the plate.

A shaft of late-afternoon sun had broken through the haze and as his ball leaped from Thomson's bat and headed for the stands, steadily climbing, it seemed to be enveloped in a golden glow, as if it marked the highway of glorious deeds and glorious dreams over which only heroes march, heroes who have lived with the gods.

His First Pitch Was Called a Strike; His Second Was Called Many Things

October 27, 1951. Charlie Dressen's reaction to an interview in which Bobby Thomson was described as having grown weary at answering questions about his historic home run indicated that there's always a livelier market for pratfalls than flawless endeavors.

"What's that guy griping about?" roared Dressen. "He was the hero, I was the bum. I meet a guy for the first time, and right away he says: 'Oh, yes, you were managing Brooklyn that year, weren't you?'"

Few managers in baseball history have been more furiously second-guessed. Most of the expert hindsight centered on the dramatic ninth inning when an entire season was capsuled into a single pitch . . . the one which Thomson lined into the left-field seats for a three-run homer. Ralph Branca, replacing Don Newcombe, threw the ball that sent all Flatbush into mourning.

The Giants had bombed Branca for nine home runs during the regular season. Thomson had hit him for the distance to help the Giants win the first playoff game; moreover, with 32, he led the club. Why, then, had Dressen called on Branca to pitch to him?

"Sukey said he was ready," was Dressen's answer to sportswriters who jammed the manager's cubicle at the Polo Grounds.

What actually happened was this: Clyde Sukeforth informed Dressen by bullpen-to-dugout phone that Branca was his best bet. . . . "He's sharp, his control is good.". . . Who would know better at such a moment? It was Sukeforth's job to know, and since all managers rely on the bullpen coach for on-the-spot pitching information, Branca came in. His first pitch was called a strike; his second was called many things, mostly blasphemous.

Generally, though, the second-guessing was as proper as it was pertinent. For instance, why hadn't Dressen, a bold manager, repudiated the book and put Thomson on, even though he represented the winning run?

"I thought of it," he admitted. "But who knows, the next guy might have knocked it out of the park, too."

The next guy happened to be Willie Mays.

[The '51 Giants, however, lost their magic and the Series to the Yankees, and maybe the real "miracle" occurred in '54, the Series best remembered for Mays' catch and throw of Vic Wertz' long ball. That year the Indians won 111 games. They had two 20-game winners and three others who had won at least a baker's dozen; they had two .300 hitters plus the powerful Larry Doby, who led the league in homers that year —and they lost to the Giants, four straight. But then the Giants had Mays.—P. W.]

37

Satchel Paige

"I just wish there was some way to paint him white"

August 25, 1944. Two or three years ago a tall, lean Negro sat in the dugout and watched Bob Feller pitch before a hometown crowd out in Iowa; he watched the strikeout king of the American League throw the ball past the hitters.

"That little white boy's fast, too," commented the 6-foot 3-inch Negro dryly.

It was Satchel Paige talking and it was his forthright way of paying tribute to another without taking anything away from himself.

Paige is coming to New York to pitch in the Stadium Sunday and he need make no apology for trodding the turf which has known the spike wounds of many of baseball's greatest, for there can be no question that if he had been tinted a less somber shade he would have been a major-league standout.

This is the one Negro pitcher about whose high talents everybody agrees. There have been others who attracted wide attention, but Paige is the first to receive unstinted and universal recognition. He has pitched against scores of big-league hitters, practically all the good ones in the last dozen years, Ruth and Gehrig somehow being exceptions, and none we ever talked

with was disposed to minimize his unusual skill. When we first started hearing about the Satchel we asked Mickey Cochrane about him. Some of Cochrane's 1935 Detroit champions had been on tour with him. Cochrane had made a point to see him pitch.

"Can he pitch?" Cochrane repeated our question. "I just wish there was some way to paint him white. I'd guarantee you I'd have a 30-game winner on my club next summer."

This was just an opinion, however competent. There is more substantial evidence available. Three times the Satchel pitched against the great Bobo Newsom and three times he beat him . . . and you can imagine how the swaggering Mr. Newsom must have liked that, can't you? A couple of winters ago in California he pitched against a major-league outfit which included Lavagetto, Lombardi, Vince DiMaggio and Hafey; they beat him 2-1 but he didn't allow an earned run—and by then he had reached the old-man stage as a pitcher. Earlier, when an organized winter league functioned on the coast, Paige pitched regularly under conditions approx-

Dizzy Dean's All-Stars took on the Homestead Grays in 1942. Cecil Travis, Dean and Satchel Paige. — *NBL*

imating the big time. His record for three seasons was: 10-2; 11-3; 9-4. And he was pitching against guys like Jimmy Foxx, Luke Appling, the Waner brothers and the top DiMaggio, meaning Jolting Joseph.

Commented Foxx: "I don't see how any pitcher could be much better."

DiMaggio: "I'm glad I don't have to swing against him all season."

Incidentally, in the aforementioned game against Bob Feller, he fanned 11 to the Cleveland ace's 10.

The Satchel has been around for some time. He claims 38. Says he started in 1924, "unless I got my dates mixed." A year-round stint is not unusual for him, that is,

pitching all summer in the States, then campaigning through Mexico, Cuba, Puerto Rico, the Dominican Republic, etc. He carries his own record around with him in a book: innings pitched, opponents, strike-outs, bases-on-balls, results of games and, a very important item to him, his end of the gate. The Satchel is a very good businessman. He knows he has box office value and deals with the promoters accordingly. He says he averages $25,000 a year, which is probably true. Few major-league pitchers have made more on straight contracts.

"I guess I would have liked to pitch against the big boys," the Satchel tells you, "but I ain't never yearned for my vittles."

Satchel Paige as a Kansas City Monarch, 1942.—*NBL*

What about the Satchels of the future? Will they be playing in the big leagues? The question becomes more pressing yearly. It has been tossed into old Judge Landis' lap more than once and the spectacularly adroit manner in which this articulate apostle of Lincoln tosses it out the window is a source of much marvel.

Fifteen Years Too Late

February 13, 1950. They lifted the color taboo about 15 years too late for Satchel Paige who, after an all too brief stint in the majors, has been handed his hat. Even so, he was around long enough to convince experts and fans alike his skills, though faded by time, were authentic. Had he got the break that came to Jackie Robinson, who hit the majors at his youthful peak, he would have ranked with the greatest pitchers, commanded opulent pay and achieved the enduring distinction of being the first of his race to make the Hall of Fame. Come to think of it, why should Old Satch be kept from the Hall of Fame simply because it takes so long to right an ancient wrong? From now on he becomes, along with Dickie Kerr, an automatic write-in on my ballot. In this way baseball, through the press box, can help make amends for the artistic recognition and fiscal rewards denied him down through the years when he was as good as any pitcher in the country. Possibly better.

[One popular trivia question illustrates the sad history of racism in baseball all too well: "Who's the only pitcher in the Hall of Fame with a losing record?" The answer: the same man who could be the greatest pitcher in history. Paige's record, once he got to the big leagues, was 28-31—not bad at that, for a guy who was at least in his mid-forties and who spent much of his time with the Browns.—P. W.]

How He Got His Name

January 27, 1962. Old Satch's honest name is LeRoy Page. . . . "I put the 'i' in 'cause Page is just somethin' you find in a book." Now 60 or so, he tells you he has no regrets about being born too soon. . . . "That's somethin' a fellow don't have much choice about."

He doesn't know how many games he's pitched, won or lost since '20, when he started. He used to pitch the year round; here in the summer, South America in the winter. . . . "One year I pitch 153 games and win most of them."

He didn't get the Satchel moniker smashing baggage as is popularly believed. . . . "They call me that 'cause I've always carried a little satchel, my bag of tricks, I call it." . . . We noticed a catcher's mitt in the bag, and asked why. . . . "I never knows when I'm gonna come across a little boy that wants to play catch," he said.

Appendix

Baseball in '47: Racism and Scapegoats

by Peter Williams

In 1950, as part of an annual series honoring the previous year's MVP, Bill Roeder wrote the first book on Jackie Robinson. In describing Robby's tense spring tour with the Montreal Royals in Daytona Beach, he singled out four teammates to whom race did not seem an issue, men who "came to accept . . . Negroes as teammates" and who felt it was "a privilege to be taking part in this pioneering venture." One of the four became the Royals' starting shortstop in the regular season, and "worked constantly with Jackie on the vital pivot maneuvers." The result was the "crack double play team" of Robinson —and Al Campanis.

That closet racism persists in baseball is cold news; we didn't really need Campanis' sad candor to tell us that. After the *Nightline* incident,* meant to honor the 40th anniversary of integrated baseball, Rachel Robinson commented that racism in the '80s "is more subtle and more disguised," and possibly worse than ever (Rossellini *et al*), and Brent Staples provided a cogent description of the modern racism, no less vicious for being "unconscious":

One hears these crypto-racist remarks from sports people all the time. A gritty, hard-working player or a smart, thinking player, one knows, is white. When an announcer speaks of a "gifted athlete" or a "natural talent," he is almost invariably speaking of a black player. . . . The implication, of course, is that hard work—the greatest of American virtues—is to be lauded more than the gift, which comes even, the inference goes, to the unworthy, the less than perfect. It is almost macabre how, in the mouths of people like Al Campanis, the expression "gifted athlete" can become a slur.

Nor does the racism of the '80s represent a pendular swing back from the liberal social climate of the '60s. Twenty years ago, just after he organized the Smith-

*In a 1987 edition of this TV interview program, Campanis said that blacks were less capable administrators than whites, arguing that this was why they had been given few jobs in baseball management.

Carlos demonstration at the '68 Olympics, Harry Edwards wrote a book contending that "the lot of black athletes is just as bad today as it was before Jackie Robinson integrated baseball in 1946." The peculiar irony of Edwards' having been appointed as an ombudsman of racial equity as a direct result of the downfall of Robinson's old teammate can't be lost on Edwards. The odd circularity of all this, the public resurfacing of one or the other of these two men at regular 20-year intervals, suggests a treadmill; worse, it suggests what a treadmill itself suggests—absolute and total lack of progress.

Campanis said a number of vile things, not rendered very much more palpable because they seemed venial rather than mortal. Why then has he been viewed sympathetically from the very start, from the point in the interview itself when Ted Koppel gave him a chance to "dig himself out"? Surely he is sympathetic because he is the sacrifice, the single victim, the scapegoat and convenient surrogate for the thousands of others in organized ball who are as bad or worse. Still, while sympathy for Campanis may be humane, or even improper, it is (like Al himself) not what's important here—what is vital is to recognize that wherever there is a scapegoat, the thousands of other guilty parties breathe a collective sigh of relief and, feeling that a plague has been lifted, comfortably return to their stereotyping.

I would like to offer another example of scapegoating at work, albeit scapegoating of a very different kind. When Robby broke into organized ball in 1945, there were eight papers in New York, the city he was being groomed to play in. The top writers on each of these papers were major figures in American sports journalism—Granny Rice, Red Smith, Stanley Woodward, Dan Parker, Dick Young, Joe Williams, Frank Graham, Bill Corum, Jimmy Cannon, Arthur Daley. Most (if not all) of these men, like Al Campanis, were closet racists; for example they all set conditions for Robinson that would not have occurred

to them had the player in question been white, and as Robby himself complained, they persisted in referring to him as a "Negro" player, while Furillo was never identified as "Italian," or Hermanski as "Polish." Although one of these writers, Dick Young, was later accused of racism by Robinson himself, Young's racist remarks were made in conversation. Only one of them, Joe Williams, has been accused of being racist in print, and these accusations (made by Jack Orr, Murray Polner and Peter Golenbock) are distinguished in two important ways: (1) they are directed at the only writer from the above list who made frequent reference to his Southern background (he often called himself "the old [Kentucky] Colonel"); and (2) they are demonstrably false. Williams, in other words, has become to sportswriters what Campanis is to baseball management.

In sketching the growth of the charges against Williams it may be best to begin, not at the beginning, but at the end. Golenbock's *Bums* came out in 1984. In it he suggests that Williams' Southern roots caused him to become a racist:

> As soon as it was announced that Robinson had signed to play for Montreal, sportswriter Joe Williams wrote, "Blacks have been kept out of big league ball because they are as race very poor ballplayers." Williams had lived in Memphis before coming to New York. . . . At the end of the 1946 season, Williams asserted that Rickey had sold second baseman Billy Herman because he wanted to lose the 1946 pennant. That way, wrote Williams, if the Dodgers won in 1947 it would be a "Negro Triumph."

Golenbock does not provide sources for these quotes, but in his biography of Rickey, published in 1982, Polner says:

> In 1946 *World-Telegram* columnist Joe Williams, who opposed the de-

segregation of baseball from the very start, wrote that Rickey deliberately had the Dodgers lose the pennant race . . . when he traded Billy Herman, a thirty-five-year-old second baseman, to the Boston Braves, thus "postponing" the victory until the year Robinson's arrival would make it a "Negro triumph."

If [Jimmy] Powers' columns had profoundly agitated Rickey, this hurt even more. He rarely entered player clubhouses, but this time he arrived unannounced, tears flowing down his cheeks, to damn the story as an unmitigated lie. Notwithstanding Williams' bigotry, he still had to deal with his players and the coming of blacks.

And in *The Black Athlete*, a 1969 history of blacks in American sport, Orr says:

Joe Williams, another eminent New York sports editor, dismissed the news by saying, "Blacks have been kept out of big league ball because they are, as a race, very poor ball players. The demands of the black often bulk larger than his capabilities."

Neither Polner nor Orr provides documentation for these comments, which are obviously Golenbock's sources.

What Williams actually wrote in the mid-'40s is dramatically at variance with what Golenbock and his predecessors report. Did he, as Polner claims, "oppose desegregation for the very start"? In the column he wrote on October 25, 1945, just after Robinson was signed by Montreal, he said:

Frank Shaughnessy, president of the International League, of which Montreal is a member, seemed to strike the most intelligent note: "After all, as long as any fellow's the right type and can make good and get along with the other players, he should be welcome in our league. There's no rule in baseball that says a Negro can't play."

This plainly is the sensible approach to the problem. . . . I would be guilty of sheer stupidity and hypocrisy if I failed to concede there has been discrimination. . . .

If only one Negro player were denied the right to play big league ball because of his race that would be evil.

Did he say, as Orr claims, that blacks are inferior players? Here is the original, mildly racist in its concern about imaginary "outside agitators," before Orr altered it significantly:

I have seen the Negro make sure and steady advances. I have also seen him cruelly victimized by pressure groups, social frauds and political demagogues. The net result, in many such cases, has been that his demands bulked larger than his capabilities. This is why I like to assume the Brooklyn outfit has signed the young Negro as a likely asset and not as a gesture to the various anti-discrimination laws. For in the end the young man must stand or fall on his ability.

Finally, did he claim that Rickey traded Billy Herman because he wanted to lose the pennant in '46 so that a '47 victory with Robby on the squad would be a "Negro triumph," thus sending Rickey blubbering like Niobe into the Bums' locker room? Here's what he said in the July 25, 1946 story:

There are times when it is profitless to go all-out in an effort to win the pennant, and this is one of the times. In the more populous sectors, especially, winning teams aren't necessary to turnstile action today. Next season it may be different. By then the customers may have become more discriminating; and it maybe to, too, they will have run out of nonsense money.

Already out of the red for this season, the Dodgers' front office, meaning brother Branch Rickey, needs no World Series. Indeed, it would probably turn out to be an expense. Members of championship teams have a way of demanding pay hoists the following spring. It is much easier for a glib talker to handle players who almost made it than it is to handle players who did make it. You are even in a position to reduce their pay. What you say is "Well, if you had hustled more and played better you would have made it." Then you slash 'em.

At the beginning of the season brother Rickey conceded the flag to the Cardinals, which seemed logical enough. But when the Dodgers began to make threatening gestures the good brother did nothing to encourage their possible success. In his book the Dodgers aren't supposed to win until 1948, and apparently he is determined to see that they don't. Could they use Mickey Owen now? Can Ray Bolger dance? And where were the Bums strengthened for a stretch drive by the release of high-salaried Billy Herman? Just the type of veteran you need to take over in a clutch, even if he can't get off a quarter, this being inflationary for the proverbial dime?

Williams, like many other writers of the time, was suggesting that the Mahatma was cheap. There is no racism in his comments here, not even any mention of Robinson, and if Rickey was looking for a "Negro triumph," why would he wait until Robby's sophomore year?

The scapegoating of Williams, then, is unusual, and very different from the case of Al Campanis, in that an image of the former has been created which seems plainly a fabrication. Campanis volunteered to have the sins of his fellows visited upon him, and in a couple of fatal minutes that was accomplished completely and with finality. Williams lost his journalistic forum in 1964, was libelled in 1969, again in 1982, and in 1984 we were given a revisionist portrait of a writer who was probably no worse than most of the others and better than some. And in 1984 Golenbock unwittingly explained why Williams had been chosen in the first place—he added the crucial detail, omitted by both Orr and Polner, that Williams had grown up in Memphis.

Works Cited

"By Joe Williams." *New York World-Telegram* 25 Oct. 1945, p. 41; 25 Jul. 1946, p. 20.
Edwards, Harry. *The Revolt of the Black Athlete*. New York: The Free Press, 1969.
Golenbock, Peter. *Bums*. New York: Putnam's, 1984.
Orr, Jack. *The Black Athlete*. New York: The Lion Press, 1969.
Polner, Murray. *Branch Rickey*. New York: 1982.
Robinson, Jackie. *Baseball Has Done It*. Philadelphia: Lippincott, 1964.
———. *I Never Had It Made*. New York: Putnam's, 1972.
Roeder, Bill. *Jackie Robinson*. New York: Barnes, 1950.
Rossellini, Lynn, with Peter Ross Range, Alvin P. Sanoff, Jeannye Thornton, Lisa J. Moore, Ira Teinowitz and Pamela Ellis-Simons. "Strike One and You're Out." *U.S. News & World Report*, 27 Jul. 87, p. 57.
Staples, Brent. "Where Are the Black Fans?" *New York Times* 17 May 1987, sec. 6, p. 56.